Brimming with creative inspiration, how-to projects, and useful information to enrich your everyday life, Quarto Knows is a favorite destination for those pursuing their interests and passions. Visit our site and dig deeper with our books into your area of interest: Quarto Creates, Quarto Cooks, Quarto Homes, Quarto Lives, Quarto Drives, Quarto Explores, Quarto Gifts, or Quarto Kids.

Inspiring | Educating | Creating | Entertaining

© 2017 Quarto Publishing Group USA Inc.
Text © 2017 Elizabeth Snoke Harris

First Published in 2017 by MoonDance Press, an imprint of The Quarto Group.
6 Orchard Road, Suite 100, Lake Forest, CA 92630, USA.
T (949) 380-7510 **F** (949) 380-7575 **www.QuartoKnows.com**

MoonDance Press titles are also available at discount for retail, wholesale, promotional, and bulk purchase. For details, contact the Special Sales Manager by email at specialsales@quarto.com or by mail at The Quarto Group, Attn: Special Sales Manager, 401 Second Avenue North, Suite 310, Minneapolis, MN 55401 USA.

ISBN: 978-1-63322-225-0

Illustrations by Jeff Albrecht Studios
Cover and interior design by Melissa Gerber

Printed in China
10 9 8 7 6 5 4 3 2 1

MIX
Paper from
responsible sources
FSC® C101537
FSC
www.fsc.org

Contents

Introduction

Have you ever wanted to…
Build a water-powered rocket?
Write secret messages in invisible ink?
Discover all the creepy-crawly insects in your backyard?

Great! You'll find easy-to-follow instructions for these and so many more awesome experiments in this book. It's chock-full of 365 of the most amazing experiments you've ever done. That means you can do a different science experiment every single day of the year!

Want S'more Catapult?, page 16

What's in this book?

You will find experiments you can do in the kitchen, the bathroom, outside, and even in the dark. Some projects will have you playing with your food or using your brain. More projects involve building and putting things together like racers, shooters, rockets, and even a light bulb. There are slime recipes, magic tricks, noisemakers, and bubbles. Not to mention the crystals, optical illusions, flyers, and spinners.

If you want to ease into things, start off with the Toothpick Star on page 215 or the Basic Air Cannon on page 119. If you are up for a challenge, check out the Elephant Toothpaste on page 173 or Hot-air Balloon on page 26. No matter what project you choose, you are guaranteed to have fun!

- Many of the experiments can be done by kids all by themselves. That's right —no adult help needed. That means no grown-ups doing all the fun stuff while you watch. You can do lots of messy, cool, mind-blowing experiments all by yourself!

- All the supplies you need for the experiments are probably already in your home. No fancy gadgets or doohickeys needed. As long as you've got some plastic bottles, rubber bands, balloons, a pair of scissors, and some other random stuff lying around, you are ready to get started.

- Science is fun! There is no better boredom buster than a science experiment. You will learn something and astound and amaze your friends and family. Many experiments offer suggestions for exploring further, so who knows where that will take you!

Bed of Tacks, page 212

Water Bottle Rocket, page 36

Bottle Ecosystem, page 186

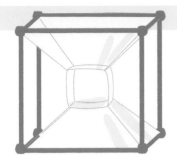

Square Bubbles, page 240

What are you waiting for?

Pick an experiment you are interested in, gather the materials, and get going! Make sure you check the safety instructions and find an adult to help if needed.

- **Supplies** includes all the stuff you need for the project. You should be able to find most things at home.
- **Do It!** has the instructions for building and performing the experiment. Try not to read past this section when doing a project. Can you figure out what is going on before you read ahead?
- **What's Happening?** Read the science behind the experiment.
- **What If?** includes ideas for making the experiment bigger, louder, longer, or just plain better.

Which weird and wonderful science experiment will you start with?

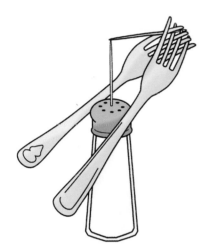

Balance Forks on a Toothpick, page 49

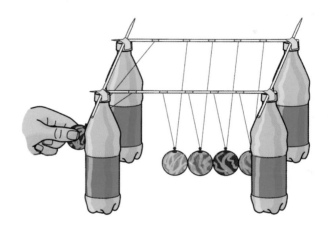

Cradle of Energy, page 85

Naked Egg, page 147

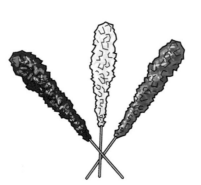

Rock Candy, page 245

Snot, page 251

Build It

Build contraptions that shoot, fly, roll, light up, tell time, and more!

Make It

1 Make Bricks

For 9,000 years, bricks have been the go-to building material. They are strong, fireproof, and waterproof. You can easily make your own mud bricks at home!

Supplies

Ice cube tray or egg carton, Bucket, Trowel, A place to dig in the ground, Straw or grass, Water

Do It!

1. Using the trowel, dig a hole in the ground (ask your parents to help pick a spot), digging down past the dark brown topsoil to the heavier soil underneath. Does the color of the soil change as you dig deeper?

2. Put several trowels full of the deeper soil into the bucket and add a big handful of straw or grass.

3. Pour in just enough water to make a very thick mud.

4. Mix the mud and grass completely with the trowel, making sure there are no clumps or rocks in the mud.

5. Pack the mud into the ice cube tray to make small bricks, making sure there are no air bubbles by slamming the tray straight down on the ground a few times.

6. Leave the tray in a bright, dry spot for several days until the bricks are completely dry.

7. Pull the bricks out of the tray and let them dry in the sun for a few more hours.

8. Once the bricks are done, take a look at the outsides. Are they smooth or rough? Are the bricks strong or do they crumble easily? What happens if you smash one on the ground? Can you build something with your bricks?

What's Happening?

The dirt deeper in your yard usually contains a very fine, sticky soil called clay. The tiny clay particles dry into a very hard material. However, without the straw, the brick would crumble to pieces. The straw gives the brick stability and helps spread out the force on the brick to make it stronger.

What If?

What if you put more or less straw in your bricks? Does adding more straw to the bricks make them stronger?

Make a Light Bulb

The first light bulbs made by Thomas Edison were incandescent, just like this one!

ADULT NEEDED

Do It!

1. Use the hammer and nail to make two holes, 1 inch apart, in the lid of the jar.

2. Cut the copper wire into two pieces about 18 inches long.

3. With an adult's help, cut off an inch of the plastic coating at each end of the strands.

4. Push a wire through each hole so that about 2 inches of the wire can be seen in the jar.

5. Make a small hook at the end of the copper wires that will be inside the jar.

6. Unwind the picture hanging wire to use the individual fine strands of iron wire.

7. Twist three strands of the iron wire together and stretch them across the gap between the two copper hooks to form the filament.

8. Put the lid with the filament on the jar.

9. Carefully use electrical tape to attach the end of the copper wires to opposite ends of the battery. Watch your bulb light up!

10. Time how long your filament glows before it burns out. The filament becomes very hot! Wait five minutes for the filament to cool before opening the light bulb jar.

Supplies

Mason jar with lid, 1-inch nail, Hammer, Three feet of insulated copper wire, 6-volt battery (or use electrical tape to tape 4 D batteries together end to end), Picture hanging wire, Wire cutter, Stopwatch, Electrical tape

What's Happening?

The electric light bulb works because you've made a complete circuit with electrons flowing out from the battery, through the filament, and back to the battery. Electrons flowing through the filament wire produce heat and make the filament glow.

Make a Chair

Become a structural engineer!

Do It!

1. Roll several layers of newspapers into very tight rolls and secure them with tape.

2. Arrange the newspaper rolls to create a chair; tape the rolls together.

3. Sit down on your chair. Does it hold you up?

4. Experiment with different shapes like squares, triangles, and hexagons.

Supplies

A LOT of newspaper, Tape

What's Happening?

Structural engineers call the weight an object has to hold "the load." Some shapes are better at bearing a load. Rectangles and squares are easy to bend and break. Triangles are less likely to bend or break.

4 Make a Dam

Dams stop or slow the flow of a river or stream and are built by people and beavers alike.

Supplies

Large, long, shallow container (large baking dish or plastic container); Sticks (from the outdoors or popsicle sticks); Small rocks; Sand; Mud; Bucket of water

Do It!

1. Fill the container with sand and make a path for a river.
2. Use the sticks, rocks, sand, and mud to build a dam in the middle of the container to block the river.
3. See if you can keep the area behind the dam completely dry.
4. When you're ready, slowly pour the water from the bucket into the container and see if the dam holds.

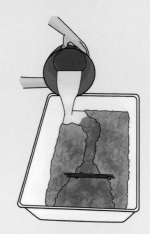

What's Happening?

When building a dam, you need to consider the materials and the shape of the dam. Sticks and rocks are strong but will not hold the water back alone. Mud and sand are needed to keep the water from leaking through the cracks.

5 Make Modeling Clay

Use your homemade modeling clay to create models of your favorite scientific discoveries!

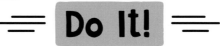

Do It!

Supplies

White school glue, Cornstarch, Flour, Salt, Water, Measuring cup, Bowl, Mixing spoon

1. Mix 2 cups of flour, 1 cup of salt, and ¼ cup of cornstarch in the bowl.
2. Mix in ¼ cup of the white glue.
3. Add water slowly, a couple spoonfuls at a time, until the clay is moldable but not too soft.
4. If you accidentally add too much water, add more cornstarch to the mixture. If the clay is too crumbly, add more glue.

Use your modeling clay to make whatever you like — a bowl, necklace, or model of your favorite scientific discovery. Make sure not to make pieces that are too thick (they will take too long to dry) or too thin (they will break easily). When you are ready, leave your piece in a warm, dry place to dry for two to three days.

What's Happening?

This clay is a polymer clay. The cornstarch and glue mix together to form long chains of molecules called polymers. This gives the clay its stretchiness. The flour and salt help the clay hold its shape while you work with the clay and when it dries.

Make Paper

Paper is the easiest product to recycle – so easy that you can recycle it into new paper at home!

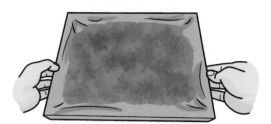

Supplies

Picture frame (one that is not going to be used again), Pantyhose (a pair that is not going to be used again), Tape, Newspaper, Large bowl or bucket, Sink, Warm water, Cornstarch, Measuring spoon, Clean cloth rags or paper towels, Spoon

Do It!

1. Remove the glass and picture from the picture frame.
2. Use the empty rectangular piece to make a strainer by stretching pantyhose over the frame, using tape if needed to hold the hose in place.
3. Tear up about six pages of newspaper into small pieces and put them into the bowl.
4. Pour warm water into the bowl to completely cover the paper, and then mix it all up.
5. Let the bowl sit for several hours or overnight, until the bowl is full of pulpy, mushy soup.
6. Mix in 2 tablespoons of cornstarch and another cup of hot water.
7. Place the frame in the sink and pour a thin layer of pulp from the bowl onto the frame.
8. Use the spoon to make sure the frame is covered evenly with pulp and to push out extra water.
9. Lay the frame on top of a dry cloth and press another cloth on top of the pulp to soak up any extra water.
10. Remove the cloth and leave the frame of pulp to dry into paper. This can take several hours, but you can use a hair dryer to speed up the process.
11. When the paper is completely dry, gently peel it off the frame. How does the paper look and feel? Can you write on it?

What's Happening?

All paper is made of millions of thin cellulose fibers from plants. When you tear the newspaper, look closely at the edges and you can see the cellulose fibers all tangled up. The fibers naturally stick together, but water breaks them apart.

Soaking the paper in water creates a cellulose pulp soup that can be made into new paper. The cornstarch helps the fibers stick back together once the water has been dried out of the pulp. A new piece of paper is born!

What If?

What if you add other items to your paper to make it more interesting? Try glitter, flower petals, or tiny pieces of colored paper.

7 Make a Stethoscope

The very first stethoscope was simply a hollow cylinder. Now you can make your own!

Do It!

Supplies

Small funnel, Large funnel, 2 feet of plastic tubing (a piece of old water hose works too), Duct tape, Balloon, Rubber band, Scissors

1. Blow up the balloon, let the air out, and then cut off the small end of the balloon.
2. Stretch the balloon over the large funnel, and use the rubber band to hold it in place.
3. Attach a funnel to each end of the tubing. If the funnels do not fit tightly on their own, use duct tape to secure them in place.
4. Place the small funnel on one ear and the large funnel with the balloon on your chest. Can you hear your heart beat? If not, make sure the funnel is under your shirt and move it around slowly until you can.
5. Do jumping jacks for 30 seconds and then listen to your heart beat again. Has it changed?

What's Happening?

The funnels on either end of the tube focus the sound of your heartbeat through the tube and to your ears. The balloon amplifies the vibrations of the very weak sound so that it's easier to hear. When you exercise, oxygen and nutrients are used up more quickly, so the heart needs to beat faster to send the blood through more quickly.

8 Make a Cantilever

A cantilever is an overhanging structure that is supported on just one end, such as a balcony or a diving board.

Do It!

Supplies

1 package of uncooked spaghetti, Masking tape, Tabletop, Scissors, Ruler

1. Tape a small handful of pasta together and then to the top edge of the tabletop, extending out.
2. Tape another handful of pasta together and then to the bottom edge of the tabletop, using tape to secure it to the previous bunch.
3. Now add another bunch of pasta to the end, using tape to secure it to the previous bunch.
4. Keep building with more pasta and tape, extending your cantilever as far off the table as possible without getting closer than 12 inches to the ground.
5. Measure your cantilever. How long can you build it?

What's Happening?

Consider a cantilever found in nature: a tree branch. A squirrel sits on a branch near the trunk. As she runs to the end of the branch, it begins to bend. Torque, or rotation caused by a force, makes the branch bend. Torque increases farther from the support, bending the branch and cantilever down.

Make a Mummy

Egyptians weren't the only peoples to mummify their dead rulers. Mummies have been found in China, Mexico, Peru, and Chile. You can make your own mummy using an apple!

Supplies

Apple, Knife, 2 plastic cups, Washing soda (found in the detergent aisle) or baking soda, Salt, Bowl, Kitchen scale, Measuring cup, Marker, Paper towels (optional), Glue (optional)

Do It!

1. Cut the apple into quarters and put two of the pieces into the two cups.
2. Weigh each cup on the kitchen scale and write the starting weight on the cup.
3. In the bowl, mix 1 cup of washing soda with ¼ cup of salt, then pour the mixture into one of the cups so it completely covers the apple.
4. Leave the other apple in the cup and put the cups in a cool, dry place for seven days.
5. Remove the apple pieces from the cups and inspect them. How does the apple being mummified compare to the other apple?
6. Weigh the apples in the empty cups and write the new weights on the cups.
7. Mix another batch of washing soda and salt and cover the apple again. Let the cups sit in a cool, dry place for another seven days.
8. Again, inspect the apples. How do the apples look different from one week ago? How do they look different from two weeks ago? How do they look different from each other?
9. Weigh the apples again. How much weight has each lost?
10. If you want to finish the mummifying process, dip strips of paper towel in white glue and wrap them around the mummified apple slice. Let the mummy wrappings dry for 24 hours before handling.

What's Happening?

The washing soda and salt mixture acts as a desiccant. It absorbs water and dries out the apple. Without water, bacteria and mold that cause the apple to rot can't grow. Wrapping the mummy in bandages and sealing it with glue protects the dried-out mummy from damp and dirt.

What If?

What if you mummified an orange slice, small squash, or even a hot dog?

10 Make a Bridge

Have you thought much about how bridges are designed?
You can build your own out of straws and paper clips.

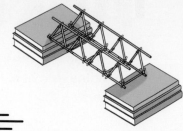

Supplies

Books, Ruler, Straws, Paper clips, Scissors, Cup, 100 pennies (or similar weight)

Do It!

1. Make two piles of books about 6 inches high and place them 12 inches apart.
2. Use the straws and paper clips to build a bridge that will span the distance between the books and hold a cup full of at least 100 pennies.
3. Use different methods to connect the straws with the paper clips. You can flatten the ends and slide them into the paper clip, or link the paper clips and slide each into a straw. You can also use the scissors to cut the straws to different lengths.

What's Happening?

You probably found that the straws were not strong enough to hold the pennies if you made a beam bridge. A truss bridge is much stronger and uses lighter materials to support a heavy load. Truss bridges use triangular shapes above or below a beam bridge for added strength. The diagonal pieces distribute the weight of the bridge and the load more evenly.

11 Make a Lava Lamp

The original lava lamp uses wax in a liquid. You can make your own
lava lamp that creates mesmerizing bubbles without heat!

Do It!

Supplies

Clear plastic bottle, Water, Vegetable oil, Food coloring, Effervescent tablets

1. Pour water into the bottle until it's about a quarter full.
2. Add a few drops of food coloring and shake the bottle gently to mix the color into the water.
3. Fill the rest of the bottle with vegetable oil.
4. Break an effervescent tablet into three or four pieces and drop them into the bottle.
5. Watch the colored water bubbles rise and fall in the oil!

What's Happening?

This lava lamp uses a chemical reaction and differences in density to create its mesmerizing bubbles. The effervescent tablets contain an acid and a base in powder form. When the tablet dissolves, these chemicals produce bubbles. The less-dense oil sits on top of the denser water and slows down the bubbles as they float up to the top. The bubbles also carry some of the colored water with them. When the bubbles pop, the denser drop of water sinks back down. The colored water bubbles rise and fall, as long as you add effervescent tablets.

Waves take many forms. Sound waves, light waves, and mechanical waves are just a few. This wave machine is a fun and mesmerizing way to explore how waves behave!

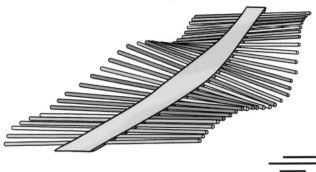

Supplies

Masking tape, 50 plastic straws, Ruler, Friend

Do It!

1. Lay 5 feet of masking tape on the ground, sticky side up.
2. Use a small piece of tape to hold each end in place, and then place straws along the entire length of the tape.
3. Leave exactly 2 centimeters between each straw and make sure the straws are centered on the tape.
4. Once all the straws are in place, lay another 5-foot-long piece of tape over the first tape to hold the straws in place.
5. Hold one end of the wave machine and have a friend hold the other (or tape it onto the back of a chair).
6. Tap one of the straws near one end. Do you see the wave travel through the straws? What happens to the wave when it reaches the end?
7. Coordinate with your friend to hit opposite ends of the wave machine at the same time. What happens to the wave? Experiment with different ways to send waves through the machine.

What's Happening?

Waves all have the same purpose: to transfer energy. In the case of the wave machine, motion energy is transferred from one end to the other by the twisting of the tape. The straws make that twisting motion more visible.

When waves collide, they travel right through each other. If the straws from one wave are down and the other straws are up, when they meet, you will see the straws stay still in that spot because the up and down motions cancel each other out.

Or if the waves in both directions are up, the motions will add together to make a larger wave at that point. The waves will also reflect or bounce back from the ends, but how they reflect depends on if the ends are loose or held in place. Try it out; what do you observe?

What If?

What if you make a wave machine with the straws spaced farther apart or closer together?

13 Popsicle Stick Catapult

Catapults have been used for centuries to hurl large rocks at enemies. This catapult hurls marshmallows!

Supplies

9 popsicle sticks, 6 rubber bands, 1 plastic spoon, Mini marshmallows or other ammunition

Do It!

1. Stack seven sticks and wrap a rubber band several times around each end to hold them tightly together.
2. Put the other two sticks together and wrap a rubber band several times around just one end.
3. Push the stack of seven sticks in between the open end of the two sticks as far as possible.
4. Use another rubber band to secure all of the sticks in place so that the rubber band makes an "X" where all the sticks meet.
5. Lay the spoon on the stick that is up in the air.
6. Use two rubber bands to secure the spoon to the stick, one near the top and another near the bottom.
7. Place a mini marshmallow in the spoon, pull the spoon down, and release. Watch the marshmallow fly!

What's Happening?

Catapults are one example of a lever. They use a beam or stick on a fulcrum, so the work done on one end is increased on the other end, making it easier to lift heavy things.

In this catapult, pulling back the spoon (lever) attached to the rubber bands (fulcrums) stores that work as potential energy. The stretched-out rubber bands store the potential energy until you release the catapult. The rubber bands then snap back into place and transfer most of the potential energy to the marshmallow as kinetic or motion energy, making your ammo fly!

14 Want S'more Catapult?

This catapult is a sweet treat!

Supplies

5 large marshmallows, 7 wooden skewers, Plastic spoon, Rubber band, Masking tape, Mini marshmallows

Do It!

1. Place three large marshmallows in a triangle and connect them with skewers.
2. Add three more skewers and another marshmallow to form a pyramid.
3. Place the spoon handle along one end of the last skewer, and secure with tape.
4. Loop the rubber band over the top of the pyramid.
5. Slide the pointed end of the skewer with the spoon through the rubber band and down into the marshmallow on the opposite side.
6. Place a mini marshmallow into the spoon, and use one hand to hold the catapult down and the other to pull back the spoon. Release and watch the marshmallow fly!

Tennis Ball Shooter

Projectile motion is the study of how objects move through the air. Make a shooter to explore how a tennis ball flies through the air – or make several and have a battle with your friends!

Supplies

Tennis ball can or cardboard tube (like a potato chip container), Plastic drink bottle that fits inside the tennis ball can, Rubber bands, Scissors, Masking tape, Pencil or skewer, Tennis ball

ADULT NEEDED

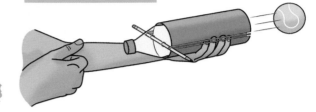

Do It!

1. Cut the bottom off of the tennis ball can so you have a long straight tube, then cut two slits on one end of the can about ½ inch apart.
2. Cut similar slits on the opposite side of the same end of the can and hook a rubber band through the slits on each side of the can.
3. Wrap masking tape around the top of the can with the slits to hold the top of the rubber bands in place.
4. With an adult's help, use the scissors to poke a hole in the drink bottle about 2 inches from the top (where the bottle stops curving).
5. Poke another hole on the opposite side of the bottle and slide the pencil through the holes so it's evenly balanced on both sides.
6. Put the bottle into the can, bottom end first, on the side opposite the rubber bands.
7. Stretch the rubber bands and slide one over each end of the pencil.
8. Now place a tennis ball in the opposite end of the can. To shoot the ball, pull back the bottle and pencil and release! How far does the ball go?

What's Happening?

Once the ball leaves the shooter, the only force acting on it is gravity. Gravity slows any upward motion of the ball until it stops going up for just an instant and then accelerates downward. However, gravity does not affect the ball's sideways motion. The combination of the constant sideways motion and gravity pulling downward causes the ball to move in a curved path, called a parabola.

What If?

What if you use different balls in your shooter? Try table tennis balls or rubber bouncy balls. What type of ball shoots the farthest?

Seed Spinners

Have you ever blown the seeds off a dandelion puff to make a wish? Did you watch the puffy white seeds float through the air? If you look carefully, you'll see that the seeds look like tiny helicopters. They are designed to float through the air for a long time to spread the dandelion seeds far and wide. Create your own spinner similar to a dandelion seed and see how long it will spin in the air!

Supplies

Paper, Ruler, Scissors, Paper clip

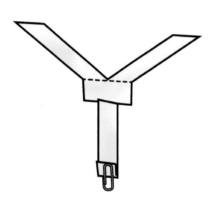

Do It!

1. Cut a strip of paper about 1½ inches wide and 8½ inches long.
2. Fold the paper into thirds, crease the folds, and then unfold the paper.
3. Cut a slit from the top almost all the way to the first fold, leaving about a ½-inch between the end of the cut and the fold.
4. Cut two small ½-inch slits on both sides, right along the first fold, and then fold the paper up on the second fold.
5. Now fold the sides inward on the two small slits you cut, and fold up the bottom toward the top, securing it with a paper clip.
6. Finally, fold the top two strips in opposite directions. Your seed spinner is complete!
7. Drop your spinner high above the ground, maybe from the top of the stairs or standing on a ladder.

What's Happening?

The shape of the seed spinner causes it to start spinning around after it falls for a second or two. The spinning motion causes lift, or an upward force on the seed spinner, which slows down its fall.

In fact, lift causes the seed spinner to fall much slower than the same paper and paper clip crumpled up in a ball — try it! For seeds, this means they spend more time in the air. Any breeze or wind can carry the seeds farther away where they can take hold in the ground and grow into new plants!

What If?

What if you change the shape of the seed spinner? Try making the wings longer or shorter, folding up a corner, or making the end rounded instead of square.

Centripetal Spinner 17

Once you get the hang of this little spinner, there will be no stopping you!

=== Do It! ===

Supplies

Wooden skewer, Scissors, Tape, Cork

1. Break the wooden skewer in half, and use the scissors to cut off any splinters.
2. Tape the skewers together in an X-shape so the two sides of the X are shorter than the other two, making sure the point of the skewer is on a longer side.
3. Push the cork onto the pointy end of the skewer and then balance the spinner on your finger between the two longer sides.
4. Move your hand so that the skewers spin around your finger.
5. Once you get it moving, point your finger upward at an angle so it doesn't slide off.
6. How long can you keep the centripetal spinner twirling around your finger?

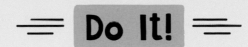

What's Happening?

Your finger pulls on the skewer, which pulls on the cork and keeps it moving in a circle. This pulling is called centripetal or "center-seeking" force and it keeps the spinner twirling around your finger instead of flying off.

Straw Spinner 18

You might look a little like an elephant with these straws in your mouth!

=== Do It! ===

1. Cut a 2-inch strip of foil and fold it so you have a piece that is 2 inches long and ½ inch wide.
2. Loosely wrap the foil strip around the short end of the straw.
3. Wrap the rubber band around the end of the straw so that the foil "bead" doesn't slide off.
4. Cut the long end of each straw in half, and then cut a 1-inch slit on the long end of one straw.
5. Squeeze that straw and slide it inside the long end of the other straw. The straws should fit together tightly but air should still flow through both straws.
6. Bend both straws so the short parts are at a right angle to the long parts.
7. Turn the straws so the bent parts are at right angles to each other, and then place the end of the straw with the foil bead in your mouth.
8. Hold the bead lightly between your lips and blow hard. The straws will spin around!

Supplies

2 bendable straws, Aluminum foil, Small rubber band, Scissors

What's Happening?

Newton's third law states that for every force, there is an equal and oppositely directed re-force. In this case, the force is the air you blow. The air pushes out of the straw, so there is a re-force of the same size, but pushing the opposite direction on the straw.

19 Straw Propeller

This propeller won't make you fly into the air, but it's still fun to spin around.

═ Do It! ═

Supplies

Drinking straw, Milkshake straw (big enough for the drinking straw to fit inside), Scissors, Tape

1. Fold the smaller straw 2 inches from the end and cut off one corner where the straw bends.
2. When you open the straw, there is a diamond-shaped hole; tape the end of the straw closed on the side closest to the hole.
3. Fold the larger straw in the middle and cut off both corners where it bends.
4. When you open this straw, there are two diamond-shaped holes; flatten both ends of the straw and tape them closed.
5. On the left side, cut off the top corner of the taped end to create a small hole.
6. On the right side, cut off the bottom corner of the taped end to create a small hole on the opposite side of the straw.
7. Slide the small straw through the hole in the large straw so the holes line up.
8. Put the open end of the small straw in your mouth and blow hard. The large straw will spin around like a propeller!

What's Happening?

When you blow into the small straw, there is nowhere for the air to go but out of the diamond hole and into the larger straw. From there, the air goes out the small holes on both ends of the large straw. Because the holes are on opposite corners and not the ends of the straw, the air blowing out pushes back on the straw, causing it to spin!

20 Pocket Slingshot

Be ready for a marshmallow battle anytime!

═ Do It! ═
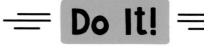

Supplies

Plastic drink bottle, Balloon, Scissors, Mini marshmallows

1. Cut the top off of the bottle just below the mouth.
2. Cut off the narrow part of the balloon, and then stretch the rest of the balloon over the mouth of the bottle, pushing it through so it folds over the opening.
3. Pull the narrow part of the balloon onto the mouth of the bottle, as well.
4. Roll up the smaller piece of balloon so that it holds the larger piece in place.
5. Put a marshmallow in the balloon, pull it back and release it. How far can you shoot the marshmallow?

What's Happening?

This slingshot shoots using the first law of thermodynamics: energy cannot be created or destroyed, only transformed. In this case, potential energy in the stretchy balloon is converted to motion energy.

Mousetrap Car

Just add wheels to a simple mousetrap and you will be ready to roll!

ADULT NEEDED

Supplies

Mousetrap, String, Straw, Cardboard, Cup, Pencil, Scissors, Tape, Bamboo Skewer, Glue or clay

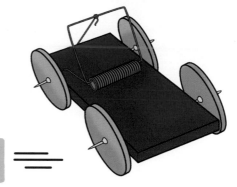

═ Do It! ═

1. Ask an adult to help you make sure the mousetrap is closed and not set, and remove the parts of the trap used to hold the bait (catch) and the long hook that keeps the rectangular hammer in place (catch lever).
2. Cut four pieces of straw about ½ inch long and tape them to the bottom of the mousetrap, two in the front and two in the back, near the outside edges of the mousetrap to hold the axles.
3. Make sure the pieces line up so the axles can spin freely.
4. Cut the bamboo skewer in half and put the two pieces through the straws.
5. Trace the cup four times on the piece of cardboard and cut out the circles to make wheels.
6. Use the scissors to poke a small hole in the center of the cardboard circles, and then slide the wheels onto the ends of the bamboo skewer axles.
7. Use glue or a small amount of clay to hold the axles in place on the wheels, making sure the wheels don't rub against the sides of the mousetrap.
8. Cut a piece of string about twice as long as the mousetrap, and tie one end to the middle of the skewer axle in the back of the mousetrap (farthest from the hammer).
9. Carefully tie the other end of the string to the top of the hammer, using a small bit of tape to hold both ends of the string in place.
10. With an adult's help, turn the back wheels so that the string winds tightly around the axle.
11. Lift the hammer to the other side and keep winding the string tightly.
12. Place the mousetrap car on the floor and let go of the hammer. It will slowly pull the string so that the car zooms!

What's Happening?

There is a lot of energy stored in the tight spring of a mousetrap. When you release the spring, that stored potential energy is converted into moving kinetic energy that pulls the string, which in turn pulls the axle and turns the wheels.

What If?

What if you make the back wheels larger than the front wheels or the other way around?

22 Balloon Car

This car uses the same science that sends rockets into space!

Do It!

Supplies

Cardboard, 2 straws, 2 bamboo skewers, 4 plastic bottle caps, Clay, Balloon, Tape, Scissors, Ruler

1. Cut a 3" x 5" piece of cardboard.
2. Cut two 3-inch pieces from a straw.
3. For the axles, tape one straw near the front and one straw near the back so the edges of the straw line up with the edges of the cardboard.
4. Fill the bottle caps with clay and cut the pointed end off of each skewer.
5. Stick one end of each skewer into the clay at the center of a bottle cap.
6. Slide each skewer through a straw and then stick wheels on the other ends.
7. Make sure the car rolls straight; adjust the placement of the skewers in the wheels as needed.
8. Place one end of the other straw in the opening of the balloon and tape it to the end of the straw.
9. Tape the straw to the top of the car with the balloon in the middle of the car and the end of the straw off the back.
10. Blow into the straw to blow up the balloon as big as you can, and then place the car on the floor and watch it zoom!

What's Happening?

When you let the air out of the balloon, it shoots out the back of the car. In the process, it pushes the balloon in the other direction with the same amount of force to make the balloon car zoom.

23 Super Spool Racer

This little racer is small enough to carry in your pocket.

Do It!

Supplies

Empty thread spool, Rubber band, Paper clip, Washer, Tape, Pencil

1. Thread the paper clip onto the rubber band.
2. Push the rubber band through the hole in the middle of the spool and then through the washer.
3. Slide the pencil through the rubber band next to the washer.
4. Use tape to hold the paper clip in place on the other end of the spool.
5. Spin the pencil around until the rubber band is tight.
6. Lay the spool (with the pencil) on the ground and watch it go!

What's Happening?

The rubber band, which holds potential energy, untwists and causes the spool to spin and roll on the ground. The washers provide a smooth surface so that friction doesn't convert the motion energy into heat energy.

Totally Tubular Race Cars

Set up a drag race with your friends to find the fastest car!

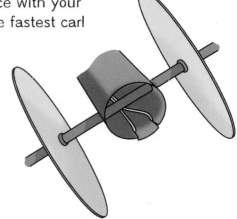

Supplies

Paper towel tube, 4 CDs or DVDs, 2 pencils, Rubber bands, Masking tape, Scissors, Glue, Hole punch

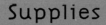

Do It!

1. Use the hole punch to make holes in the paper towel tube exactly opposite each other on both ends. Make sure the holes line up across the tube opening and lengthwise so the wheels all sit on the ground and roll straight.
2. Slide pencils through the holes in the front and the back for axles, making sure the pencils spin freely in the holes.
3. Wrap several layers of masking tape around one end of a pencil, using enough tape that it will slide into the opening on a CD and not slide out.
4. Use a small amount of glue to make sure all of the CD wheels are secure.
5. Loop several rubber bands together to make a chain that is at least as long as the paper towel tube, and loop or tie one end of the chain to the back axle of the car.
6. On the other end, cut two slits about an inch apart on the bottom of the tube.
7. Feed the rubber band chain through the tube and hook the end of the chain onto the slits.
8. Make sure the rubber band chain is underneath the front axle, and then use a piece of tape to hold it in place.
9. Turn the back wheels to wind the rubber band tightly around the axle. When you can't wind the wheels anymore, let them go and watch the car zoom!

What's Happening?

Stretch out a rubber band and let it fly. The stretching adds energy to the rubber band, which is released when you let go and it goes flying with kinetic or motion energy.

The exact same thing happens inside the CD tube race car. Except in this case, the rubber band is attached to the axle of the car. To stretch the rubber band, you wind it around the axle. When it is released, instead of flying, the rubber band spins the axle and the race car zooms!

What If?

What if you make the tube shorter or longer? What else can you change to make your CD tube car move faster and farther?

Basic Paper Airplane

Flying

Many of the earliest flight scientists, from Leonardo da Vinci to the Wright Brothers, used paper models to design airplanes. Now you can make one too!

Supplies

Paper (8½ x 11 inches)

Do It!

For all of the steps in folding a paper airplane, make sure you crease each fold well by running your finger along the fold several times.

1. Fold the paper in half longways and then open it up again.
2. Fold the top right corner down so the top of the paper meets the first fold in the center, and then do the same on the left side. You should now have a folded triangle above a rectangle.
3. Fold the top side of the triangle to meet the first fold in the center of the paper.
4. Do the same on the left side, and then fold the paper in half longways along the center fold, so the folded parts are on the outside.
5. Lay the folded paper on its side, and then fold the long open edge of the top part so it meets the closed side (the center fold).
6. Turn the folded paper over and repeat the process, and then open the last fold to a right angle, creating the wings.
7. To fly the airplane, hold the center fold so the wings are on top, and then pull back your arm and throw the plane just slightly upward. How far does it fly?

What's Happening?

Paper airplanes, like real airplanes, are under four different forces. When you throw the airplane, you apply a forward moving force called thrust. You can give the airplane more thrust by throwing it harder. In a real airplane, the engines provide thrust.

Air pushing against the airplane as it moves is called drag. Drag works against thrust to slow down the airplane. Lift keeps the airplane up in the air. Air moving over and under the wings provides this upward force. The weight of the airplane, or gravity, pulls the airplane down toward the ground.

When designing a paper airplane, the goal is to provide the greatest lift with the smallest drag, so the airplane stays in the air for a long time and moves through the air quickly!

What If?

What if you adjust the folds on the airplane to increase the lift and decrease the drag? Can you design a paper airplane that flies faster or a greater distance?

Paper Glider

Can you build a glider that stays in the air longer than 30 seconds - the world record?

Supplies

Paper (8½ x 11 inches)

Do It!

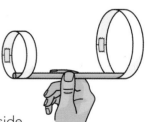

For all of the steps in folding a paper airplane, make sure you crease each fold well by running your finger along the fold several times.

1. Fold the paper in half longways and then open it up again.

2. Fold the top right corner down so the top of the paper meets the first fold in the center, then do the same on the left side. You should now have a folded triangle above a rectangle.

3. Fold the top half of the triangle down so the point meets the bottom, and then fold the triangle down along its bottom edge. The paper should now be a rectangle with the folded parts at the top.

4. Fold the top corners of the rectangle down to the center fold. Then fold the entire plane in half toward you, along the center fold so the folded parts are inside.

5. Create wings by folding each side out ½ inch from the center fold. This is where you will hold the plane.

6. Finally, fold up about ½ inch along the outside edge of each wing.

7. To fly the airplane, hold the center fold so the wings are on top and throw the plane almost straight up.

What's Happening?

A glider is designed to increase lift so that it stays in the air longer — even if it doesn't travel as quickly.

Straw Glider

This glider may not look like much, but it can fly farther than most paper airplanes.

Do It!

Supplies

Straw, Paper, Ruler, Scissors, Tape

1. Cut a strip of paper 10 inches long and 1 inch wide.

2. Cut another strip 5 inches long and 1 inch wide, and then tape the strips into a hoop.

3. Tape a hoop to each end of the straw, making sure the straw is inside the hoops and the hoops are on the same side of the straw.

4. Hold the straw in the middle, with the hoops on top, and throw it like a spear. How long does the straw glider stay in the air? How far does it glide?

What's Happening?

This glider's hoops provide lift to keep it in the air, and with no wings, there's practically no drag.

28 Balloon Flinker

When an object floats and sinks at the same time, it's called a flinker.

═ Do It! ═

Supplies

Helium balloon with a string or ribbon; Paper cup; Scissors; Small objects of different weights; Clock or stopwatch

1. Use the scissors to poke small holes on opposite sides of the cup near the top.
2. Thread the string from the helium balloon through both holes and tie the end back to the string above the cup. The cup should hang from the balloon like a hot-air-balloon basket.
3. Add small objects to the cup until the balloon can flink — or hang mid-air — for at least 30 seconds.

What's Happening?

A flinker equalizes the forces so that gravity pulls down just as much as the buoyant force pushes up. So the flinker just stays where it is, stuck in mid-air!

29 Hot-air Balloon

Use an ordinary toaster to turn a garbage bag into a hot-air balloon. **ADULT NEEDED**

═ Do It! ═

Supplies

Toaster, 2 pieces of poster board, Tape, Lightweight kitchen-size garbage bag

1. Unplug the toaster and clean out any crumbs, and then put the toaster on the floor and plug it back in.
2. Tape the poster board together to make a tube that fits around the toaster but does not touch it.
3. Turn on the toaster and place the poster board tube over it. Be careful, the toaster will get hot!
4. Slide the garbage bag over the tube and wait for the toaster to heat up the air in the bag. The bag will gradually inflate, lift up off the poster board, and fly up to the ceiling! If the bag tips over, put a couple pieces of tape on opposite sides of the bag to give weight and balance to the bottom of the bag. Don't forget to turn off the toaster after the hot-air balloon lifts off!

What's Happening?

As the toaster heats up the air in the bag, the air molecules move farther apart and push some of that air out of the bag. Soon, the air in the bag is less dense than the air in the rest of the room, and the bag begins to float. As the air cools, the bag falls back to the ground.

Sled Kite

A sled kite is the easiest to get up into the air and keep flying in even the lightest breeze.

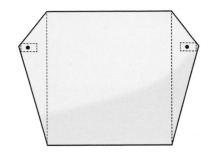

Supplies

White plastic garbage bag, Pen, Ruler, Scissors, Tape, Hole punch, 2 12-inch bamboo skewers or straws, Paper clip

Do It!

1. Cut off the bottom of the garbage bag and down one side so you have a large single layer of white plastic.
2. Use the ruler and pen to draw a 12" x 9" rectangle in the center of the plastic, with the shorter side on top.
3. Measure 4 inches down from the top and draw a line across the rectangle so it extends exactly 4½ inches past the longer sides on each end.
4. Connect this point to the corners on that side of the rectangle, so you have a six-sided shape.
5. Cut out the shape.
6. Tape the skewers to the long sides of the rectangle, and then place a small piece of tape on both sides of the corners of the flaps outside of the skewers.
7. Use the hole punch to carefully put a hole in the tape, just in from the corner.
8. Cut a 36-inch piece of string, and tie one end of the string to each of the holes.
9. Tie one end of the rest of the string onto the stick and wrap all the string onto the stick.
10. Tie a paper clip onto the loose end of the string, and then hook the paper clip onto the loop of string tied to the holes. You're ready to fly your kite!

What's Happening?

To launch a kite, hold it up in the air and run as fast as you can as you let go of the kite. If you're lucky, a breeze will catch the kite and carry it up to the sky.

With a sled kite, the air inflates the kite, giving it a rounded shape like a wing. The air flowing over the kite has to go farther to get over the curve, so it moves faster than the air under the kite. Thanks to Bernoulli, we know that the still air has higher air pressure and pushes up harder than the fast-moving, low-pressure air pushes down. As long as there is wind or moving air, the kite will stay high in the sky!

What If?

What if you make your kite twice as big? Or even three times as big? Will it still fly?

Cool Diamond Kite

Did you know Benjamin Franklin tied a kite string to his foot while floating in a pond to see if the kite could pull him across the water?

Supplies

2 bamboo skewers, String, Tape, Scissors, Plastic bag, Stick, Paper clip

Do It!

1. Lay the bamboo skewers in a T shape so the crosswise skewer is about ⅓ of the way from the top of the lengthwise skewer.

2. Tie the skewers together securely with string.

3. Cut open the plastic bag so you have a single layer, lay the skewers on top of the bag, and cut out a diamond shape slightly longer and wider than the skewers.

4. Use string or tape to securely attach the corners of the bag to the ends of the skewers.

5. Cut a piece of string 20 inches long and tie one end to the top of your kite and the other to the bottom of the kite.

6. Cut another piece of string 36 inches long and tie it to the bottom of the kite.

7. Cut six 6-inch strips from the rest of the plastic bag. Tie the strips onto the string several inches apart to make the tail of your kite.

8. Tie one end of the rest of the string onto the stick, and then wrap all the string onto the stick.

9. Tie a paper clip onto the loose end of the string.

10. Hook the paper clip onto the loop of string attached to the top and bottom of the kite. You are ready to fly your kite!

11. Take your kite outside in an open space, hopefully on a day with a good breeze. Never fly your kite during a thunderstorm or near electrical lines. Slowly unroll the string as the wind takes your kite up, up, and up!

What's Happening?

The key to keeping a kite in the air is the tail. Wind gives the kite lift, but it can also cause the kite to roll and turn. A tail adds weight to the bottom of the kite to keep it from rolling or spinning, which can tangle up the string or cause your kite to crash. Most kite flyers recommend a tail that is three to eight times longer than the length of the kite.

What If?

What if you use a long ribbon for a tail? What about more than one ribbon? What other materials or configurations can you use for a kite tail?

Paper Bag Kite

Have a blast with this easy-to-assemble flyer!

Supplies

Large brown paper grocery bag, 2 straws, String, Scissors, Tape, Glue, Stick, Paper clip, Paper streamer or tissue paper, Markers or crayons (optional)

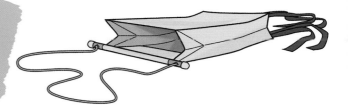

Do It!

1. Make a slit about 1 inch long on one end of a straw, then squeeze the straw and slide it into the other straw.
2. Use tape to secure the two straws together.
3. Cut the two short sides and one long side of the paper bag so you have a flap left on the bottom.
4. Fold the flap out and lay the straws where the flap meets the bag, centering the straws so there is at least an inch sticking out on either side of the bag.
5. Glue the straws in place, and then fold the flap into the bag and glue it down, as well.
6. Cut a length of string three times longer than the width of the paper bag.
7. Squeeze one end of the straw and use the scissors to snip a tiny triangle out of a side of the straw, near the middle.
8. Thread one end of the string through the hole and out the end of the straw and tie the string in place, and then use a piece of tape or some glue to hold it in place.
9. Repeat this process with the other end of the straw and the other end of the string.
10. Cut eight streamers from tissue paper or other lightweight material you might have handy. The streamers should be about three times longer than your kite.
11. Glue or tape two streamers inside each corner of the top of the bag.
12. Tie one end of the rest of the string onto the stick and wrap all the string onto the stick.
13. Tie a paper clip onto the loose end of the string, and hook the paper clip onto the loop of string attached to the straws. You're ready to fly your kite!
14. Take your kite outside in an open space, hopefully on a day with a good breeze. Slowly unroll the string as the wind takes your kite up, up, and up!

What's Happening?

As long as there is some wind, faster-moving air moves over the kite and slower-moving air moves inside and under the kite. Bernoulli's principle states that the slower-moving air pushes harder than the faster-moving air, giving your kite lift and keeping it in the air.

What If?

What if you use a paper lunch bag? Does the smaller bag fly more easily?

33 Perfect Parachute

Have you ever wondered how a parachute can allow someone to jump from a plane at astounding heights and land safely on the ground? Make a parachute yourself to figure it out!

Supplies

Large plastic garbage bag, Scissors, Ruler, String, Tape, Action figure or another toy with similar weight, Stopwatch, A friend to run the stopwatch

Do It!

1. Cut down one side of the garbage bag and open it up to make a large sheet of plastic.
2. Cut out a 24" x 24" square from the plastic, then cut four pieces of string, each 24 inches long.
3. Tape one string to each corner of the square.
4. Gather the other ends of the string and tie a knot at the end.
5. Use another piece of string and tape if needed to attach the action figure to the end of the four strings.
6. Find a high place to drop the parachute from, such as over a staircase or from the top of a jungle gym, and hold the parachute open so the action figure hangs down.
7. Drop the parachute and time how long it takes to reach the ground.
8. Remove the action figure and drop it from the same height without a parachute. What is the difference between the times with and without a parachute?

What's Happening?

Gravity pulls the parachute and action figure downward. At the beginning of the fall, the parachute expands and fills with air. As they fall, air continually pushes out the edges of the parachute and new air pushes in as everything moves downward.

The effect is air pushing upward on the parachute, called air resistance, which acts against gravity and slows the fall of the action figure. The force of air resistance increases as the parachute falls faster until it exactly equals gravity. From then on, the parachute and action figure will fall at a constant speed, called terminal velocity, until they reach the ground.

What If?

What if instead of an action figure you attach a raw egg? Can you drop the egg with a parachute so that it does not break?

Dragonfly Helicopter

The Chinese invented this toy thousands of years ago and called it the "bamboo dragonfly."

Do It!

Supplies

Straw,
Scissors,
Cardstock
or light
cardboard like
a cereal box,
Stapler, Ruler

1. Cut two pieces of cardstock ¾ inch wide and 4 inches long.
2. Flatten one end of the straw and cut a ½-inch slit down the center.
3. Slide the two pieces of cardstock together into the slit and staple them to the straw.
4. Fold and crease the cardstock down and at an angle to make the propeller.
5. Open the blades of the propeller up so the two sides are straight out but slightly angled.
6. To launch the helicopter, hold the straw between your open hands with the propeller on top. Slide your hands in opposite directions to spin the straw and watch the helicopter take off!

What's Happening?

As a helicopter propeller moves through the air, the air underneath the wing pushes up more than the air on top pushes down. Unlike airplane wings, a propeller can hover.

Homemade Hovercraft

No need to search the skies for alien ships - you can build your own hovercraft!

Do It!

Supplies

CD or DVD
(that doesn't
need to be used
again), Pop
top bottle top
(from a sports
drink bottle or
dishwashing soap
bottle), Craft
glue, Balloon

1. Glue the bottle top onto the CD directly over the hole in the center.
2. Once the glue is dry, blow up the balloon.
3. Pinch the balloon closed with one hand while you use the other to stretch the opening over the bottle top.
4. Place the hovercraft on a flat surface, such as a hard floor.
5. Pull open the bottle top and let go of the balloon. Watch your hovercraft glide smoothly over the floor! How long does it glide before the balloon runs out of air?

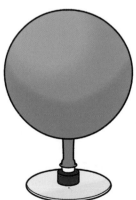

What's Happening?

Hovercrafts don't hover far off the ground, but they do move around easily with very little friction. In this experiment, the air from the balloon pushes down through the bottle top to create a thin layer of air between the hovercraft and the floor. This air eliminates almost all the friction between the floor and CD so it can glide around.

Stomp Rocket

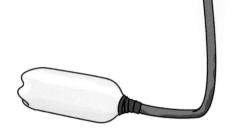

Shoot off a paper rocket with this bigger version of the squeeze rocket on page 39.

Rockets & Explosions

Supplies

Empty 2-liter bottle, Bicycle inner tube, Duct tape, 2 pieces of printer paper, Scissors, Clear tape

Do It!

Make the Launcher

1. Cut the valve off of the bicycle tube so you have a long, straight tube about 2 feet long.
2. Stretch one end of the tube over the mouth of the bottle.
3. Wrap duct tape around the tube and bottle so that it's secure and won't pop off when you stomp on the bottle.
4. Roll up one piece of paper longways as tight as you can so that you have a long, thin tube.
5. Use the clear tape to tape the paper along the length of the tube so that it stays securely in place.
6. Slide the paper tube into the end of the inner tube.
7. Use duct tape to hold it in place and seal the connection so no air can escape.

Make the Rocket

1. Cut the second piece of paper in half longways.
2. Wrap one half around the paper tube on the launcher.
3. Tape the rocket tube so it doesn't unroll and slide it off of the launcher tube.
4. Cut 2 inches off the rocket tube so that it is a bit shorter than your launcher tube.
5. Use the other half of the paper to make a nose cone and fins.
6. To make a nose cone, cut out a half circle, roll it up into a cone and tape it to the top of your rocket.
7. To make fins, cut out three triangles, and fold a tab on one side that you can tape to the rocket.

To launch your rocket, slide the rocket onto the launch tube. Have your friend hold the bottom of the launch tube (but not the rocket!) pointed upward. Stomp as hard as you can on the bottle and watch your rocket fly!

What's Happening?

This rocket uses Newton's first law of motion. When you stomp on the bottle, air is pushed very quickly through the tube and into your rocket, pushing it up. Because your rocket is so light, this large force on a small mass makes your rocket accelerate to a great speed. The more force you use when you stomp, the faster your rocket flies, and the higher it will go.

Underwater Volcano

Not all volcanoes are on mountaintops. In fact, there are millions of underwater volcanoes in oceans all over the world!

ADULT NEEDED

Supplies

Glass measuring cup, Small candle, Sand, Water, Stove or hot plate

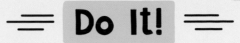 **Do It!**

1. Place the candle in the bottom of the cup. Carefully cover the candle with sand.
2. Pour water into the cup so that it's almost to the top.
3. Place the cup on the stove or hot plate and turn the heat on medium.
4. Watch your sand volcano erupt! (Don't forget to turn off the stove when your volcano is done.)

What's Happening?

As the wax heats up and melts, you will see a bump form in the sand layer. When the wax gets hot enough, the bump will erupt and hot wax will flow through the sand and float to the top of the water. This is exactly what happens in a real volcano. Magma from the hot core of the Earth heats up and expands so that it pushes up through the earth and becomes lava. When the lava, just like the wax, hits the water, it cools and hardens.

Ketchup Volcano

Use ketchup to make your lava and eruption look more like the real thing!

Supplies

Plastic cup; Newspaper, tape, clay and paint (optional); Baking dish; Ketchup; Baking soda; Dish soap; Bowl; Mixing spoon; Measuring spoon; Measuring cup

 **Do It!**

1. Use a plastic cup, newspaper, and tape to make the form for your volcano. Cover this with clay if you want.
2. Put your plastic cup volcano in a baking dish.
3. In a bowl, mix a cup (or more) of ketchup, a squirt of dish soap and ½ cup of water. Pour this into the plastic cup volcano.
4. Add 2 tablespoons of baking soda.

What's Happening?

Ketchup is made with vinegar, which reacts with the baking soda to make carbon dioxide gas. The gas gets trapped in the soap, creating a bubbly volcano!

39 Drink Bottle Rocket

Do this experiment outdoors, as a powerful explosion really sends this rocket flying.

ADULT NEEDED

Supplies

Sports bottle with pop-open cap, Ceramic mug, Effervescent tablet (such as Alka Seltzer), Water

Do It!

1. Have an adult help you find a safe outdoor place to launch your rocket.
2. Fill the bottle about half full with warm water.
3. Put half of an effervescent tablet in the rocket, and shake it up for just two seconds. Quickly place the bottle upside down in the mug.
4. Wait. In about 10 to 30 seconds, your rocket will shoot. Warning: Do not pick up the rocket or place your face or any body part above the rocket. You could get hurt.

What's Happening?

The tablet is made of citric acid, the same acid found in lemons and oranges, and sodium bicarbonate, also known as baking soda. When these two chemicals mix in the water, they react to create carbon dioxide gas inside your rocket. As more and more gas is created, the pressure builds. When the cover can't hold anymore, it pops out and all the gas goes rushing out.

40 Geyser

When it comes to eruptions, volcanoes get all of the attention, but geysers can produce some pretty amazing explosions too!

Supplies

Funnel, Pot (that's as tall as the funnel), 3-foot-long plastic tubing, Water

Do It!

1. Put the funnel in the pot with the large end facing down.
2. Fill the pot with water.
3. Slide one end of the tube under the funnel. You may need to hold the funnel down if it floats.
4. Blow into the other end of the tube, and watch the water fly up out of the geyser! How high can you make the water shoot out of the spout?

What's Happening?

Real geysers are caused by funnel-shaped cracks underground that are filled with water. When water at the bottom of the funnel gets so hot that it boils, the bubbles of steam rise to the surface and shoot out of the geyser, along with the water at the top of the funnel.

Experi-mint Explosion

You've probably shaken up a bottle of soda and opened it up to watch it spray all over the place. (And if you haven't, you should!) In this experiment, you will add mint candies to the soda for an explosion that will blow you away. This experiment is very messy and best performed outdoors.

Supplies

2-liter bottle of soda, 12 Mentos mints, Paper, Index card, Tape, Measuring cup, Rain poncho (optional)

═ Do It! ═

1. Find an outside area to launch your rocket. Roll and tape the piece of paper into a tube about 1 inch wide. Make sure the mints fit in the tube. Slide 12 mints into the tube and put the index card under the tube so they don't fall out.

2. Do the next steps quickly to get a larger explosion. You can put the poncho on now if you are worried about getting sprayed with soda!

3. Carefully open the bottle of soda. Place the index card and tube of mints on top of the bottle opening.

4. Quickly slide out the index card so the mints drop in the soda bottle. Make a run for it or you will be covered with soda!

5. After the soda explosion, carefully pour the soda that's left in the bottle into a measuring cup. How much soda was left in the bottle?

6. A 2-liter bottle has about 8.45 cups of liquid. Subtract the amount left in the bottle from 8.45 cups to get the amount of soda that exploded out of the bottle.

What's Happening?

Soda gets its fizz from the carbon dioxide gas dissolved in the soda. When you open a bottle of soda, you can hear the fizz and see the bubbles of gas. If you shake up the bottle first, there's more fizz and bubbles because the gas is released faster. Adding the mints just makes the bubbles come out of the soda even faster. The gas comes out so fast that it takes most of the soda with it, making an awesome explosion.

If you look closely at the outside of the mints, you can see tiny little holes that feel chalky. This texture and the ingredients in the mints help break up the hold that the soda has on the carbon dioxide gas. Other flavors of mints don't work as well because they have a smooth, waxy coating that keeps them from dissolving and freeing the carbon dioxide gas.

What If?

What if you use a different type of soda? Try different flavors, including regular and diet.

Do different flavors of mints also cause explosions? Other materials give similar (or even bigger!) explosions. Try rock salt, table salt, and Wintergreen LifeSavers.

42 Water Bottle Rocket

Pump up this rocket with a ball pump and it will fly past the treetops!
Fair warning: You're likely to get wet with this one!

ADULT NEEDED

Supplies

Empty 2-liter soda bottle; Cork that fits tightly in the bottle (if your cork is too small, wrap tape around it); Ball pump with a needle; Garden pitchfork, rake, or shovel with a handle; Water

═ Do It! ═

1. With an adult's help, push the needle of the ball pump all the way through the cork so that it comes out the other end.

2. Push the rake or pitchfork into the ground so that the handle is near the ground at a slight angle. If you don't have a tool with a handle, you can use branches or something similar to make a launch pad for your rocket.

3. Fill about a quarter of the bottle with water. Seal the bottle with the cork.

4. Place your rocket on the launch pad so that the neck of the bottle goes through the handle, which supports your rocket. The cork and ball pump will be underneath the handle.

5. Carefully and steadily pump up your bottle while keeping the bottle lined up on the launch pad.

6. Keep pumping until the cork pops off and the rocket shoots into the air!

What's Happening?

As you push air into the bottle rocket with the pump, the air pressure builds up until the cork can no longer hold it in. The air and water come rushing down and the rocket goes shooting up. This demonstrates Newton's third law: every force (the air and water rushing down) has an equal and opposite force (the rocket shooting up).

Newton's second law is also at work here: acceleration equals the force divided by the mass. The bottle and water feel the same force, but because the bottle has a much smaller mass than the water and air, it has a much greater acceleration.

What If?

What if you add more or less water to the bottle? What is the ideal amount of water for the highest flight?

Add a nose cone and fins to your rocket to make it more aerodynamic. Does this make it fly higher? You can even add a parachute so that the rocket will stay in the air longer on the way down.

Balloon Rocket

You can launch this rocket indoors. Make two or more and have balloon rocket races with your friends!

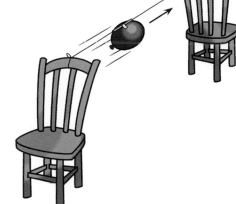

Supplies

Long piece of string (10 to 15 feet long), 2 chairs (or other objects about the same height and 10 to 15 feet apart), Straight straw, Tape, Balloons, Scissors

Do It!

1. Tie one end of the string to one of the chairs.
2. Slide the straw onto the string, and then tie the other end to the other chair, 10 to 15 feet away. Make sure the string is taut and straight.
3. Put a piece of tape across the top of the straw.
4. Blow up one of the balloons. Hold the end closed but do not tie it off.
5. Put the balloon under the straw and use the tape to attach the balloon to the straw.
6. Slide your balloon rocket all the way to one end of the string so that the open end of the balloon is close to one of the chairs.
7. Release the balloon and watch it fly! Does it get all the way to the other chair?
8. Blow up the balloon and try again, or set up two strings and have balloon rocket races with a friend.

What's Happening?

When you blow up a balloon, you're creating a much higher air pressure inside the balloon than outside. When you release the balloon, the air rushes out and pushes the balloon in the opposite direction. If you just blow up a balloon and let it go, the balloon will fly all over the room in all directions (try it!). By attaching the balloon to the straw and string, you can control which way the air flies out of the balloon and which direction the balloon flies. The balloon rocket will keep moving until all of the air is out of the balloon.

What If?

What if you use different sizes and shapes of balloons? Use a stopwatch to see which balloon makes it to the other end of the string in the shortest amount of time.

Can your balloon rocket carry cargo? Use a cereal box to make a small, lightweight box to carry small toys or even candy from one end of the string to the other.

44 Lemon Juice Bottle Rocket

Ready for a rocket launch with a bang? Prepare for lift-off!

Supplies

Empty 16-ounce plastic soda or water bottle, Cork that fits tightly in the bottle (if your cork is too small, wrap tape around it), Toilet paper, Lemon juice, Baking soda, Measuring spoon, Water, Scissors, Funnel

Do It!

1. Find a place outdoors to launch your rocket.

2. Use the funnel to pour lemon juice into the bottle so that it's about an inch deep.

3. Then pour water into your bottle so that it's half full.

4. Put 1 teaspoon of baking soda into the center of a square of toilet paper.

5. Fold up the toilet paper to make a little packet.

6. Drop the baking soda packet into the bottle and close it up with the cork.

7. Shake up the bottle and stand back. Within a few seconds your cork rocket will lift off!

What's Happening?

As the water and lemon juice soak through the toilet paper, the acid in the lemon juice reacts with the baking soda to produce carbon dioxide gas. As the gas pressure builds up in the bottle, it pushes the cork out with a bang and sends it shooting into the air!

What If?

What if you use more lemon juice? Or more baking soda? Try other acids, such as soft drinks and vinegar. What if you use a different-sized bottle?

Tea Bag Rocket

This gentle rocket is more like a hot air balloon than a space rocket, but it's still fun to launch!

ADULT NEEDED

Supplies

Tea bag,
Matches,
Ceramic plate,
Scissors

Do It!

1. Cut open the top of the tea bag and dump out the tea.
2. Open up the empty tea bag to a tube shape, and stand it on the ceramic plate.
3. Have an adult use the lighter to light the top of the tea bag. The bag will burn down to the bottom and then fly up into the air!

What's Happening?

When you light the tea bag at the top, it traps air inside the bag. The hot air expands so that the hot air inside the bag is less dense than the cooler air outside the bag. The more dense air outside of the bag pushes up through the bottom of the bag, causing the air inside the bag to move upward. This movement of hot and cool air is called convection. As the bag burns completely into ash, it becomes light enough to be launched upward by this air current.

Squeeze Rockets

This portable rocket is powered simply by the strength of your hands!

Do It!

Supplies

Plastic bottle,
Modeling clay, 2
straws of different
sizes (one should fit
inside the other)

1. Put one end of the smaller straw in the opening of the bottle so that most of the straw is out of the bottle.
2. Use a bit of the modeling clay to hold the straw in place and seal the top of the bottle.
3. Put a small piece of modeling clay in one end of the larger straw to seal it off, as well.
4. Slide the larger straw over the smaller straw and squeeze the bottle as hard and quickly as you can.

What's Happening?

This rocket makes use of Newton's first law of motion: An object will stay at rest (or moving in a straight line and constant speed) unless a force acts on it. In this case, when you squeeze the bottle, you're applying force to the bottle, which then pushes the air inside the bottle, which in turn pushes out the rocket straw.

47 Chemical Clock

Molecules mingle in a chemical reaction. You can see it happen right before your eyes!

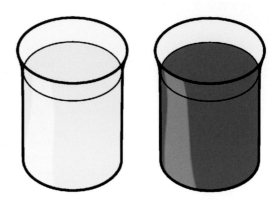

Supplies

3 clear cups, 1 non-chewable Vitamin C tablet (1000 mg, or two 500 mg tablets), Tincture of iodine (2%), Hydrogen peroxide, Liquid laundry starch or corn starch, Warm water, Measuring spoon, Measuring cup, Resealable plastic bag, Spoon, Masking tape, Marker, Safety goggles

═ Do It! ═

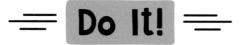

1. Wear safety goggles for this experiment. Be careful handling iodine because it stains.
2. Place the Vitamin C tablet in the plastic bag and seal it tightly. Crush the tablet into a powder with the back of a spoon.
3. Pour the powder into one of the cups and mix it with ¼ cup of warm water. Stir until the powder is dissolved. Use the masking tape and marker to label the cup "Vitamin C."
4. In the second cup, add 1 teaspoon from the "Vitamin C" cup, ¼ cup of warm water, and 1 teaspoon of the tincture of iodine. Label the cup "Vitamin C + Iodine."
5. In the third cup, mix ¼ cup of warm water, 1 tablespoon of hydrogen peroxide, and ½ teaspoon of liquid laundry starch. Label this cup "Hydrogen Peroxide + Starch."
6. Pour the liquid from the "Vitamin C + Iodine" cup into the "Hydrogen Peroxide + Starch" cup. Quickly pour the mixture back and forth between the cups until they're mixed well.
7. Set the cups down and watch. After several seconds, you will see a big change in the liquid!
8. After the experiment, pour the liquids down the drain with plenty of water. Do not keep the liquids.

What's Happening?

This chemical reaction is known as the "iodine clock reaction," because you can control the amount of time it takes the solution to turn blue, also known as the reaction time. When you mix the solutions together, there are two chemical reactions occurring at the same time. Iodine reacts with both the Vitamin C and the starch. Iodine and Vitamin C creates a clear liquid, but iodine and starch creates a blue liquid. As soon as all the Vitamin C has been used up, the rest of the iodine immediately reacts with the starch to create a dark blue liquid. Increasing or decreasing the amount of Vitamin C is one way to control the reaction time.

Hourglass

In the Middle Ages, an hourglass was an accurate measure of time. Now you can make your own.

Do It!

1. Remove the labels from both bottles.
2. Fill one bottle half full of sand.
3. Trace a circle on the cardboard using the opening of the other bottle.
4. Cut out the circle. Punch a hole in the middle.
5. Place the circle on top of the sand-filled bottle. Put the empty bottle upside down on top of the circle.
6. Secure the bottles together with tape.
7. Flip the hourglass and watch the sand drain from one bottle into the other. How long does it take for the sand to fall?

Supplies

2 2-liter bottles, Cardboard, Pencil, Scissors, Hole punch, Sand, Duct tape

What's Happening?

The size of the bottle, the hole, and the size of the sand all affect the accuracy of an hourglass. Large-grain sand won't flow as quickly as fine-grain sand.

Equatorial Sundial

What time is it? Time to create a sundial clock and find out!

Do It!

Supplies

Cardboard, Scissors, Ruler, Protractor, Pencil, Modeling clay, Map or the Internet, Compass

1. Cut out a 6" x 6" cardboard square.
2. Draw a line across the center of the square using a ruler.
3. With a protractor, draw lines every 15 degrees on one side of the line. Turn the square. Now the lines are on the bottom half.
4. Label both ends of the center line "6." On the left, label the lines in descending order (6, 5, 4…).
5. Label the center line at the bottom "12." Continue in descending order (12, 11, 10…) until you reach 6 on the other side.
6. Poke a pencil through the center of the square where the lines meet.
7. Use a map or the Internet to find your latitude. With a protractor, adjust the pencil so that the angle between the cardboard and the surface it's sitting on is the same angle as your latitude.
8. Hold the cardboard and pencil in place with clay. When your sundial faces north, the pencil will point at the North Star.
9. Set the sundial outside facing directly north. The pencil's shadow will indicate the time. How accurate is your sundial?

What's Happening?

The angle of this sundial is parallel to the Earth's equator. The sun takes a different path through the sky depending on how far away you are from the equator.

50 Liquid Hourglass

This timer is like a sand hourglass, except it uses two liquids instead of sand and air.

Supplies

2 water bottles with caps, Scissors (or a hammer and nail),
Glue, Straw from a drink box, Tape, Food coloring, Water,
Vegetable oil, Stopwatch, Masking tape, Marker

Do It!

1. Remove the labels and caps from the bottles.
2. Glue the two caps together, top to top. Wrap tape around them to secure them.
3. With the scissors or a hammer and nail, poke two holes inside the caps that go all the way through.
4. Cut the straw in half. Poke one piece of straw through each hole. One straw should stick out more on one side, and the other more on the other side.
5. Fill one bottle to the top with water. Add a couple drops of food coloring and shake the bottle gently to mix the color.
6. Screw one side of your glued-together caps onto the bottle of water.
7. Fill the other bottle to the top with vegetable oil.
8. Quickly flip the bottle of water and screw the other side of the glued-together caps onto the bottle of oil. Once the bottles are secured tightly together, you will see bubbles of oil float upward, and bubbles of water sink to the bottom.
9. Place a strip of masking tape along the length of the bottom bottle. Mark the water/oil level each minute. Does the same amount of water and oil bubble through each minute?

What's Happening?

Water is denser than oil. As the water in the top bottle bubbles down, the lighter oil bubbles up. Because there is no extra space in the bottle, the water and oil switch places at the same rate. As more oil and water switch places, the weight of the liquid changes too. This causes the bubbles to move up and down more rapidly until all the oil is in the top bottle and all the water is in the bottom bottle.

What If?

What if you use wider or narrower straws, or different-shaped bottles? What if you use different liquids with the oil, such as corn syrup or soap? Do these factors affect the rate that the bubbles move between the bottles?

Pendulum Timer

Galileo was the first to see the potential of pendulums for keeping time. Today, we use pendulums in grandfather clocks.

Supplies

2 chairs, Broom, String, Scissors, Washers or small weights, Stopwatch

Do It!

1. Place the chairs back to back about 2 feet apart. Lay the broom across the backs of the chairs.
2. Cut a piece of string 18 inches long. Tie one end to the middle of the broom.
3. Tie three washers to the end of the string. Pull the string back and watch it swing.
4. Time how long it takes to swing back and forth once. Adjust the length of string, number of weights, and how far back you pull so that it takes one second to swing back and forth.

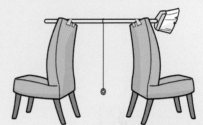

What's Happening?

It doesn't matter how much weight you use or how far back you pull the pendulum. Those two factors don't change how fast it swings. The length of the string is what makes a difference. A longer string will swing slower, and a shorter string will swing faster.

Water Timer

In ancient Greece, a clepsydra —or water timer—was used to time short events.

Do It!

Supplies

2 2-liter bottles with straight sides, Scissors, Water, Marker, Masking tape, Stopwatch

1. Remove the bottle labels. Cut the top off one of the bottles so only the straight sides remain.
2. Place a strip of tape along the length of the bottle.
3. Poke a small hole in the bottom of the other bottle.
4. Fill the uncut bottle with water and place it inside the cut bottle.
5. Start timing as soon as the water drips. Mark the water level on the tape each minute. Time the drips for five minutes.
6. Remove the top bottle and dump out the remaining water. To use your water timer, pour the water from the bottom bottle into the top. Then wait for it to drip down.

What's Happening?

The weight of the water and the outside air pressure push the water through the hole. The amount of water that drips in one minute depends on the size of the hole. Stop the water by tightening the top bottle lid. Water will drip just until the air pressure outside the bottle balances with the weight of the water inside the bottle. The water will stop dripping until you loosen the top.

Perception of Time

Time flies when you're having fun, but why does it seem to drag when you're taking a math test?

Supplies

Stopwatch or clock, At least 5 friends, A game or book that your friends enjoy

Do It!

1. You will need to do this experiment with each friend separately. Make sure everyone is out of the room except you and one of your friends.

2. Have your friend sit down. Ask them to remain quiet and tell you when one minute has passed. Start the stopwatch and tell your friend to start. When your friend tells you that a minute is up, make note of the actual time on the stopwatch.

3. Next, play a game with your friend or have them read a book they enjoy. Ask them to tell you again when one minute has passed. Start the stopwatch and tell your friend to start. When your friend tells you that a minute is up, make note of the actual time on the stopwatch.

4. Repeat this process with your other friends. How close were they to one minute? Did they guess longer or shorter when they were sitting still? How about when they were playing a game or reading a book?

What's Happening?

Scientists have come up with a theory for why time flies when you are having fun — and drags when you are bored. Brain scans have shown that brain activity changes depending on how we focus on a task. Concentrating on time passing, like when you're bored, will trigger brain activity, which will make it seem as though the clock is ticking more slowly. When you concentrate on an activity you enjoy, the brain focuses on that activity instead of the passing of time. This means that time doesn't just fly when you're having fun, but even when you're busy doing something you don't enjoy, like homework or mowing the lawn.

What If?

What if you compare boys and girls? Are girls better or worse at estimating time than boys? What if you compare kids and adults? Do strategies for measuring time work, such as counting seconds with "1-Mississippi, 2-Mississippi, 3-Mississippi"? Does time estimation change with the time of day, or with certain activities like reading or doing math problems?

Brain & Body

Do experiments on your own body! Explore your senses, fool your brain, keep your balance, and make some noise.

Touch Your Toes

54

Can you touch your toes without falling on your face?

Do It!

Supplies

Wall

1. Stand away from the wall and bend forward to touch your toes. You can bend your knees if you want. Did you have any trouble?

2. Stand with your back against the wall. Place your heels all the way against the wall and keep your feet flat on the ground.

3. Bend forward and touch your toes. You can bend your knees but keep your feet flat and against the wall. Can you do it without falling on your face? Can you bend your body another way to touch your toes without falling over?

What's Happening?

When you bend over to touch your toes without a wall, your bottom pushes out behind you to keep your center of gravity over your feet. When you are up against the wall and bend forward, you can't move your center of gravity back over your feet and you fall over. This means you need to find a different way to reach your toes. Try bending your knees and sliding your hands down your side.

55 Balancing Butterfly

Make your own pet butterfly that balances on your finger.

Supplies

Cardstock, Scissors, 2 large coins or washers, Toothpick, Tape, Crayons or markers

═ Do It! ═

1. Cut out a butterfly shape on the cardstock. Use crayons or markers to decorate it.
2. Tape the toothpick under the body so that one end sticks out slightly above the head.
3. Tape the coins near the top of each wing.
4. Place the end of the toothpick on your finger. The butterfly balances!

What's Happening?

The shape of the butterfly is made so that the tops of the wings are much higher than the head. The weight of the coins bend the wings downward just slightly so that the wings hang down just below the head. The added weight of the coins also moves the center of gravity of the paper butterfly to just below the tip of the toothpick. This allows the butterfly to balance perfectly on the tip of your finger. You can even bounce your finger gently up and down and the butterfly won't fall off.

Leg Lift

How well can you balance on just one leg?

Do It!

Wall

1. Stand away from the wall. Lift one leg a few inches out to the side, away from your body. Did you have any trouble balancing?
2. Stand with one side of your body as close as you can to the wall. Press your arm against the wall while you lift the leg that is away from the wall out to the side. Are you able to keep your arm against the wall and your leg raised?

What's Happening?

When you stand on the ground with two feet, your center of gravity is in the middle of your feet. When you lift one foot outward, you need to shift your center of gravity over so it is over the foot on the ground. However, by raising your foot out away from the wall, you are moving your center of gravity even farther from the foot that's still on the ground. This means you must lean in the other direction to keep from falling. When you are against the wall, this is not possible and you fall over.

Chair Pickup

Standing up while holding a chair is not as easy as it sounds!

Do It!

Supplies

Wall, Chair
that you can
lift easily

1. With your shoes on, stand two shoe lengths from the wall. Place the chair between you and the wall.
2. Bend at the waist so that your body makes a right angle and your head is resting against the wall.
3. Hold onto the seat of the chair and lift the chair.
4. Keep both feet flat and try to stand up. Can you stand up with the chair, or are you glued to the wall?

What's Happening?

When you bend over and pick up the chair, the chair becomes a part of you. Scientists call this a system. The you-chair system's center of gravity is no longer your belly button. Because you now have a weight in front of you, your center of gravity shifts to somewhere between your belly button and the wall. Chances are, this spot is not over your feet and you need the wall to keep you from falling forward. That is why it feels like your head is glued to the wall when you try to stand up.

58 Bottle Bump

Can you touch a bottle with your nose?

 ## Do It!

Supplies

Empty plastic bottle

1. Kneel on the floor and place one elbow in front of your knee so that your hands point straight out in front of your body along the floor.
2. Place the empty bottle right at your fingertips.
3. Place both of your hands behind your back.
4. Without using your hands, lean forward and nudge the bottle with your nose. Can you reach the bottle, or do you fall on your face?

What's Happening?

In this situation, your center of gravity is at the edge of your knees. If your center of gravity is just the smallest bit above your belly button, you will not be able to touch the bottle without falling on your face. If your center of gravity is lower, you will just be able to reach the bottle with the tip of your nose *and* keep your center of gravity over your knees. In general, adult women have a lower center of gravity and can touch the bottle, while men have a higher center of gravity and usually fall. Try this with some grown-ups to see if it is true!

59 Balancing Sculpture

Use your knowledge of center of gravity to create a beautiful and delicious balancing sculpture.

Supplies

Toothpicks; Bamboo skewers; Carrot or apple cut into 1-inch pieces; Marshmallows, gummy candies, and similar foods that can easily be stuck on a skewer; Full water bottle

Do It!

1. Poke a toothpick into a marshmallow. Can you balance the toothpick on top of the water bottle? Of course not! It is very difficult to get the center of gravity of the marshmallow directly over the toothpick.
2. Poke more toothpicks and skewers into the marshmallow, and then add items to the end. Can you create a "sculpture" that balances on top of the bottle?

What's Happening?

Balancing a marshmallow with a toothpick on the bottle is nearly impossible. The small point of the toothpick and the large marshmallow makes it extremely difficult to line up the high center of gravity (in the marshmallow) over the tiny base (point of the toothpick) so that it doesn't fall over. As you create the sculpture, you will notice that hanging skewers and candies on either side of the marshmallow makes it balance much better. In this configuration, the weights on the long skewers moves the center of gravity down, under the toothpick. Instead of balancing on top, the sculpture now hangs stably below.

Balance Forks on a Toothpick

Thrill and amaze your family at dinner with this gravity-defying fork balancing trick.

Supplies

2 forks, 2 toothpicks, Saltshaker

Do It!

1. Push the forks together so that the tines are intertwined and the handles hang down.

2. Push one end of a toothpick into the center of the two forks so that the forks are almost at a right angle to the toothpick.

3. Stick one end of the other toothpick into the center hole of the saltshaker.

4. Place the tip of the toothpick in the forks on the tip of the toothpick in the saltshaker so that they balance in midair.

What's Happening?

When you combine the two forks so that their handles hang down, the center of gravity, or balance point, is somewhere just below the fork tines. If you adjust the angle of the toothpick to the forks just right, the center of gravity will be right below the other end of that toothpick. When you balance the forked toothpick on top of the toothpick in the saltshaker, the center of gravity ends up right near the lid of the saltshaker so the balancing toothpicks are very stable.

With a steady hand and a little knowledge of center of gravity, these challenges will be a piece of cake!

61 Balancing Nails

Can you balance 14 nails on the head of one nail?

Supplies

15 large nails with large heads, Wood block, Hammer

Do It!

1. Hammer one of the nails straight into the wood block so that it sticks up at least 2 inches.
2. Now balance the remaining 14 nails on the head of the nail in the block. Can you do it without reading ahead?

What's Happening?

The center of gravity of an object (or group of connected objects like nails) is the balance point, or where the weight of the object is centered. Arrange the nails symmetrically so that the center of gravity of the nails is the middle of their symmetric arrangement.

Start by laying down a single nail. Lay 12 nails across the first, alternating sides, so that the heads of the nails lie on the body of the first nail. Place the last nail over the first nail and the tops of the other nails. Pinch the top and bottom nails together at each end and lift them. You will see the other nails hang down, but they are held in place by the nail heads pulling on the top nail. Place the center of the bottom nail on top of the nail in the block. It balances!

The solution to this challenge is not to balance the nails, but to hang the nails so that the center of gravity is below the head of the single nails. Most of the weight of the 12 nails hanging down is below the head of the nail in the block.

What If?

What if you make many hanging nails and stack them on top of each other? How many nails can you fit on the head of a single nail? The world record is 255. Can you beat it?

This can looks like it's about to tip, but it's actually perfectly balanced.

Supplies

Empty soda can, Water

Do It!

1. Try to balance the soda can on its bottom edge. Can you do it without reading ahead?

What's Happening?

If you try to balance the can on its edge while it is empty, you will find that it cannot be done. Most of the mass of the can will not be over the balance point when you tilt the can. Instead, pour a small amount of water into the can and try to balance it on its edge again. Now there is more mass over the balance point, and the can will rest on its edge. Because the water keeps the shape of the can, you can even spin the can around and it will stay balanced.

Balancing a Coin　63

Can you balance a coin on the edge of a dollar?

Supplies

Dollar bill, Quarter

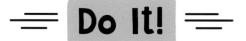
Do It!

1. Try to balance the quarter on the edge of the dollar bill while the bill is held straight out. Can you do it without reading ahead?

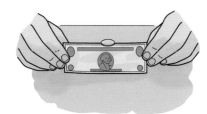

What's Happening?

Fold the bill in the middle of the long side and set it on the table. Balance the coin where the bill is bent. Grab the short ends of the bill and slowly pull outward until the bill is straight. As you pull, the coin shifts as gravity and friction push and pull on the coin. The weight of the coin pushes down on the part of the bill closest to its center of gravity. This causes more friction, so that part of the coin doesn't move until the bill supports a part of coin even closer to the center of gravity. Eventually, the edge of the bill is straight and supporting the weight of the coin right under its center of gravity. The coin is balanced on the edge of the bill! You can even lift the bill upward into the air.

What If?

What if you use a smaller or larger coin? What other objects could you balance on the edge of a dollar bill?

64 Find Your Center of Gravity

Knowing the location of your center of gravity will keep you from falling over!

Supplies

2 chairs, 2 bathroom scales, Measuring tape, 6-foot long plank, Marker, Friend, Masking tape (optional)

═ Do It! ═

1. Place the bathroom scales on the two chairs and move the chairs about 5 feet apart with the chair backs away from each other.
2. Place the plank so that each end rests on the scales and you can still read the values on the scales.
3. Carefully shift the board so that the readings on each scale are the same.
4. Measure the distance between the edges of the scales where the board is no longer supported.
5. Carefully mark the center of this distance on the board. It will be easier later if you mark all around the outside of the board.
6. Have a friend lie on their back on the plank and carefully adjust their position until the reading on both scales is equal and no part of their body is resting on anything besides the board. Where does the halfway mark on the board fall on your volunteer's body? This point is their center of gravity. If you like, mark it with a piece of masking tape.
7. Measure your friend's height and divide it by 2. Measure the distance from the floor to their center of gravity. How do these two numbers compare? Is their center of gravity high (above the halfway height) or low (below the halfway height)? How does the location of their center of gravity compare to the location of their belly button? Have your friend help you find your center of gravity too.

What's Happening?

Your center of gravity is the center of your weight distribution — the center of where gravity pulls you down. In general, toddlers have a higher center of gravity because their heads are bigger and their legs are shorter. Men generally have a higher center of gravity because they have larger shoulders, and women generally have a lower center of gravity because they have larger hips. In any case, if your center of gravity is over your base (like your feet when you are standing), you won't fall over.

Long & Thin Object

To find the center of gravity for a long and thin object, simply balance it!

Do It!

Supplies

Yardstick, Clay

1. Stick out one finger on each hand, and hold the yardstick on top of the two fingers.

2. Slide your fingers toward each other while keeping the yardstick balanced. Your fingers will meet at the balance point. Because the yardstick is uniform, its center of gravity is in the middle at 18 inches.

3. Place some clay anywhere on the yardstick except the center. Repeat the process to find the new center of gravity. Is it still in the center?

What's Happening?

Any object will balance at its center of gravity. To find the center of gravity of a long, thin object, find the point where it balances. When you slide your fingers under the yardstick, the finger closer to the center holds most of the weight until the other finger slides closer. Your fingers take turns until they are both under the center of gravity and supporting the weight together.

Flat Object

Where is the center of gravity in an odd-shaped, flat object?

Do It!

Supplies

Empty cereal box, Scissors, Hole punch, String, Key, 2 pencils

1. Cut a flat, wacky shape out of the box. Punch a hole at the top. Make another hole a quarter of the way around. Stick a pencil through one of the holes.

2. Cut a piece of string a few inches longer than the longest part of the shape. Tie the key to one end of the string. Tie the other end to the pencil that is stuck through the hole. Let the shape and string hang on the pencil. Mark the line that the string makes across the shape.

3. Move the pencil with the string to the other hole. Let the shape and string hang. Again, mark the line that the string makes. The shape's center of gravity is where the two lines cross.

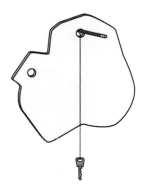

What's Happening?

An object's center of gravity is the average of where gravity pulls down. When you hang the object, this point will always go straight down, just like a small weight hanging on a string. The string shows you exactly where straight down is.

Blind Spot

Senses

Everyone has a blind spot – a point in your vision that each eye can't see. You probably don't notice because your two eyes cover for each other. Where is your blind spot and what happens when you look there?

Supplies

Index card, Markers, Ruler

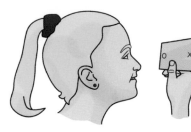

═ Do It! ═

1. On an index card, write an X on one end and make a circle near the other end.

2. Hold the card at arm's length with the X on the left. Close your left eye. Focus on the X but be aware of the circle.

3. Slowly move the card closer to your eyes until the circle disappears.

4. Use the ruler to measure how far away the blind spot is from your right eye.

5. Turn the card over, close your right eye, and repeat the process to find the blind spot for your left eye. Are the blind spots the same distance from your face?

6. Draw thick, red lines on either side of the circle, but leave some space around the circle. Use the same method as above to find your blind spot. What happens to the circle and red lines when you hold the card at your blind spot?

What's Happening?

The retina in the back of your eyeball is full of nerves connected to light and color sensors that allow you to see. However, those nerves must connect to the brain through the optic nerve to be of any use. In that small area where the optic nerve is attached to the retina, there are no light receptors. So, when you look at the exact spot that focuses on that point, you don't see anything!

Each eye's blind spots are not in the same place, so your brain combines the information from both eyes to figure out what should be there. That's why, when you hold up the card with the red lines at your blind spot, it looks like one continuous red line. Your brain is guessing that there is no break in the line because it can't see what's there with just one eye.

What If?

What if you make bigger or smaller circles? What if you put the X and O closer together or farther apart?

# Get Dizzy

Being dizzy means you cannot tell if you are moving, or still, or which direction you might be going. Some people really like the feeling of being dizzy, and others avoid it as much as they can!

Supplies

Chair that spins around, Blindfold, Friend

Do It!

1. Blindfold a friend and have them sit in the chair.
2. Quickly spin your friend around once, and then carefully stop the chair.
3. Ask your friend if they are stopped or moving. If they say moving, ask which direction. Let your friend sit for one minute or until any dizziness wears off.
4. Repeat the process, increasing the number of spins until your friend is unable to identify when the chair stops. How many spins does it take for your friend to get dizzy? Was the direction the chair was spinning the same direction your friend thought they were moving?

What's Happening?

The dizzy feeling starts in your ears. Your inner ear contains three semicircular canals that are filled with fluid. These canals don't help you hear, but they do detect how your head moves. The cupula, which is a flap in your inner ear, senses which way the fluid is moving.

The fluid starts out at rest. As you spin around on the chair, it flows through the canals and pushes open the cupula flap. When you spin around for a while, your inner ear and the fluid move together and the cupula swings back down. At this point, you do not really feel like you are moving. However, when you stop spinning, the fluid keeps going and pushes the cupula open the other way. This is what creates the feeling of spinning in the opposite direction. Your brain is confused because your ears say you are moving, but your eyes say you are still!

What If?

What if you put in earplugs? Does this affect how quickly you get dizzy? Now that you know how to get dizzy, how can you get undizzy? Try just a quarter or half a turn in the opposite direction immediately after spinning. If you are sitting still, how much time does it take for the dizziness to go away?

69 Hear Here

How well can you locate sounds?

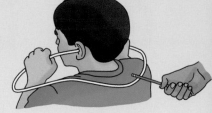

Supplies

Flexible tubing about 3 feet long, Pencil, Friend

Do It!

1. Hold the tube to each ear with the curved part behind your head.
2. Have your friend stand behind you and tap the tube with the pencil slightly closer to one ear.
3. Tell your friend which side you think the tapping sound is on. Were you right? Try tapping other places on the tube. How well can you locate which side your friend is tapping?

What's Happening?

When a sound is closer to one ear, it reaches the closer ear first and the farther ear a bit later. Your brain uses this time difference to figure out the direction of the sound. If someone on your right calls your name, the sound reaches your right ear first. Tapping on the tube does the same thing. As you tap closer to the middle of the tube, the time difference for the sound to reach your ears is smaller, so it's harder to tell which side your friend is tapping.

70 Can You Smell Well?

Smells such as popcorn or lemons are unmistakable. Other smells are subtler. How sensitive is your sniffer?

Do It!

1. In the first cup, add 1 cup of water.
2. In the second cup, add ¾ cup of water and ¼ cup of vinegar.
3. In the third cup, add ½ cup of water and ½ cup of vinegar.
4. In the fourth cup, add ¼ cup of water and ¾ cup of vinegar.
5. In the fifth cup, add 1 cup of vinegar.
6. Label each cup in order from most to least vinegar.
7. Place the cups in front of your friend, labels facing away from them.
8. Have your friend pick up a cup and hold it 6 inches from their nose.
9. Ask them to rank the cups in order from strongest smell to weakest. Do they order the cups correctly?

Supplies

5 cups, Measuring cups, Vinegar, Water, Friends

What's Happening?

Everything with scent releases chemicals, called odorants, into the air. The odorants travel into your nose and interact with smell receptors. When an odorant interacts with a receptor, it sends a signal to your brain to identify the smell. The odor intensity depends on how much odorant is in the air.

Peripheral Vision

Have you ever seen something out of the corner of your eye but couldn't quite figure out what it was? That's peripheral vision at work. How well do you see off to the side?

Supplies

Colored paper, Black marker, Scissors, Masking tape, Friends, Table

== Do It! ==

1. Cut out three different shapes from different colors of paper. For example, a red triangle, blue circle, and green square.

2. Write a different three-letter word on each shape. Make sure your friends don't see the shapes!

3. Have one friend sit at the table. Ask them stretch out one arm and make the thumbs-up sign.

4. Do the same with the other hand, but hold it off to the side, out of their vision. Tell your friend to stare straight at the thumb in front of them.

5. Tape one of the shapes to their outer thumb so that it faces them. Ask them to slowly bring their outside arm around to the front. Have them tell you when they first notice the motion of the paper, the color, the shape, and the word. Mark those on the table with tape. Your friend should only look at the thumb in front of them during the experiment. If they accidentally look at their other thumb, try again with a different color, shape, and word.

6. Write your friend's initials on the tape. Repeat this with several friends. How do their peripheral visions compare?

What's Happening?

Your peripheral vision depends on the arrangement of rods and cones on the back of your eye. Rods are sensitive light sensors that help you see light and dark. Cones detect colors. The center of your eyeball has the most rods and cones. The very center, or fovea, is almost all cones. That's why you see best when looking straight ahead. The sides have fewer rods and almost no cones.

Your friend sensed motion first, as this is just a change in light and dark. As their arm swings around closer to the front, they next noticed color, and then the shape as their eyeballs had enough cones and rods to pick up these features. However, they can't read the word on the paper until it's almost directly in front of them. You can only pick out details, like words, when an object is right in front.

72 Remodel Your Ears

Animal ears come in all shapes and sizes. If you had animal ears, could you hear better?

Supplies

Construction paper, Scissors, Radio

=== Do It! ===

1. Play music at a low volume. Stand several feet in front of the radio and turn around. What happens to the sound? In what direction is the music the loudest? Quietest?
2. Make two narrow cones. Hold a cone up to each ear and stand in front of the radio. Slowly turn around. What happens to the sound? Where is the music loudest? Quietest?
3. Make two wide cones. Hold them to your ears and stand in front of the radio. What happens to the sound? Where is the music loudest? Quietest?
4. How did your hearing change with different ears? Which animals have ears these shapes?

What's Happening?

Sound travels in all directions. Your outer ear, or pinna, collects sound before it goes into your inner ear where it is translated and sent to your brain. Pinnae sense the direction of sounds. Animals have different shaped pinnae to help them survive. For example, bats have large ears to amplify sound so they can fly in the dark.

73 In the Dark

Your eyes contain sensors that help you see color and brightness. How well do these sensors work in dim light?

=== Do It! ===

Supplies

Colored paper (6 different colors, including black and white), Dimly lit room, Pen

1. Shut the door, turn off the lights, and close the curtains. The room should be almost completely dark. Keep the papers and pen handy.
2. Close your eyes until they are adjusted to the darkness.
3. Open your eyes. Look carefully at each paper in the dim light. Write down the color on the paper.
4. Turn on the light. Did you correctly label the colors in the dim light?

What's Happening?

The sensors that help you see are nerve cells at the back of your eyeball called rods and cones. Rods send the brain information about light and dark; cones send information about color and brightness. Rods work best in dim light and can become overwhelmed by bright lights, such as oncoming car headlights at night. Cones don't work as well in dim light, so it's difficult to tell colors apart when lights are low. How well did your cones figure out the color of the papers in the dim light?

How Much Touch?

A punch on the arm feels way different than a kiss on the cheek. How sensitive are your different body parts to these touches?

Supplies

Scissors,
Ruler, Tape,
5 craft sticks,
Monofilament
fishing line
in 5 different
diameters, Pen,
Friend

Do It!

1. Cut a 2-inch piece of each size fishing line. Tape each piece to a craft stick so that about 1½ inches hangs off the end of the stick. Label each stick with the size of the fishing line.

2. Ask your friend to wear short sleeves and shorts for the experiment. Have them sit with their hand face up on a table and their eyes closed.

3. Hold the stick with the smallest diameter fishing line over your friend's index finger. Carefully lay the fishing line on their fingertip so that the line bends slightly. Ask your friend if they feel anything. Repeat this on their palm, back of their hand, forearm, inside forearm, cheek, neck, back of neck, elbow, and back of leg. Then move on to the next size fishing line. Which body parts are most sensitive to touch and can feel the smallest size fishing line? Which could only feel the larger size fishing line?

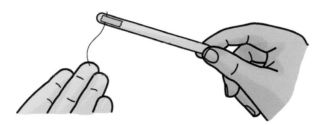

What's Happening?

The technical term for the fishing line taped to the stick is a Von Frey device. They are used to detect the smallest amount of touch that you can feel, called the detection threshold. Your skin is full of many receptors that send signals to your brain through nerves. The signals let your brain know that something is touching you and how hard or strong that touch is. However, not all parts of your body have the same number or type of receptors, so different body parts are more sensitive than others. For example, your face is about 500 times more sensitive than your legs.

What If?

What if you try this experiment when it is very warm or cold? What if it is very dry or humid? How do these conditions affect the sensitivity of your skin?

75 One Touch, Two Touch

Your skin feels all sorts of touches, from a sharp poke to a gentle brush. Can you tell if that poke comes from one finger or two?

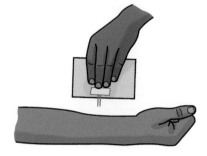

Supplies

22 toothpicks, 11 index cards, Tape, Pen, Ruler with millimeter markings, Friend

Do It!

1. Use the ruler to mark different distances on the index cards. Start with 50 mm (5 cm). Then decrease the distance on each card by 5 mm (.5 cm) so that the next card is 45 mm, then 40 mm, and so on. Mark a final card with lines that are 2.5 mm apart. Label each card with its distance.

2. Tape toothpicks over the lines, with 1 inch of toothpick hanging over the edge of the card. Keep the ends of the toothpicks even.

3. Ask your friend to wear short sleeves and shorts for the experiment. Have them sit with their hand face up on a table and their eyes closed.

4. Choose the card with the toothpicks closest together. Gently press the toothpicks to the tip of your friend's finger. Make sure both toothpicks touch at the same time. Ask your friend if they feel one touch or two. If they say one, try again with the next larger set of toothpicks. Continue until your friend feels two touches.

5. Repeat this on different parts of their body. Which body parts can tell one touch from two when the toothpicks are close together? Which can only tell one touch from two when the toothpicks are far apart?

What's Happening?

Each type of touch has a different receptor in the skin that lets the brain know what is happening. In this experiment, the Merkel's disk receptor lets your brain know that the skin is feeling pressure from the toothpicks. In some areas of your skin, these receptors are closer together; in others, they are farther apart. Each receptor can only send one signal to the brain at a time. In areas with spread out receptors, such as your back, the toothpicks must be farther apart to send signals from two different Merkel disks to let your brain know that there are two touches. If the toothpicks are close, only one Merkel disk is activated and one signal is sent to the brain. Your fingertips have many receptors, so it's much easier to tell when there is one touch or two.

What If?

What if you try this experiment on young kids and grown-ups? Does your ability to feel more than one touch change with age?

Two Eyes or One?

Just how handy it is to have two eyes instead of one?

Supplies

3 pencils, Cardstock, Scissors, Tape

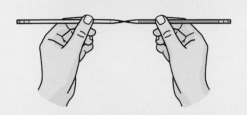

Do It!

1. Hold a pencil in each hand and close one eye. Touch the tips of the pencils together. Did you do it? Now open both eyes and try again. Was it easier this time?

2. Cut a 1-inch donut shape out of cardstock. The inside circle should be just big enough for a pencil to slide through. Tape the donut shape to the end of one pencil.

3. Hold the donut pencil in one hand, with the hole facing sideways. Close one eye. Use the other hand to stick a pencil through the hole. Could you do it? Now open both eyes and try again. Was it easier?

What's Happening?

Each eye sees a slightly different view of the world. Hold this book in front of you, close one eye, and then the other. You will see the world behind the book shift from side to side as you switch eyes. Your brain uses this difference in view to see how far away things are. We call this depth perception. With just one eye, it's difficult to stick the pencil in the hole or touch the ends of two pencils together.

Which Is Heavier?

Use your muscles to sense the weight of an object.

Do It!

Supplies

Blindfold, 2 large cups, Marbles, Friend

1. Fill both cups halfway with the same number of marbles.

2. Blindfold your friend. Hand them a cup for each hand. Ask your friend if the cups weigh the same. The answer should be yes.

3. Take away the cups. Add five marbles to one of the cups. Hand the cups back to your friend. Again, ask if the cups weight the same. If different, which is heavier? If they say that the cup with added marbles is heavier, remove two marbles and try again. If they say no difference, add five marbles and try again.

4. Repeat the process until you find the smallest number of marbles to add to the cup for your friend to recognize that one cup is heavier.

What's Happening?

Muscles are constantly sending your brain information about what they are doing. In this experiment, you found the detection threshold — the point at which your muscles tell your brain that something has changed.

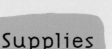

78 Air Horn

Nothing gets attention like the ear-piercing scream of an air horn.

Make Noise!

= Do It! =

Supplies

Plastic cup, Balloon, Straw, Tape, Scissors

1. Cut the bottom out of the cup and the top off the balloon.
2. Stretch the bottom part over the cup so that the opening of the balloon is on the edge of the cup.
3. Tape the balloon tight across the bottom of the cup.
4. Cut the straw in half and insert one piece into the opening of the balloon.
5. Tape the straw to the balloon to hold it in place.
6. Blow into the straw to sound the horn!

What's Happening?

Blowing into the straw causes the stretched balloon to vibrate and make a sound. The cup amplifies, or makes the sound louder, and focuses the sound out the top of the cup.

79 Balloon Amplifiers

Need some helping hearing? Just stick a balloon on your ear.

= Do It! =

Supplies

Balloon

1. Blow up the balloon and tie it off. Tap it with your finger. What do you hear?
2. Put the balloon up against your ear. Tap on the balloon with your finger. What do you hear now?

What's Happening?

When you blow up a balloon, you force air into it. The air molecules are packed together much more tightly inside the balloon than out in the rest of the room. This means the sound vibrations travel more quickly without losing as much energy or volume (loudness). The sound is also focused through the balloon toward your ear, making a louder sound.

What If?

What if you blow up the balloon as large as you can without popping it? What happens to the sound? What happens if you only blow it up a little bit?

Bottle Organ

Some instruments make sounds when you hit them; others by blowing into them. This one makes sounds both ways!

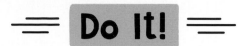
Do It!

Supplies

4 identical glass bottles, Metal spoon, Water

1. Fill the bottles ¼, ½, and ¾ full. Leave one bottle empty.
2. Tap the bottles on the side with the spoon. Which bottle makes the lowest sound? Which makes the highest?
3. Hold the top of a bottle to your lower lip and blow across the top. Make slight adjustments to how you hold the bottle until you hear a loud sound. Blow on each of the bottles. Which makes the lowest sound? Highest?

What's Happening?

When you tap the bottles, the glass vibrates, and those vibrations are sound. Adding water to the bottles slows down the vibrations, making lower sounds. The empty bottle vibrates the fastest and makes the highest sound.

Blowing across the top of a bottle vibrates the air inside instead of the bottle. Bottles with less air have less space to vibrate, so the air vibrates faster with a higher pitch. The empty bottle has the most space, and vibrates slower and produces the lowest pitch.

Chicken in a Cup

This experiment produces a chicken sound so realistic, you'd swear you were on a farm.

Do It!

Supplies

Plastic cup, Nail, Cotton string about 18 inches long, Paper clip, Paper towel, Water, Scissors

1. Poke a hole in the bottom of the plastic cup with the nail.
2. Tie a paper clip to one end of the string. Thread the string through the hole into the cup.
3. Hold the cup upside down so the string hangs down.
4. Fold the towel in half twice and wet it. Squeeze out any extra water.
5. Hold the cup in one hand and the wet paper towel in the other. Wrap the paper towel around the string, squeeze tight, and pull downward with a jerking motion on the stretched-out string. Do you hear the chicken?

What's Happening?

Tiny vibrations are created as you pull down on the string, and vibrations cause sound. They are too faint to hear until you add the cup. The cup acts as a sounding board to make the sounds louder.

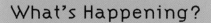

Corrugahorn

Musical instruments can be found in the most unlikely places. You'll need to head out to the garage to find this sound maker.

Supplies

3-foot or longer piece of corrugated plastic drainpipe (must be flexible and corrugated or bumpy on the inside), Leaf blower or hairdryer (optional)

Do It!

1. Find a wide-open outside space.
2. Grab the drainpipe in both hands and swing it in a circle over your head as fast as you can. You should hear a low-pitched sound coming from the pipe. As you swing faster, the sound will get higher in pitch and louder.
3. Instead of whirling the drainpipe overhead to force air through the tube, you can use a leaf blower or hairdryer. Set up the leaf blower so that it blows through the drain pipe. Hold the tube close to the blower and then move it farther away. What happens to the sound?

What's Happening?

As air moves through the corrugahorn, it hits the corrugation or bumps inside the pipe. The bumps cause the air to vibrate, and vibrating air is simply sound. You may have noticed that the corrugahorn only plays specific notes. These notes match the soundwaves that fit exactly inside the pipe. Faster-moving air produces faster vibrations, which correspond to shorter waves and higher pitches.

What If?

What if you use a shorter or longer pipe? Can you find other pipes that are corrugated on the inside? Some convenience stores and fast-food restaurants use straws for their frozen drinks that are corrugated on the inside. You can play these by blowing in the straws.

Try taking your drain pipe corrugahorn on a car ride and holding the end of the pipe out the window. How do the notes correspond to the speed of the car? Do you get a louder sound if you hold the end of the pipe facing forward, backward, or straight out the window?

Drums

Are you the kind of kid who wants to bang on a drum all day? Make your own collection of drums with a variety of sounds.

Supplies

Round containers of various sizes and shapes, Shrink-wrap window insulation (with double-sided tape) or plastic wrap, Balloons, Hair dryer, Masking tape, Spoon

Do It!

1. Cut a piece of shrink-wrap (or plastic wrap) that is a few inches larger than the opening at the top of a round container.

   If you are using shrink-wrap, place the double-sided tape around the outside of the container about 2 inches from the top. Put the shrink-wrap on the container and press the edge along the double-sided tape so that it is tight. Wrap masking tape around the bowl to hold the shrink-wrap in place. Blow a hairdryer set on high about 2 inches from shrink-wrap until the top of the drum is tight.

   If you are using plastic wrap, lay the plastic wrap on top of the bowl. Place masking tape around the edge of the bowl to hold the plastic wrap in place. Make sure the plastic wrap is as tight as possible.

   For smaller drums, stretch a balloon over the top and secure it with masking tape.

2. Repeat the process for the different containers. Use a spoon to bang on the drums. How do the different shapes affect the sound the drums make? How do the wide drums sound different from the narrow drums? How do the tall drums sound different from the short drums?

What's Happening?

When you bang on a drum, the top or head of the drum vibrates. The vibrations have a higher sound and travel more easily through a tight drumhead than a loose one. The body or shell of the drum acts as an amplifier, making the sounds louder. The shell also affects the pitch, or how high or low the sound is. Narrow drums have higher pitches and wider drums have lower pitches.

What If?

What if you use other materials for a drumhead? Try aluminum foil, paper, or a disposable tablecloth. How do they sound different or similar?

Guitar

If you've always wanted to be in a rock-and-roll band, this guitar is a good place to start.

Supplies

Empty tissue box, 6 rubber bands of different sizes and thicknesses, 2 pencils, Tape (optional)

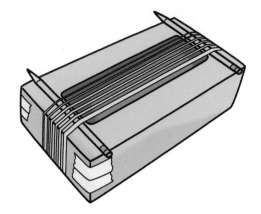

= Do It! =

1. Carefully remove any plastic that's in the hole of the box. Make sure that the only hole in the box is the one on top that the tissues come out of. Tape up any other holes.
2. Stretch the rubber bands long ways over the box so that they are over or near the hole. The rubber bands should be equally spaced.
3. Slide a pencil under the rubber bands above the hole and slide the other pencil under the rubber bands below the hole.
4. Use your fingers to pluck the rubber bands. How do the sounds made by the thick rubber bands compare to the thin rubber bands? Does the amount the rubber band is stretched affect the sound it makes?

What's Happening?

When you pluck the rubber bands, they vibrate and produce a sound. Thicker, less stretched rubber bands vibrate slower and make lower sounds. Thinner, more stretched rubber bands make higher sounds. The pencils make what is called a bridge so that the rubber bands can vibrate without bumping into the box. They also transfer the vibration of the rubber bands to the box, which also vibrates and makes the sound louder.

What If?

What if you change the position of the pencils? How does this change the sound of the guitar? Take one or both pencils off completely and see what happens to the sound. How does the shape and size of the guitar box affect the sound? Try using a large box and a very small box. Change the size of the hole, as well.

Hanger Gong

This could be the quietest sound experiment ever.

Supplies

Wire hanger, 2 pieces of string each 1 foot long, Wall

Do It!

1. Tap the hanger against a wall. What do you hear?
2. Tie the two strings to the bottom ends of the hanger.
3. Hold the hanger by its handle. Wrap the end of one of the strings around your index finger twice. Wrap the end of the other string around your other index finger twice.
4. Keep the strings wrapped on your fingers while you stick your fingers in your ears. Bend over so that the hanger hangs free. Let the hanger tap against a wall. What do you hear? How does it compare to the tapping before you put your fingers in your ears?

What's Happening?

When you tap the hanger, vibrations travel through the air to your ears as soundwaves. When you tie a string to the hanger, attach the strings to your fingers, and put your fingers in your ears, the vibrations travel to your ears through the string instead of through the air. The string is denser than air and vibrates differently.

Harmonica

This harmonica sounds more like a kazoo, but it is easy to make and play.

Do It!

Supplies

1 straw, 2 large craft sticks, 1 large rubber band, 2 small rubber bands, Scissors

1. Cut two 2-inch pieces from the straw.
2. Wrap the large rubber band longways around one stick.
3. Place one of the straw pieces crosswise on the stick, under the rubber band and near one end.
4. Place the other straw piece on top of the rubber band near the other end.
5. Place the other stick on top. Wrap the small rubber bands tightly on each end of the stick sandwich to hold it together.
6. Blow between the straws. Slide the straws closer together or farther apart to make different sounds.

What's Happening?

When you blow into the harmonica, the air flowing around the rubber band causes it to vibrate and make a sound. The pitch depends on how fast the rubber band vibrates. If the straws are far apart, the longer rubber band will vibrate slower and make a lower pitch. If they are close together, the shorter rubber band will vibrate faster and make a higher pitch.

87 Megaphones

Have you ever yelled at a friend far away and put your hands up to your mouth to make your voice louder? You were using a megaphone!

Supplies

Large outdoor space, Friend, Small paper plate, Large paper plate, Poster board, Scissors, Tape

 **Do It!**

1. Cut a slit in the small paper plate from one edge to the very center of the plate. Slide one edge of the slit over the other so that the plate makes a cone shape. Tape the edges of the plate in place so that it stays in a cone shape.

2. Cut just a little bit off the pointy end of the cone so that there is a hole at least 1 inch across for you to speak into.

3. Repeat this for the large paper plate and for a very large circle cut from the poster board.

4. Go outside with your friend and the megaphones. Have your friend stand facing away and 10 steps in front of you. In your regular speaking voice, say their name. If they can hear you, they should raise their hand and take another 10 steps and stop. Say their name again and see if you are heard. Repeat the process every 10 steps until your friend cannot hear you say their name.

5. Do the experiment three more times using each of the three megaphones. Did the megaphones help your friend hear farther away? Which megaphone carried your voice the farthest?

What's Happening?

Megaphones help your voice go farther in two different ways. First, a megaphone focuses your voice. When you talk without a megaphone, the sound comes out of your mouth in all directions. A megaphone focuses the sound waves so that they all go forward and not off to the sides, up high, or down low. Second, a megaphone acts as an extension of your mouth. This means the sound moves more gradually from your small mouth to the wide-open world. More of the sound goes out instead of getting caught in your mouth or vocal chords, which makes your voice louder.

Rain Stick

Some people think rain sticks were used in rituals to call rain from the clouds during dry spells.

88

Supplies

Paper towel tube; Aluminum foil; Tape; Paper grocery bag; Scissors; Ruler; ¼ cup of dried beans, Markers, construction paper, glue, paint (optional)

Do It!

1. Cut a piece of foil about 6 inches wide and 18 inches long. Scrunch up the foil into a long snake and then twist it into a spiral shape. Slide the spiral into the paper towel tube. Use a piece of tape to hold it in place on both ends.

2. Trace one end of the tube onto the grocery bag. Draw another circle around the traced circle twice as big around. Cut out the larger circle. Place it over one end of the tube, scrunch down the sides around the tube, and wrap tape around it to hold it in place.

3. Pour the dried beans into the tube.

4. Make another large circle from the bag and attach it to the other end in the same way using tape.

5. Slowly turn the rain stick upside down. What do you hear? Keep turning the stick over and over for a continuous rainfall sound.

What's Happening?

As the beans fall down the tube, they bump into the foil. Each bump causes vibrations that make a soft tapping sound, like a raindrop falling on the ground. As the beans fall down the tube, they continue to tap on the foil so that one raindrop becomes a deluge.

Screaming Balloon   89

Vibrations can cause surprising sounds!

Do It!

Supplies

Balloon, Hex nut

1. Place the hex nut inside the balloon. Blow up the balloon and tie it off.

2. Hold the balloon with the palm of your hand. Swirl it around so that the hex nut rolls around the balloon. What do you hear?

3. Twirl the balloon as fast as you can and then hold it still. How does the sound change as the hex nut rolls faster?

What's Happening?

Each time a corner of the hex nut hits the side of the balloon, it causes a tiny vibration. As the nut spins around, it causes thousands of vibrations and a loud, whirring "scream." Twirling the balloon faster causes faster vibrations and a higher-pitched sound. As the hex nut slows down, so do the vibrations and the pitch becomes lower.

90 Singing Glasses

The next time you are at a dinner party with fancy glassware, wow the guests with a singing wine glass!

Supplies

Wine glass, Water

═ Do It! ═

1. Wash your hands with soap and water. This experiment works best with very clean hands.

2. Place the wine glass on a table and hold down the base of the glass with one hand. Rub your clean, dry index finger of your other hand along the rim of the glass with firm pressure. Do you hear a sound?

3. Dip your finger in water and try rubbing the rim of the glass again. You don't want to push so hard that you break the glass but don't be too gentle, either. You should hear a clear ringing sound. If not, adjust the speed and pressure of the rubbing motion on the rim of the glass.

4. Add a small amount of water to the cup and repeat the process. How does the ringing sound of the glass with water compare to the sound from the empty glass? Continue to add water to the glass and observe changes in the ringing sound. Are you still able to get a sound from the glass when it is completely full?

What's Happening?

The key to making a wine glass sing is the right amount of friction. A dry finger has too much friction, but a wet finger has just a little bit of friction. As you slide your wet finger along the rim of the glass, that little bit of friction causes your finger to stick and slide as it moves. You might have even felt it on your fingertip. This sticking and slipping causes the glass to vibrate and vibrations cause sound. Look carefully at the surface of the water near the glass while it is singing. You should be able to see these vibrations in the water. You can also cause the glass to vibrate by tapping with a metal spoon. Try it! You should hear the same pitch as when you make the glass sing.

As you add water to the glass, the vibrations are slowed down by the weight of the water on the glass. Slower vibrations have a lower pitch. As you add more water, the pitch of the singing glass gets lower.

Singing Rod

Almost anything can be used to make sound!

Supplies

Smooth, thin, aluminum rod (2 feet long); Wax (wax paper, a candle, or crayon will work)

Do It!

1. Rub one half of the rod with wax all the way around the rod.
2. Find the center of the rod by balancing it on your index fingers. Slowly slide the fingers together without dropping the rod. Where they meet is the center. Hold onto the rod with one hand at the exact center.
3. Use your other hand to pinch the waxed side of the rod between your thumb and index finger. Firmly slide your fingers outward from the center to the end. Repeat the process several times until you hear a ringing sound.

What's Happening?

When you slide your fingers over the rod, the wax causes your fingers to slip and stick as they move along. These cause tiny vibrations that add up every time you slide your fingers. You will hear a high ringing sound as the whole rod vibrates.

Singing Straw

Make your straw sing.

Do It!

Supplies

Straw, Scissors, Glass of water

1. Make a cut partially through the straw about 2 inches from the end of the straw. Don't cut all the way through. The straw should still be attached by a small piece.
2. Bend the straw at the cut so that it is a right angle. Place the longer piece of straw into the glass of water.
3. Blow gently into the smaller end to hear a whistling sound. Slowly move the straw up and down in the glass of water. What happens to the sound?

What's Happening?

Sound is vibrations, and scientists call those vibrations "sound waves." When you blow through the short part of the singing straw, air moves over the opening at the top of the long part of the straw. This air vibrates and causes the singing sound. As you move the straw up and down in the water, you change the length of the straw with vibrating air or sound waves. Longer straws have longer sound waves, which make lower-pitched sounds. Shorter straws have shorter sound waves, which make higher-pitched sounds.

93 Soda Straw Oboe

Make one of these at a restaurant when you've been waiting for a very long time!

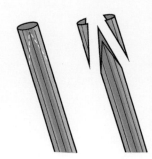

═ Do It! ═

Supplies

Straw, Scissors

1. Chew one end of the straw so that it is flat but not mangled. Cut a pointy triangle on the flattened end of the straw. Pinch the straw to open the flattened end of the straw so air can flow through again.
2. Hold the pointy end of the straw loosely in your mouth and blow hard. The straw should make a sound not unlike a duck call.
3. Cut an inch off your straw. Blow again. Is the sound different? Keep shortening your straw and listen to how the sound changes.

What's Happening?

An oboe makes sound by the vibrations of two thin, wood-like reeds. Your straw makes sound in the same way except instead of reeds, you have two pointy straw triangles. When you chew on the straw, the plastic is softened so that it vibrates more easily. Shortening the length of your straw also shortens the length of the sound vibrations. Shorter vibrations, or waves, make higher pitches. As the straw gets shorter, the pitch of the sound gets higher and squeakier.

94 Wind Chime

Wind can make music too.

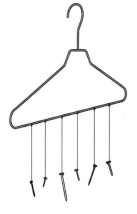

═ Do It! ═

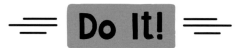

Supplies

Clothes hanger, 6 nails of different lengths, Another nail of any size, String, Scissors

1. Cut six pieces of string about 6 inches long. Tie one end of a string to the hanger and the other end to the top of the longest nail. Do the same for each nail, in order from longest to shortest.
2. Hold the hanger so the nails hang freely. Use the extra nail to tap each of the hanging nails. Do the nails sound the same?
3. Hang your wind chime outside and let the wind make music. Or hang the chime on your bedroom door and use it as an alarm to know when your little brother is trying to sneak in.

What's Happening?

When you tap the nails, they vibrate and make sounds. The longer nails vibrate slower and create a lower pitch, while the shorter nails vibrate faster and have a higher pitch.

Floating Cube

Fool your friends with this gravity-defying illusion!

Supplies

Square piece of paper,
Ruler, Scissors, Tape,
Markers or crayons

= Do It! =

1. Use the ruler to draw two lines across the center of the paper that divides the paper into four equal squares. Draw a line from one corner to the center of the paper. Decorate the other three squares however you like. You can write a message, draw dots to look like dice, or color them a solid color. Just make sure that your drawings don't overflow into the other squares.

2. Cut along the diagonal line and fold the two triangles back along the sides of the square. Fold along the edges of the square inward and bring the two triangles together to make half of a cube. Tape the triangles together in the back to hold the cube in place and make a handle.

3. Hold the triangle so that the cube is facing you, and close or cover one eye. Does it look like the inside of a box or the outside? Tape the triangle to your littlest finger and slowly move your fingers to make the cube appear to float above your hand.

What's Happening?

When you look at something with one eye closed, you are seeing a flat two-dimensional (2D) world, which is slightly different than the three-dimensional (3D) world we usually see with two eyes. Our brain must convert information from a 2D world to a 3D image. Because our brains are more likely to expect to see the outside of a box than the inside, that is what it tells us we see.

What If?

What if you make other shapes? Can you make a floating pyramid or a floating octahedron?

96 False Memories

Does your brain create memories of something that isn't there?

Supplies

At least five friends, Paper, Pencils, Clock

== Do It! ==

1. Give each of your friends a copy of the word list. Give them one minute to memorize the list.

2. Take away the list and explain that they will write down all the words they can remember from the list. Did your friends remember all the words? Did they miss words? Did they add extra words?

Word List

bed
rest
awake
tired
dream
wake
snooze
blanket
slumber
snore
nap
yawn

What's Happening?

Scientists use variations of this memory game to explore how our brain remembers. At least one friend probably added the word "sleep" to their remembered list of words. If you ask them, they are probably quite confident that "sleep" was on the list because they created a false memory of that word. Of course, all the words on this list are related to sleep, called the critical word, on purpose to try to make the brain remember a word that isn't there. The associative model of memory explains how that happens. When we remember something, we group that memory with similar memories. When we need to pull up or recall a memory, some associated memories get included, as well. For example, if you were to remember your last birthday, you might also remember some of your earlier birthdays, as well. For some of your friends, the words on the list were stored in the brain along with the associated word "sleep."

What If?

What if you come up with other lists of words with a critical missing word to try on your friends? What if you try the test early in the morning, late in the evening, or right after school? What if you try the test on kids and adults? Do these changes affect how well people remember the list and make false memories?

Floating Arm

Are you in control of your body, or does your arm have a mind of its own?

Supplies

Wall

Do It!

1. Stand next to a wall and push the back of your hand and arm against the wall as hard as you can while you count slowly to thirty.

2. Step away from the wall and relax your arm. How does your arm feel? Does anything odd happen?

What's Happening?

Pushing against the wall on purpose is known as a voluntary motion. You are in control of how hard and how long you push your arm. However, when you step away from the wall and relax, your arm has an involuntary motion as it rises upward. You did not tell your arm to move; rather, it moved on its own. Scientists are still exploring why this happens, but most agree that it is a combination of the signals from your brain and muscles. Research as to why this happens can help doctors treat diseases like Parkinson's disease and Tourette syndrome that involve involuntary motion.

Arch Illusion

In this optical illusion, two identical socks suddenly appear to be different sizes.

Supplies

Pair of socks

Do It!

1. Lay the socks next to each other flat on a table.

2. Move the socks so that one is about an inch above the other and the open ends of the socks line up like the picture. Do the socks look the same size, or does one appear bigger than the other? Move the socks so that they are centered one above the other. Do they appear the same size now? Rotate the socks so that now the open ends are lined up and pointed down with the toes pointed up. Do they appear the same size now?

What's Happening?

The arch illusion depends on one property of the arch: the outside edge of the arch is longer than the inside arch. When you line up the arches so that the longer outside arch is above the shorter inside arch and the ends match up, the top arch appears to be larger. In reality, the arches are exactly the same size but our brain is fooled! When you turn the arches so they stretch up and down or move them farther apart, it is easier for our brain to see that they are indeed the same size.

99 Impossible Triangle

Create an illusion of a triangle that appears to be lying flat and standing up at the same time!

Supplies

12 dice or square blocks, Piece of paper

≡ Do It! ≡

1. On the paper, place five dice in a row right next to each other. On one end, stack four dice straight up. On the other end, place four more dice to make a corner.
2. Slowly rotate the paper and move your head until it appears that the top dice in the stack lines up exactly with the last dice on the other row. You are looking at what appears to be an impossible triangle that is flat on the paper and standing up at the same time!

What's Happening?

This illusion relies on perspective, or the angle and direction that you look at an object. Move your head just a small bit and the illusion is broken. M.C. Escher made impossible objects popular with his two-dimensional drawings of staircases and buildings that are impossible in the three-dimensional real world.

100 Invisible Triangle

It's a triangle … or is it?

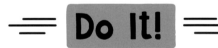

Supplies

Round fruit (kiwi, oranges, or some other colored fruit works best), Knife, White plate

≡ Do It! ≡

1. Cut three round slices from the fruit of about the same size.
2. Cut a triangle out of each slice as shown. Arrange the fruit on a plate so that the holes line up to make the corners of a triangle.
3. Look at the plate of fruit. Do you see the triangle? Does it appear brighter or a different color than the rest of the white plate?

What's Happening?

This illusion was created in 1955 by Italian psychologist Gaetano Kanizsa and is known as Kanizsa's Triangle. It is an example of illusory contours, or lines that aren't there but appear to be. Your brain sees that the fruit is not quite whole and fills in a shape that must be covering the missing pieces. The result is that your brain sees a triangle that is not really there.

X-ray Tube

Look straight through your hand using only a sheet of paper!

Supplies

Paper (8½ x 11 inches), Tape

Do It!

1. Roll the paper into a tight tube about 1 inch across, and tape it to keep the paper in place.

2. This experiment works best in a well-lit room where you can look at a wall or furniture that is not white. First, hold your hand in front of your face. Close or cover one eye and then the other. What do you notice? Does it appear that your hand is moving? Or is the rest of the room moving?

3. Hold up your left hand and rest the tube between your thumb and index finger. Hold the tube up to your right eye so that your hand covers your left eye. Slide your left hand to about 2 or 3 inches from your face. Do you see anything odd? If not, tilt the tube a bit to the left. You are looking

What's Happening?

Having two eyes is very useful. It allows you to see in three dimensions and gives you a wider field of view. Two eyes also lead to some pretty crazy illusions. In the first part of the experiment, without the tube, you may have noticed that each eye sees a slightly different view. Your brain combines these views together so that you see more than you would with just one eye. When you put the tube up to your eye, you only see what is at the end of the tube. The sides of the tube block out everything else. When your hand is next to the tube, your brain combines one eye's view of your hand with the other eye's view through the tube. It looks like there is a hole in the middle of your hand!

What If?

What if you use a longer or shorter tube? Or a tube that is smaller or bigger around? What if you move your hand or the tube closer or farther from your eyes?

102 Muller-Lyer Illusion

The pipe cleaners are the same length, but it sure doesn't look that way!

Supplies

4 pipe cleaners, Scissors

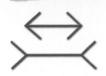

Do It!

1. Lay two pipe cleaners side by side, 6 inches apart. Cut the other two pipe cleaners in half.
2. Slightly bend the four pipe cleaners in the middle. Place two bent pipe cleaners on the ends of one long pipe cleaner, like arrows bent out from the center. Place the other two on the ends of the other long pipe cleaner, like arrows bent in from the center. Look at the two long pipe cleaners. Do they look the same length?

What's Happening?

There are several theories about this illusion. One theory is that the arrows on the end suggest 3D images. Our brain interprets the inward arrows as part of a smaller, farther away cube, and the arrows bent outward as part of a closer, larger cube.

Another theory depends on the way our eyes move when looking at the lines. When the arrows bend outward, our eyes travel farther away from the center of the line. When they bend down, our eyes move back in toward the center, making the line appear shorter. Why do you think one line appears shorter than the other?

103 Proprioception

Do you *really* know where your fingers are?

Do It!

1. Raise both hands in the air so you can't see them. Make a pointer with your right hand, and leave the fingers of your left hand spread out. (Reverse the hands if you are left handed.)
2. With your eyes open, touch the tip of your pointer to your nose, and then touch the tip of your pointer to the tip of your left thumb. Touch your nose, and then the tip of your index finger. Touch your nose, and then the tip of your middle finger, and so on to your pinky. Always use the tips of your fingers. Did you have any trouble?
3. Do the same thing, but with your eyes closed. Was it harder to find your fingers? Do it again, but wiggle your fingers each time you touch your nose. Is it easier?

Supplies

You

What's Happening?

Proprioception is an awareness of the position of your body parts and what they are doing. Your muscles, joints, and even inner ear have sensors that help your brain keep track of your body. However, your eyes and the visual information they collect are the most important tool your brain has for proprioception. That's why when you close your eyes, your brain briefly loses track of your fingers and you have trouble finding them. If you wiggle your fingers, the proprioceptors in your muscles send signals to your brain to help track them down.

Stroop Effect

What if you saw a big, red octagon with the word GO in white letters? Your brain might be confused, because a red octagon usually means stop. See if you can confuse your friend's brain in the same way.

Supplies

Paper, Crayons or markers, Friend, Stopwatch

Do It!

1. With crayons or markers, write the names of at least 10 different colors, and make sure the color you write with matches the color of the word you write. For example, use the red crayon to write "RED."

2. On another piece of paper, write the exact same words, but this time, write the words in a color that does not match the name of the color you are writing. For example, use a blue crayon to write the word "RED."

3. Tell your friend to name the color of each of the words you show them. With a stopwatch, measure how long it takes your friend to name the colors on the first paper where the words match the colors. Then give your friend the other paper, where the words don't match the colors, and time how long it takes them to name all the colors. Did they make any mistakes? Which paper took them longer to read?

What's Happening?

J. Ridley Stroop found that in this situation, the words have a strong effect on your ability to say the color. Your brain is receiving conflicting information. What the words say is not the same as the color of the words. So, your brain takes longer to figure out the right answer. Some scientists think this is because the words are read faster than the colors are named, and others say that naming colors requires more attention than reading words. Which do you think is right?

What If?

What if you ask your friend to read the words instead of naming the colors? Can they read the words faster? What if you compare kids to adults? Who can name the colors faster?

Yellow Blue Red Green Orange Red Black Blue Purple

105 Size-weight Illusion

In this experiment, your friends will lift two boxes with the same weight and claim that one is much lighter than the other. How can that be?

Supplies

Shoe box, Large box (at least three times larger than the shoe box), 6 cans of soup (or other canned food), Scale, Packing tape, Friends

═ Do It! ═

1. Put three cans in the shoe box and three cans in the large box. Weigh each box on a scale and add items to the smaller box until both boxes have the same weight. Use packing tape to hold the cans in the center of each box so they don't roll around.

2. Close the boxes and place them in front of your friends. Ask them to lift each box and tell you which is heavier. Did your friends notice that they both weigh the same, or did they say one box was heavier than the other? Ask them to lift the boxes again just to be sure. Do they still give the same answer?

What's Happening?

Scientists think this illusion works because our brain takes size into account when preparing to lift a box. We assume that larger boxes must be heavier so we use more muscle power to lift them. But when we lift the box, it feels lighter than expected, so our brain tells us that the large box is lighter than the small box. However, if you keep lifting the boxes, your muscles figure out that they weigh the same and use the right amount of force to lift them. Your brain, however, continues to think that the larger box is heavier.

What If?

What if you lift a warm box and a cold box? Or a light-colored box and a dark-colored box? Or boxes made of different materials, such as metal or Styrofoam? Do these factors affect how heavy a box feels?

Thaumatrope

The name of this optical illusion means "wonder turner."

Do It!

Supplies

Straw, Index card, Scissors, Tape, Markers

1. Fold the index card in half. On one half, draw a cross. On the other half, draw a circle slightly larger than the cross.

2. Tape one end of the straw to the back of the card behind the cross. Fold the card over with the pictures on the outside, and tape the card together. The straw forms a handle and the card has a cross on one side and a circle on the other.

3. Hold the straw between your palms. Move your hands in opposite directions so the straw and pictures spin back and forth. Can you make the straw spin fast enough for the circle to "capture" the cross?

What's Happening?

The retina, in the back of your eyeball, converts images into signals that are sent to your brain. But this takes time. Your retina holds onto the image less than 0.1 second. If the thaumatrope spins faster than that, your brain is tricked into seeing two pictures at once. Cartoons work the same way. The pictures change so quickly that your eyes and brain think they are continuous.

Upside-down Faces

How good are you at recognizing faces?

Do It!

Supplies

3 copies of a photograph of a face, Scissors, Tape, Friends

1. Cut the eyes and mouth out of one copy of the photo and tape them upside down onto another copy. Leave the third copy as is.

2. Turn both faces upside down. Does anything look strange? Turn the faces right-side up. Does anything look strange now? Show the photo with the taped mouth and eyes to your friends upside down first. See if they can figure out what is wrong before turning it right-side up and showing the original photo.

What's Happening?

This illusion shows how our brain recognizes faces. We are used to seeing faces right-side up and expect eyes and mouths to look right-side up, as well. Our brain also sees the whole face instead of individual features. We recognize faces by the position of the eyes, mouth, and nose relative to others. When the face is upside down, this all goes out the window, and our brain must focus on individual features, such as the expression of the eyes or mouth, which look fine until you flip the face right-side up!

Energy & Forces

Harness the energy of science to discover how things roll, slide, bounce, push, attract, and repel.

Balls

108 Galileo's Ball Drop

Historians are pretty sure that Galileo didn't drop a feather and a cannonball off the Leaning Tower of Pisa, but that doesn't mean you can't drop some balls off the top of a ladder.

This experiment is best done outdoors where the falling balls won't do any damage.

Do It!

Supplies

2 balls that are the same size but different weights (for example a tennis ball and a field hockey ball, or a basketball and a medicine ball), Ladder, Friend

1. Set up the ladder outside, in an area where the balls will hit a hard surface (so you can use the sound of them hitting the ground to help figure out which lands first).

2. Ask your friend to hold the ladder, and then carefully climb up a few steps and hold the balls out in front of you.

3. Drop the balls at the same time, being careful not to push or throw them.

4. Listen and watch to see which ball hits the ground first. Repeat this two or more times to make sure the results are consistent. If you want, use a video camera to record the balls falling so you can watch it back and see what happened.

What's Happening?

When two balls of the same size but different weights fall, they accelerate or speed up at the same rate. Gravity pulls down the heavier ball with a bigger force, but the heavy ball has more mass, so it takes a bigger force to accelerate it. The lighter ball needs a smaller force to accelerate, so both balls speed up the same amount and hit the ground at the same time!

This is actually true for any object, even a feather and a cannonball, but air gets in the way. The air resistance pushing up will slow down the feather much more than the cannonball, so it appears that gravity pulls the feather less and it falls slower.

If you could remove the air, you would see the feather and bowling ball fall together.

What If?

What if you drop two balls that are the same weight but different sizes or shapes?

Fun Fact

Galileo actually did his experiments by sliding objects down a ramp so they moved slower and could be timed with a water clock—there were no digital stopwatches or smartphones then!

Double Ball Drop

A ball bouncing on the ground is nothing special, but when you put one ball on top of another ball and let them bounce together, something surprising happens!

This experiment is best done outside on concrete or another hard, flat surface.

Supplies

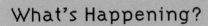

Large ball (basketball, soccer ball, or similar size), Smaller ball (tennis ball or similar size)

Do It!

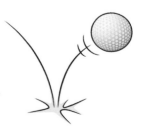

1. Hold the large ball out at shoulder height and drop it. How high does it bounce?
2. Hold the small ball out at shoulder height. How high does this ball bounce?
3. Now place the small ball directly on top of the large ball.
4. Hold them out at shoulder height and drop them together. Now how high do the balls bounce?

What's Happening?

When you hold the ball out, ready to drop, the ball has potential or stored energy. When you release the ball, gravity pulls it downward, turning that stored energy into motion, or kinetic energy. When the large ball hits the ground, it compresses or squishes, and its motion energy gets stored as elastic energy, like a spring. As the ball releases, it pushes up on the small ball on top, passing on that stored elastic energy.

Why does the small ball go SO high? The small ball has much less mass than the large ball so that extra energy causes it to go even faster than the large ball, which means it bounces much higher than it would on its own.

The Way the Ball Bounces

If you've ever played a ball sport when it's very cold outside, you may have noticed that the balls don't bounce as high or travel as far as when it's warmer. Find out why!

This experiment is best done outside on concrete or another hard, flat surface.

Supplies

6 golf balls, Yardstick, Freezer, Friend

Do It!

1. Put three golf balls in the freezer for at least two hours and leave the other three out at room temperature.
2. Have a friend hold the yardstick straight up from the ground.
3. Drop the balls one at a time from the top of the yardstick, and make a note of how high each of the balls bounces. Which ball bounced higher: the frozen golf balls or the room-temperature balls?

What's Happening?

The bounciness of a ball depends on its elasticity, and a golf ball is fairly elastic. When you hit the ball with a golf club, most of that energy goes into the motion of the ball. However, if you freeze the golf ball, it becomes more rigid and brittle, and less elastic. The ball doesn't squish as much when it hits the ground, so less energy goes into the bounce and the ball doesn't get as high as a warmer, more elastic ball.

111 Racquetball Popper

Cut open a rubber ball to make a popping fun toy!

= Do It! =

POP!

Supplies

Racquetball (or another hollow rubber ball), Scissors, Table tennis ball

1. Use the scissors to cut the racquetball in half down the middle.
2. Choose a side without any tears or trim the tears off.
3. Trim off about ¼ inch so the popper is slightly less than half a ball.
4. Hold the sides and push the middle out so the popper is inside out; you may need to squeeze the sides together a few times to get it to stay inside out.
5. Hold the popper, curved side up, out in front of you and drop it on the ground. The popper will "pop" when it hits the ground and bounce up higher than it was dropped from!
6. Turn the popper inside out again, then turn it upside down so the curved side is down and place the table tennis ball in the popper cup.
7. Drop the popper and watch the ball shoot up!

What's Happening?

Elastic energy is stored in the popper by pushing it inside out. Holding the popper out over the floor stores gravitational energy. When you drop the popper on the floor, this turns into kinetic motion energy. The release of that stored energy sends the popper into the air. When you put the ball on the popper, the same thing happens, except a table tennis ball is much lighter than the popper. So the ball shoots up even higher!

112 Shoot the Moon

Roll a ball all the way to the top of a hill using gravity alone.

= Do It! =

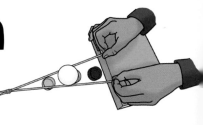

Supplies

Table tennis ball, 2 bamboo skewers (or other long sticks), Book (about 1 inch thick), Rubber band, Bottle caps (optional)

1. Line up the two bamboo sticks next to each other and wrap the rubber band around one end to hold them together. You should be able to easily open the sticks into a V shape.
2. Lay the book on the table and place the open end of the V at the edge of the book.
3. Place the table tennis ball at the point of the V.
4. Adjust the sticks back and forth to change the shape of the V so the ball rolls uphill toward the book. Can you get the ball to roll to the book without falling through the sticks?
5. To make the game, place bottle caps in a row between the bottom point of the V and the top near the book.
6. Each cap is worth a different number of points, with the cap near the point worth the least, and near the book worth the most. Drop the ball into the bottle cap closest to the book to get the most points!

What's Happening?

The ball doesn't really roll uphill—it just looks that way! As the ball rolls, the center of the ball lowers, and it appears to roll up when actually the ball is rolling down!

Cradle of Energy

How does energy transfer from one object to another?
You'll find out in this experiment!

Supplies

5 bouncy balls, 5 pushpins, Thread, 4 identical bottles (at least 8 inches tall), 4 bamboo skewers, Ruler, Tape

═ Do It! ═

1. Stick a pushpin into each of the bouncy balls, then cut four pieces of thread 17 inches long.
2. Tie the center of each thread around a pushpin in the bouncy balls.
3. Fill the bottles with water and put the caps on to make them more stable.
4. Place the bottles at four corners of a rectangle that is 6 inches wide and 10 inches long.
5. Tape bamboo skewers to the lids of the bottles to hold them in place, making sure the sides of the rectangle are straight.
6. Tie the ends of the thread for each bouncy ball to the bamboo skewers on opposite long sides of the rectangle, making sure each ball hangs at the exact same height.
7. The balls should line up perfectly, hung so they are almost touching and as low as possible.
8. Use a small piece of tape to hold each string to the bamboo skewer so it doesn't slide around.
9. Pull back a ball from one end and let it go. Watch the ball on the other end fly out!
10. Try pulling back two balls and letting go. How many balls come out the other side?

What's Happening?

Whenever two objects collide, the total momentum and kinetic energy stay the same. Both of these depend on the mass and the speed of the objects that collide. So, if a fast-moving object hits an object of the exact same mass that is sitting still, the momentum and energy is transferred from the fast object to the still object.

If the collision is elastic, energy is not lost to friction, heat, sound, or anything else, and the still object will zoom off with the same speed as the fast object and the fast object will stop.

This is exactly what happens in this example, also called Newton's cradle. The balls all have the same mass, and the hard rubber makes for a mostly elastic collision.

What If?

What if you add more balls to the Newton's cradle? What if you use marbles or some other ball?

114 Fun with Friction

What material heats up the most from friction?

= Do It! =

Supplies

Washcloth, Wire coat hanger, Wooden skewer, Plastic pen, Cardboard, Tape

1. Cut a piece of cardboard 8 inches long and 3 inches wide. Roll it up like a pencil and tape it together.
2. One at a time, hold the hanger, skewer, pen, and cardboard. Do they each feel cool or warm?
3. Hold the washcloth tightly around a straight part of the hanger and rub it at least 30 times. Feel the wire where you rubbed the cloth. Does it feel cool or warm?
4. Repeat this with the skewer, pen, and cardboard. Which material changed temperature the most?

What's Happening?

The amount of heat produced by friction depends on the materials and how hard they're pressed together. Even though the hanger is smooth, it gets hot because metals absorb heat easily. That's why we use metal pots and pans to cook.

Plastic and cardboard are insulators, so they do not hold onto the heat as well. All the materials gain some heat energy when the friction converts the energy of motion into heat.

115 Ball Bearings

What makes the wheels on a bicycle spin so fast? Ball bearings!

= Do It! =

Supplies

Soup can, Jar lid that fits over the soup can, Pencil, Modeling clay, 12 marbles

1. Put a ball of modeling clay on each end of the pencil.
2. Lay the pencil across the middle of the jar lid and hold it in place with clay.
3. Push one end of the pencil to make the jar lid spin around on the soup can. How many times does it go around?
4. Remove the jar lid and put the marbles on top of the soup can.
5. Put the jar lid back on top of the marbles and spin the pencil and jar lid again. How many times does it go around now?

What's Happening?

Wheels spin around an axle. Without ball bearings, the wheel would rub against the axle, and sliding friction would convert all the motion energy into heat energy. The wheels would heat up and your toy would stop moving. With ball bearings between the wheel and axle, the ball bearings — like the marbles— roll around. Rolling friction is much smaller than sliding friction, so the pencil and jar spin more before friction slows everything down.

Rollin' with Friction

How can you reduce the effect of friction?

Do It!

Supplies

Shoebox,
Balloon,
Scissors,
Straws, Tape,
Ruler

1. Cut a hole in one end of the box. Push the balloon through the hole, leaving the opening outside the box.
2. Blow up the balloon and hold the end closed. Place the box on the floor and let go of the balloon. Measure how far the box moves.
3. Try other surfaces, such as carpet and sidewalk. On which surface did the box slide the farthest?
4. Lay the straws side by side to make a 3-foot-long row.
5. Blow up the balloon and place the box on one end of the straw runway, then let it go. Measure how far the box moves. Does it move farther with the runway or without?

What's Happening?

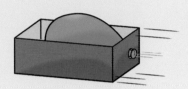

When two surfaces move against each other, there is sliding friction. Sliding friction converts motion energy into heat energy and slows things down. More force between the surfaces, and rough surfaces, cause more friction. The box slides farther on smooth surfaces than on rough surfaces.

When the box is on the straws, it creates rolling friction. Rolling friction is many times smaller than sliding friction, so the box moves farther before the rolling friction slows it down.

Phonebook Friction

Legend has it that if you interweave the pages of a phonebook, it is impossible to pull apart!

Supplies

2 phonebooks,
Friend

Do It!

1. Weave the pages of the books together by turning over one page at a time from alternating books. Keep going until you've weaved all the pages.
2. Have your friend grab the spine of one book as you grab the spine of the other. Pull as hard as you can. Can you pull the books apart?

What's Happening?

The force holding the books together is static friction. Static friction depends on the force between the two objects and the properties of the two materials in contact. Heavy objects with rough surfaces have more friction than light objects with smooth surfaces. When you weave together the pages of a book, the weight of the pages adds up. The pages also become bent at an angle, especially with thicker books. When you hold the spines to pull the books apart, you squeeze the pages together. All these factors create a LOT of force and make it nearly impossible to pull apart.

118 Sticky Rice

Can you lift a bottle of rice using just a pencil?

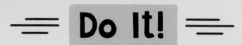

═ Do It! ═

Supplies

Glass or plastic soda bottle, Rice, Funnel, Pencil

1. Funnel the rice into the bottle to the very top. Use the pencil to pack the rice down into the bottle, and add more rice to the top. Keep packing and adding rice until it is difficult to pull the pencil out of the rice.
2. Push the pencil down as far as you can, but leave enough of the pencil sticking out of the bottle to hold on to.
3. Hold the pencil and slowly pull it up. Can you lift the bottle of rice?

What's Happening?

When you first pour the rice into the bottle, there's a lot of space between the grains of rice. As the rice is packed into the bottle, this extra space is removed. When the pencil is pushed into the bottle, there is nowhere for the rice grains to go to make room for the pencil, so they push against the pencil. The rice pushing on the pencil provide enough friction force to prevent you from pulling the pencil out!

119 Science Friction

For something to slide, it must overcome static friction. How does weight affect this?

═ Do It! ═

Supplies

Shoe, Rubber band, Scissors, Rocks, Ruler

1. Cut the rubber band into one long piece. Attach one end to the back of your shoe and put the shoe on a flat, smooth surface.
2. Pull the rubber band until the shoe is just about to move. Measure how far the rubber band stretches.
3. Place some rocks in the shoe. Pull the rubber band again until the shoe is just about to move and measure how far it stretches. How much longer did the rubber band get when you added weight to the shoe?

What's Happening?

To slide the shoe, you need to pull harder than the static friction that holds the shoe in place. Once the shoe slides, sliding friction takes over. Static friction is many times bigger than sliding friction. Once the shoe moves, it's easier to pull because the sliding friction pulls back with less force. The heavy shoe has more friction than the lighter shoe. More static friction means a bigger force is needed to move the shoe, and bigger forces stretch the rubber band longer.

A Penny for Your Bottle

Your challenge: Put a coin inside a bottle using just one finger.

Supplies

Bottle, Index card, Coin (must fit through the bottle opening)

= Do It! =

1. Place the index card on top of the bottle.
2. Place the coin on top of the card over the bottle opening. Check all sides to make sure it's right in the center.
3. Now put the coin inside the bottle using just one finger. Can you do it without reading ahead?

What's Happening?

Inertia is the tendency for an object, like the coin, to stay put until a force acts on it. The only thing keeping the coin from going in the bottle is the card. If you apply a force to the card, and only the card, to remove it from under the coin, the coin will fall into the bottle. Just use your finger to quickly flick the card straight out from under the coin. Make sure the card moves straight and doesn't flip to push the coin up and away from the bottle.

Change-ing Tower

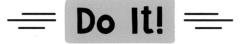

121

Your next challenge: Remove the bottom level of a coin tower without toppling it.

Supplies

10 coins, Plastic knife, Tabletop

= Do It! =

1. Stack the coins to make a small, straight tower.
2. Now remove the bottom coin from the tower using only the knife without knocking over or moving the rest of the tower. Can you do it without reading ahead?

What's Happening?

To solve the challenge, hold the tip of the plastic knife flat on the table. Slide the knife quickly and smoothly so that you just kick the bottom coin out from under the tower. The key is to move fast and not hesitate. Because you are only applying a force to the bottom coin, that's the only coin that will move. The inertia, or tendency to stay at rest, of the other coins in the tower will hold it in place.

What If?

What if you use more or fewer coins? What if you use coins of different sizes or weights? Does this make it harder or easier to remove the bottom coin?

122 Don't Drop This Egg

You'll have "egg drop" soup if you don't do this one right!

Supplies

Egg (raw if you dare, but hard-boiled works too), Toilet paper tube, Pie plate, Glass of water

Do It!

1. Place the pie pan on top of the glass of water.
2. Place the toilet paper tube on the pan directly over the glass of water.
3. Place the egg on top of the paper towel tube.
4. Now get the egg into the glass of water with just one hand. Can you do it without reading ahead?

What's Happening?

Because of inertia, the egg will stay where it is unless a force acts on it. To make it work, you just need to remove the pan and tube so the egg falls straight down into the glass. To do this, just give the pan a quick chop sideways. It will fly off the glass. The edge of the pan will hook the tube so that it gets out of the way, as well. Without the tube to hold it up, gravity will pull the egg down into the glass.

123 Streak of Beads

These beads keep going and going, with some surprising effects.

Do It!

Supplies

4 strings of round plastic beads, Scissors, Glue gun, Jar that will hold the beads

1. Make one cut to each string of beads.
2. Glue the end of one string of beads to the next, until you have one long chain of beads.
3. Feed one end of the chain into the jar carefully so there are no tangles or knots.
4. Once the beads are in the jar, hold on to the end of the chain at the top.
5. Hold the jar up high and let go of the end of the chain of beads to watch them streak out!

What's Happening?

As soon as you let go of the end of the chain of beads, gravity pulls them downward. The beads at the bottom pull on the ones above, and once they start moving, the beads will keep moving until they hit the floor because of inertia. Inertia is the tendency of an object to keep moving at the same speed and in the same direction until a force acts on it. These beads keep moving, and pulling along the beads behind them, until the floor applies a force to stop them.

Balancing Stick

Can you make a stick stand on its end?

Do It!

Supplies

Yardstick, Clay

1. Cup your hand and put the end of the stick on your palm. Let go of the stick with your other hand. Are you able to keep the stick upright?
2. Place a fist-sized lump of clay around the stick, about 8 inches from one end.
3. Try to balance the stick in the same way with the clay end up high. Now try to balance it with the clay end down low. Which situation is easiest to balance the stick?

What's Happening?

The tendency of an object to spin is called rotational inertia. It depends on the amount of mass and how far the mass is from the pivot point. In this case, the pivot point is the end of the stick in the palm of your hand. When the clay is up high, far from the pivot point, the stick has more rotational inertia than when it is down low. This means the stick turns more slowly when the clay is high, and tips over easier when it is low.

Buckets of Dryness

Amaze your friends by swinging water over your head and staying completely dry!

Do It!

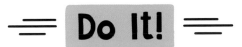

Supplies

Bucket, Water, Outdoor space

1. Fill the bucket with a few inches of water, making sure it's not too heavy and you can lift it easily.
2. Hold the bucket in front of your body and swing it back and forth, getting a little faster each time.
3. When you feel confident, swing the bucket all the way around over your head. Move the bucket fast and do not slow down until you reach the bottom of the swing. After some practice, try swinging the bucket in a circle several times without stopping.

What's Happening?

The water stays in the bucket because of inertia. Inertia is the tendency of a moving object to keep moving in a straight line. When you swing the bucket back and forth, that straight line is to the left or the right. But the bucket pulls the water into a curved path using centripetal force.

When you swing the bucket over your head, the same thing happens. The inertia of the water is sideways, but the bucket pulls it into a circle. If the inertia of the water is greater than gravity, you will stay dry!

126 Sticky Balloons

You might want to get several balloons and have a party, because this experiment will really get you charged up about static electricity!

Supplies

Balloons, Your hair or a wool sweater, Mirror, Wall

═ Do It! ═

1. Take a balloon and rub it on your hair or a wool sweater for at least 15 seconds.
2. Look in the mirror and hold the balloon a few inches from your head. Your hair should jump up and reach for the balloon.
3. Give the balloon a few more rubs on your head and then stick it on the wall. It should hang right there for quite a while: up to 30 minutes on a very dry day!

What's Happening?

Electrons are the key to electricity! Electrons are tiny, negatively charged parts of the atom that swarm and spin around the central, positively charged nucleus. For some materials called conductors (like most metals), these electrons can easily move from one atom to another. Other materials are called insulators because they hold onto their electrons more tightly, such as plastics, hair, and fur. The electricity that we use to power our appliances and electronics is just a flow of electrons through a wire. But static electricity involves electrons that are stuck in one place. We can create a static charge by rubbing together two insulators, such as a balloon and your hair.

Friction moves the electrons from one insulator to another, leaving the balloon negatively charged (it gained some electrons) and your hair positively charged (because it lost electrons). Opposites attract and likes repel. So, when the negatively charged balloon is placed near your positively charged hair, they will attract each other, causing your hair to stand up.

You can even have a charged object pull toward a neutral object like a wall. The wall is made of atoms just like everything else, and placing the balloon on the wall will polarize or move more positive charges toward the balloon and negative charges away, so that there is a pull between the negative balloon and the positive charges in the wall that holds the balloon in place.

What If?

What if you use something else to charge up your balloon? Try blankets and fabrics of different types, such as wool, cotton, nylon, and silk. You can even try furry pets! How about metal, plastic, wood, or other hard surfaces?

Use the power of static electricity to move a stream of running water.

Do It!

Supplies

Plastic comb,
Your hair,
Water faucet

1. Turn on the faucet and adjust the flow until there's just a thin stream of water flowing.
2. Comb your hair at least 10 times with the plastic comb.
3. Slowly bring the comb near the stream of flowing water without touching the water. The water should bend its direction of flow toward the comb! Move the comb around and watch what happens to the water.

What's Happening?

When you comb your hair, you not only get a sharp-looking hairdo, you also scrape electrons off your hair and onto the comb, giving it a negative charge. The water has both negative and positive charges. When you hold the comb near the stream of water, the positive charges in the water are attracted to the negative charges on the comb, and the stream of water bends.

Dancing Balloons   128

This experiment is truly repulsive! The negativity of these balloons keeps them from ever coming together.

Do It!

Supplies

2 balloons, 2 pieces of string at least 2 feet long, Your hair or a wool sweater

1. Blow up both balloons.
2. Tie a string to the end of each balloon. If you'd like, draw faces on your balloons with a marker.
3. Rub the balloons on your head or a wool sweater to charge them with electrons.
4. Hold the ends of the strings together so the balloons hang down together, and watch the fun! The charged balloons should dance around each other without touching.

What's Happening?

Rubbing the balloons on your head scrapes electrons off your hair and onto the balloons. This leaves your head with a slightly positive charge and the balloons both with a negative charge. Like charges repel. Because the balloons are both negatively charged, they will dance around each other but never touch — at least not until the electrons have escaped into the air.

129 Levitating Tinsel

Make something fly with the magical power of static electricity!

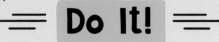 **Do It!**

Supplies

Seven 6-inch strands of tinsel, Scissors, Balloon, Your head

1. Lay out six pieces of tinsel together in a long bundle.
2. Cut two small pieces from the extra piece of tinsel and tie both ends of the tinsel bundle together.
3. Charge up a balloon by rubbing it on your hair.
4. Hold the tinsel above the balloon and drop it onto the balloon. What happens?

What's Happening?

When you rub the balloon on your hair, electrons are scraped off and transferred to the balloon, and the balloon is negatively charged. At first, the tinsel has no charge. When you drop it onto the balloon, some of those electrons are transferred to the tinsel. Now both the balloon and the tinsel are negatively charged! Objects with the same charge repel each other. The tinsel hovers above the balloon with gravity pulling it down, and the repelling electrostatic force of the electrons pushing it up. Eventually, the extra electrons on the tinsel escape into the air, but for a few seconds, it can defy gravity!

130 Spark Zapper

Static electricity can be shocking! Use this tool to make your own sparks whenever you want.

 **Do It!**

Supplies

Metal pie tin, Styrofoam plate, Styrofoam cup, Scissors, Masking tape, Your head

1. Tape the Styrofoam cup to the center of the pie tin.
2. Rub the Styrofoam plate all over your head for five seconds.
3. Put the plate down on the table, upside down.
4. Pick up the pie tin by the cup and drop it onto the plate.
5. Touch the edge of the pie tin. You will get zapped by a spark!

What's Happening?

When you rub the Styrofoam plate on your hair, you're scraping negative electrons off your head and onto the plate. The pie tin has a bunch of free electrons that can move around. When you put the pie tin on the foam plate, those free electrons are repelled by the extra electrons on the Styrofoam and try to get away. As soon as you put your finger near the pie tin, they jump onto your finger. Zap!

Salt & Pepper Pick-up

Use the force of static electricity to separate salt from pepper.

Supplies

Salt, Pepper, Paper plate, Spoon, Balloon, Your hair or a wool sweater

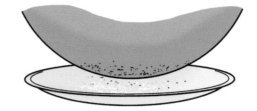

Do It!

1. Pour 1 teaspoon of salt and 1 teaspoon of pepper on the paper plate. Use the spoon to mix them up so you have a pile in the center of the plate.

2. Blow up the balloon and tie off the end.

3. Rub the balloon on your hair or a wool sweater to charge it up with electrons.

4. Hold the balloon about an inch above the salt and pepper mixture and watch what happens! You should see the pepper jump off the plate and onto the balloon, leaving the salt behind.

What's Happening?

There are two reasons the pepper sticks to the balloon and the salt does not. First, the pepper polarizes much easier than the salt. That's because its electrons move mostly to one side of the pepper flake, leaving one end positive and the other with a negative charge. The positive end is attracted to the negative balloon. Salt does not polarize quite as much, so it doesn't feel as much of a pull. However, it will jump up on the balloon if you hold it very close to the plate. Also, the pepper flakes are much lighter than the salt crystals. So even if the salt does jump up onto the balloon, it's too heavy to stay and it falls back down.

You will also see some of the pepper and salt jump up to the balloon and then fly off. This is because it grabbed an electron off the balloon and suddenly became negatively charged – just like the balloon. The like charges repel, throwing the tiny particle away.

What If?

What if you try to separate other mixtures? Try sugar and cinnamon and any other mixtures you can make from the spice cabinet.

Gelatin Pick-up

Build tiny towers of gelatin powder with static electricity!

Supplies

Unflavored gelatin, Salt, Pepper, Paper plate, Spoon, Balloon, Your hair

Do It!

1. Pour 1 tablespoon of gelatin in the center of the plate.
2. Blow up the balloon and tie off the end.
3. Rub the balloon on your hair to charge it up with electrons.
4. Hold the balloon just above the plate but not touching the pile of gelatin.
5. Slowly pull the balloon up. You should see the gelatin form tiny towers as it reaches up toward the balloon!

What's Happening?

When the balloon is held near the gelatin particles, they become polarized. Electrons move mostly to one side of the gelatin particle, leaving one end positive and the other with a negative charge. The positive end of the particle is attracted to the negative balloon. As the balloon moves away from the plate, the gelatin particles form a chain with the negative ends attached to the positive ends. These chains look like tiny towers on the plate of gelatin powder. When the balloon moves too far away, the gelatin is no longer polarized and the towers collapse.

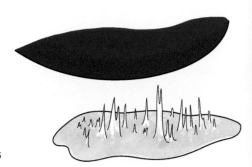

133 Static Slime

Can you stop slime in mid-flow? You sure can, with the help of static electricity!

Supplies

Cornstarch, Vegetable oil, 2 plastic cups, Spoon, Balloon, Your hair

Do It!

1. Pour ¼ cup of oil into one of the cups. Mix in 3 to 4 tablespoons of cornstarch with the spoon until the liquid looks like thin gravy.
2. Blow up the balloon and rub it on your hair to charge it.
3. Pour the mixture from one cup into the other while holding your charged balloon near the flow of liquid. The liquid should stop flowing, and you might even see solid-looking chunks jump onto the balloon!

What's Happening?

When the cornstarch particles are in the electric field caused by the charged-up balloon, they link up like a net, which slows down the flow of the oil. As soon as you remove the electric field, the oil flows normally.

Sticky Statics

Electric charges cause all sorts of objects to attract and repel—even tape!

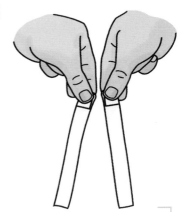

Supplies

A flat, smooth surface (a binder cover or countertop); Clear plastic tape; Scissors (optional)

═ Do It! ═

1. Place a 10-inch-long piece of tape onto the flat, smooth surface. This is the base tape.
2. Cut a 4-inch-long piece of tape and fold over a small amount on one end to make a handle.
3. Place the piece on top of the base tape.
4. Make another 4-inch piece in the same way and add it to the base tape.
5. Use the handle on the two smaller tapes and pull them off the base tape.
6. Hold these tapes so that they hang near each other. Do the tapes repel or attract? Try holding the tapes in different ways: non-sticky to non-sticky side, sticky to non-sticky side, and sticky to sticky side. Does the way you hold the tape affect whether they attract or repel?
7. One at a time, gently rub your fingers over both sides of the tapes. Bring them together again. Do they act differently now?
8. Stick the two pieces of tape together (non-sticky to sticky side) so that you have a double-thick piece of tape. Run your fingers over the tape to remove any leftover charges.
9. Pull the two pieces of tape apart by their handles. Hold the tapes so that they hang near each other. Do the tapes repel or attract? Try all the different combinations of holding the tapes as above.

What's Happening?

In the first part of the experiment, you pulled two separate pieces of tape off the base tape. Pulling the tapes off the base tape charged the tapes in the same way. Because they have like charges, they will repel each other, no matter how you hold them.

However, in the second part of the experiment, you pulled the tapes apart from each other. This left one tape with a positive charge and the other with a negative charge. The different-charged tapes attracted each other.

What If?

What if you use your charged tape to see if other household objects have a charge? Try holding a charged tape near a TV or computer monitor (when they are turned on), refrigerator, cell phone, lamp, or any other object you think might be charged.

135 Soda Can Electroscope

Make your own electroscope so you can immediately detect an electric charge!

Supplies

Empty soda can, Masking tape, Styrofoam cup, Aluminum foil, Scissors, Balloon, Your hair or wool sweater

 **Do It!**

1. Pull the tab of the can out so that it's perpendicular to the top of the can.
2. Turn the Styrofoam cup upside down and tape the can on top, so it lies sideways on the bottom of the cup and the tab on the can is vertical.
3. Cut two strips of aluminum foil about 2 inches long and ¼ inch wide.
4. Make a hook on the end of each strip, and use the hook to hang the strips from the tab of the can. The strips should hang right next to each other. Your electroscope is now ready to use!
5. Charge up a balloon by rubbing it on your hair or a wool sweater for several seconds.
6. Hold the balloon close to, but not touching, the soda can. What happens to the foil strips as the balloon gets closer to the can? What happens as you move it away?
7. Touch the charged balloon to the soda can. What happens to the foil strips when you touch the can? What happens when you take the balloon away?
8. Touch the soda can with your hand and observe what happens to the strips.

What's Happening?

When you move the charged balloon close to the can but don't touch it, the electroscope becomes charged by induction. The negative balloon repels the negative electrons to the other side of the can, so that one side is negatively charged and the other is positive. The foil strips are next to each other, so they will have a like charge and repel each other or move apart. When you move the balloon away, the charges spread out on the can and the foil strips hang down again.

When the charged balloon touches the electroscope, the can is charged by conduction. The extra electrons on the balloon move over to the can. The whole can is negatively charged, including the foil strips, so they repel each other. However, when you move the balloon away, the electroscope is still charged and the foil strips stay separated. When you touch the can with your hand, you ground the electroscope so that the extra electrons leave through your finger.

N-il- It El-ctrom--n-t

Unlike refrigerator magnets, which are always on, electromagnets only work when connected to a source of electricity.

Supplies

Long iron nail, Magnet wire (with an enamel coating), D battery, Electrical tape, Scissors, 12 small paper clips

What's Happening?

The coiled wire around the nail is called a solenoid. When electric current runs through the solenoid, it creates a magnetic field inside the metal coils. Iron has atoms that become magnetized in a magnetic field, which makes your electromagnet stronger.

Do It!

1. Wrap the wire around the nail 20 times, leaving 6 inches of wire on each side.
2. With scissors, remove 1 inch of the plastic coating from both ends of the wire.
3. Tape each piece of exposed wire to one end of the battery. You've made an electromagnet! Hold it over a pile of paper clips. How many paper clips stick to your electromagnet? Make sure to disconnect the wires from the battery when you are done experimenting, but be careful, as the wires can get hot.

Floating Paper Clip

Defy gravity by levitating a paper clip in mid-air!

Do It!

Supplies

Strong magnet, Paper clip, Thread, Scissors, Tall glass, Screwdriver, Tape, Test materials: penny, paper, cloth, etc.

1. Place the magnet on the end of the screwdriver, and then balance the screwdriver across the glass, so the magnet hangs 3 inches out from the edge of the glass.
2. Cut 12 inches of thread and tie it to the paper clip. Stick the paper clip to the magnet.
3. Slowly pull the thread downward until you pull the paper clip off the magnet and it floats a centimeter or two from the magnet.
4. Tape the thread down firmly so the paper clip stays put. Now you can test what materials block the magnetic field.
5. Place a penny between the paper clip and the magnet without touching the paper clip. What happens? Repeat the process for the other test materials. Which materials block the magnetic field and make the paper clip fall?

What's Happening?

Magnetic forces happen when the electrons spinning around atoms line up. This happens easier in some materials, like iron or nickel, than it does in other materials, like plastic or wood. When the paper clip touches the magnet, it becomes magnetized. The force between the magnet and paper clip keep it magnetized. The paper clip is caught between the upward force from the magnet and the downward force from the thread and gravity.

Magnetic Compass

Make a compass so you'll always know which direction you're headed!

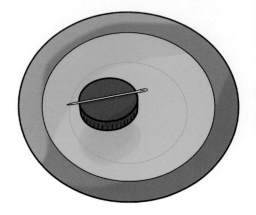

Supplies

Small bowl of water, Sewing needle, Magnet, Plastic bottle top, Tape, Compass or smartphone, Marker

═ Do It! ═

1. Magnetize the needle by rubbing it at least 50 times with one end of the magnet (the north end if it is labeled). Make sure you rub the needle in only one direction and lift the magnet off the needle each time.

2. Use a small piece of tape to secure the needle to the top of the bottle cap.

3. Float the bottle cap, with the needle on top, in the water. The needle will automatically turn to point north!

4. Use the compass or a smartphone with a compass app to figure out which end of the needle is pointing north, then use the marker to mark "N" near the north side of the bottle cap. Use your compass to figure out which direction the front door faces, which directions the street you live on runs, and which direction you go to get to school.

What's Happening?

Earth is a giant magnet! A compass is just a magnet that is free to move so it can align with the Earth's magnetic field. The bowl of water provides a low friction surface for the needle to float on and turn freely. Exposing the iron in the needle to the strong magnetic field in the magnet lines up the spin of the electrons in the needle's iron atoms, which then creates a magnetic field in the needle. Over time, the spinning electrons will fall out of line. You will then need to "recharge" your compass needle each time you use it.

What If?

What if you use a paper clip or nail instead of a needle? What if you hung the needle by a thread inside a jar so you can carry your compass around without spilling water? How else can you improve the design of this compass?

Magnet Gun

Can you hit a target with the power of magnets?

Supplies

2 neodymium magnets, 3 steel ball bearings, Ruler with a groove in the middle, Strong tape, Scissors, Table

Gauss: a unit of magnetic induction

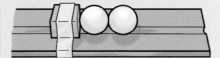

Do It!

1. Place two ball bearings at the end of the ruler. Tape one magnet next to the balls.
2. Slide the ruler so the ball and magnet are at the edge of the table. Trim extra tape off the magnet.
3. Roll another ball along the ruler toward the magnet. The ball on the end will shoot out!
4. Roll the ball at different speeds and from different distances. What happens?

What's Happening?

When the ball rolls toward the magnet, it speeds up because the magnet is pulling on it. As it accelerates, it gains kinetic energy. When the first ball hits the magnet, that energy is transferred to the magnet and the balls. The ball at the end shoots off with almost the same kinetic energy that the first ball had when it hit the magnet. Some of the energy is lost to sound and heat, but most is transferred to the ball at the end.

Electromagnetic Train

Make a train that zooms!

Do It!

1. Make two stacks of three neodymium batteries. Point the stacks toward each other so that they repel. Place each stack on either end of the battery.
2. Tape one end of the wire to the end of the dowel. Tightly wrap wire around 4 inches of the dowel. Slide the coil off.
3. Stretch the coils apart so that each loop does not touch.
4. Place the battery-magnet train into the coil. Watch it zoom to the other end! If your train doesn't move, flip it around or turn over the stack of magnets on one end.

Supplies

Copper wire (16 gauge, uncoated), AAA battery, 6 neodymium magnets slightly bigger than the battery, Dowel, Tape

What's Happening?

When you place your train into the coil, it creates an electric circuit. Electricity travels from one end of the battery, through the magnet into the wire, where it travels around the battery and back in through the magnet on the other end. The electricity creates its own magnetic field. The magnets on the battery are lined up so that the magnetic field in the wire pushes the train through the coil.

141 Minute Motor

This electric motor is so simple, it can be put together in about a minute!

Supplies

AA battery, Screw (that will stick to a magnet), Neodymium battery, Insulated wire, Electrical tape, Scissors

Do It!

1. Remove some of the plastic insulation from each end of the wire.
2. Tape one end of the wire to the negative end of the battery.
3. Place the magnet on the flat end of the screw, and then put the pointed end of the screw on the positive end of the battery.
4. Hold the battery so the screw and magnet hang downward.
5. Touch the loose end of the wire to the magnet and watch the screw spin around!

What's Happening?

When the end of the loose wire touches the magnet, you give the electric current in the battery a path to follow. The current flows out of the battery, through the wire, into the magnet, through the screw, and back to the battery. Any object with a current flowing through it in a magnetic field is pushed on by the Lorentz force, which causes the screw to spin around.

142 Magnetic Fruit

Can magnets stick to food?

Do It!

Supplies

Large toothpick, Thread, Scissors, Tape, Fruit, Strong magnet, Ruler

1. Tape a ruler to a countertop with 6 inches hanging over the edge.
2. Cut an 18-inch piece of thread. Tape it to the ruler longways down the ruler.
3. Tie the middle of the toothpick to the other end of the string.
4. Slide a grape onto each end of the toothpick so the toothpick is balanced. Let the grapes hang until they stop turning.
5. Slowly move the magnet toward the grape. Does the grape move? Does it move toward or away from the magnet? Try other grape-sized pieces of fruit. Do they move near the magnet?

What's Happening?

The reason why the fruits moved slowly away from the strong magnet is because of a weak magnetism that repels objects, known as diamagnetism. When some non-metals are in an electric field, the electrons spinning in the atom line up opposite of the magnetic field in the magnet, which creates a repelling force so weak that you can only see it when you hang the fruit on a string. If you put the grape on a table near a magnet, it won't move at all.

This Battery Is a Lemon

Create your own electricity with fruit!

Supplies

6 lemons, 6 nails or large paper clips, Heavy copper wire (with or without plastic coating), Wire cutters or heavy scissors, 1 LED or light bulb from holiday lights (with wires attached), Electrical tape

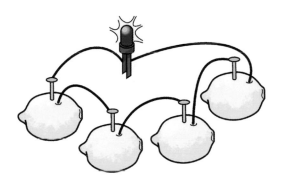

═ Do It! ═

1. Cut the copper wire into six 8-inch lengths and two 10-inch lengths. Cut off about an inch of the plastic insulation from both ends of each wire.

2. Squeeze and roll the lemons on the table so they are good and juicy on the inside without breaking the skin.

3. Stick a nail about halfway in each of the lemons.

4. Connect the lemons in a row with the short copper wires.

5. Stick the ends of the copper wire into the lemon close to the nail, but not touching.

6. Connect a long wire to each wire or lead on the light bulb using electrical tape.

7. Stick the other ends of the copper wire into a lemon on each end of the row. Watch the light bulb light up! If you are using an LED and it doesn't light up, just switch the leg of the LED that each wire is attached to so the electricity flows in the right direction to light the bulb.

What's Happening?

Usually, your lights would be plugged into an electrical socket or would be powered by a battery, right? Batteries are made of two different metals and an acid. In this case, the lemon provides the acid. The nail and copper wire are the two different metals. The nail and wire are electrodes, where the electricity enters and leaves the battery. Electrons flow from the nail into the lemon juice acid to the copper wire, and then to the next lemon, gathering more and more electrons until there are enough to light up the bulb!

What If?

What if you use other fruit in your battery? Try other acidic fruits and vegetables, such as oranges, limes, tomatoes, and potatoes, and see what happens.

Holiday Light Circuits

Why do some holiday lights go out when one bulb goes out, but other lights stay lit?

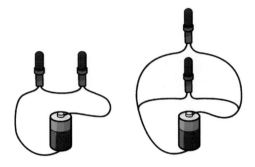

Supplies

Strand of holiday lights, Scissors, D battery, Electrical tape

Do It!

1. Cut two lights off the strand, making sure each light has two long wires attached.
2. Remove an inch of plastic coating from the end of each wire.

Make a Series Circuit

1. Twist one light's wire to the other light's wire to attach them in a row. Tape them together.
2. Tape the wires at both ends of the lights to opposite ends of the battery. Do the bulbs light up? How bright are they? What happens if you take a bulb out?

Make a Parallel Circuit

1. Cut two extra pieces of wire, about 4 inches long, from the strand of lights.
2. Remove an inch of plastic coating from the end of each wire. Twist one light's wires to the other light's wires to create a circle.
3. Attach an extra wire where the wires from the light connect. Tape the wires together.
4. Touch the loose ends of the extra wires to opposite ends of the battery. Do the bulbs light up? How bright are they? What happens if you take a bulb out?

What's Happening?

For electrical current to light up a light bulb, it must have a complete circuit that connects from one end of a battery back to the other end. Both the series and parallel circuits make at least one loop for the electrical current to flow through. In a series circuit, there is one big loop for the current to flow through. The current flows through both lights in the circuit and the bulbs light brightly. If you take one bulb out, the loop is broken so the current stops flowing and the bulb that is left does not light up.

In a parallel circuit, there are two connected loops. Half the current goes through one light bulb and half goes through the other. Both bulbs light, but are half as bright as the bulbs in the series circuit. When one bulb is removed, there is still a path for the current and the other light bulb stays lit.

While light bulbs in a series circuit burn brighter, one burned-out light will make the whole strand of lights go out. In a parallel circuit, one burned-out light bulb does not take out all the lights in the strand.

Gassy Water

Break apart water atoms to make hydrogen gas and oxygen gas!

Supplies

Water, Salt, Measuring spoons, 2 cups, Clear glass, 2 lead pencils sharpened on both ends, two 8-inch lengths of plastic-coated copper wire, Scissors, 9-volt battery, Electrical tape, Outdoor space

═ Do It! ═

1. Do this experiment outdoors. In one cup, mix ¾ tablespoons of salt into 1 cup of water to make a 5% saltwater solution.

2. In the other cup, mix 1½ tablespoons of salt with 1 cup of water to make a 10% saltwater solution. Label each cup.

3. Remove 1 inch of plastic coating from each end of both pieces of copper wire.

4. Wrap the end of one wire around the end of a pencil, making sure the wire touches the black graphite in the pencil.

5. Tape the wire in place, and do the same with the other pencil and wire.

6. Wrap the loose ends of the two wires around the leads on the battery: one on the positive end and one on the negative. Tape the wires in place.

7. Fill the glass halfway with water, and place the pencils in the glass. After several seconds, bubbles should cover the ends of the pencil. The bubbles on the pencil on the negative lead of the battery are hydrogen, and the other lead is oxygen.

8. Take the pencils out of the glass and empty the water.

9. Pour in the 5% saltwater solution and put the pencils back in. What happens? Repeat the experiment with the 10% saltwater solution. Which liquid created the most bubbles?

What's Happening?

On the pencil connected to the positive lead of the battery, water is oxidized. The water is broken into oxygen gas (O_2) and charged hydrogen ions. On the pencil connected to the negative lead of the battery, water is broken into hydrogen gas (H_2) and hydroxide ions. There are a lot more hydrogen bubbles on the positive lead than there are oxygen bubbles on the negative. Water (H_2O) has twice as many hydrogen atoms as oxygen. This means it releases twice as much hydrogen gas.

Salt is an electrolyte and helps the water conduct electricity more easily so more energy is available to break up the water molecule quicker. Once you add salt to the solution, the gas bubbles on the anode aren't just oxygen, but also contain some chlorine from the salt.

Homopolar Motor

How many motors do you have in your house? Refrigerators, blenders, computers, and toys that move all have motors. Can you make your own electric motor?

Supplies

AA battery, Neodymium magnet,
Copper wire (16 gauge, uncoated),
Pliers, Wire cutters

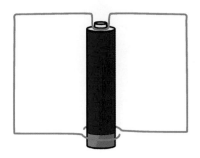

≡ Do It! ≡

1. Cut off a 10-inch piece of copper wire.
2. Bend the wire into a square that is even on both sides, with a small dip at the top.
3. Curve the bottoms of the wire in opposite directions, making sure they touch the magnet but do NOT touch each other.
4. Put the magnet on the flat end of the battery.
5. Slide the wire onto the battery and magnet so the point at the top touches the bump on the top of the battery, and the curves at the bottom wrap around the magnet. As soon as the wire is in place, it will spin around! If the motor doesn't work, try turning the magnets upside down. If that doesn't work, try a fresh battery. Also make sure the wire is not getting stuck to the magnet or battery, and that the bottom of the wire is touching the magnet only.

What's Happening?

When you put the wire onto the battery and motor, an electric current flows through the wire, down to the magnet, and back to the battery on both sides. There is also a strong magnetic field from the magnets. Whenever there is an electrical current in a magnetic field, the wire carrying the current feels the Lorentz force, that is at a right angle to both the current and the magnetic field. The Lorentz force pushes the wire so that it spins around the battery.

What If?

What if you bend the wire into other shapes that spin around? Just make sure the shape is symmetrical so it doesn't fall off the battery when it spins around.

Electromagnetic Motor

This electric motor harnesses the power of a magnetic force to make it go!

Supplies

D or C battery, 2 large safety pins, Electrical tape, Magnet wire (wire with an enamel coating), Scissors, Strong magnet, Marker or other round object about ½ to 1 inch in diameter, Sandpaper

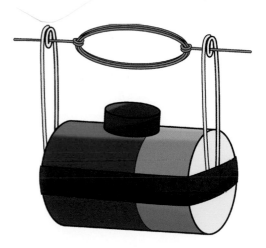

≡ Do It! ≡

1. Tape the top of a safety pin to each end of the battery so that the bottom ends are pointing straight up in the same direction.
2. Wrap the magnet wire tightly around the marker 15 times.
3. Leave a 2-inch length of wire on each side of the loops.
4. Slide the loops off the marker and wrap the end pieces tightly around either side of the loop several times to hold the loop together. The rest of the end pieces should stick straight out from opposite sides of the loop.
5. Use the sandpaper to remove all the enamel coating from the end piece on one side of the loop. Then use the sandpaper to remove the enamel from just one side of the end piece on the other side of the loop.
6. Stick the end pieces of the loop through the holes at the bottom of the safety pins so the loop is now suspended over the battery.
7. Place the magnet on the battery, directly below the center of the loop. Watch the loop spin around!

What's Happening?

An electric motor uses the attracting and repelling properties of magnets to change electromagnetic energy into motion energy. This motor has two magnets: the strong magnet you placed on top of the battery and the electromagnet you created from the magnet wire. When electrons, in the form of electrical current from the battery, pass through the wire, it creates a weak magnetic field. By wrapping the wire several times into a loop, the magnetic field is stronger. The magnetic force from the strong magnet pushes and pulls on the loops of the electromagnet, causing it to spin around.

What If?

What if you use more or fewer loops in the electromagnet? What if you change the shape from a circle to a square or triangle? What if you make bigger loops? What is the biggest motor you can make?

148 Air Lift

Use the power of air to lift a heavy book off the table.

Supplies

Heavy book, Straw, Gallon-size resealable bag, Tape, Scissors

═ Do It! ═

1. Seal the bag and make sure there is no air inside. Cut a small hole through one side of the bag about an inch below the seal. Stick the straw in the hole and push it in a couple of inches. Use tape to seal the straw in the hole.

2. Lay the bag on a table so that the straw sticks out over the edge. Put the heavy book on top of the bag. Blow into the straw and watch the book rise off the tabletop.

What's Happening?

If you lift the book over the table, there is air between the book and the table. But if you drop the book, it falls and pushes the air out of the way as if it wasn't even there. Most of the time, you don't notice the air around you. We move through it almost effortlessly. But if you pack a bunch of air into a small space, like blowing up a balloon or a plastic bag, you can see the air molecules taking up space.

The bag between the book and the table holds the air in place. As you blow into the bag, the air becomes pressurized. The air molecules are pushed together and out equally in all directions. The bag pushes down on the table and up on the book, lifting it up!

What If?

What if you use a garbage bag? Can you lift a friend off the table? Have them sit on a flat piece of cardboard on top of the bag. Use duct tape to seal the open end of the bag and attach several straws so that other friends can help you blow up the bag.

Upside-down Glass of Water, Part 1

Air pushes against your body with a force of 15 pounds per square inch! Imagine a bowling ball pushing against every inch of your body. You are so used to this air pressure that you don't even notice it. Is air pressure enough to keep water in a glass, even if you turn it upside down?

Supplies

Drinking glass, Water, Index card

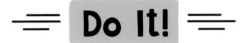

Do It!

1. Fill the glass at least half full of water.
2. Place the index card on top of the glass. Hold the glass with one hand and put your other hand flat over the index card. Quickly flip the glass upside down. Remove your hand from the index card. The water stays in the upside-down glass!

What's Happening?

The secret to this water trick is air. The air surrounds you and constantly bumps into you. There are also miles of air above you that are pulling downward onto you and the glass of water by gravity. All of this adds up to a force of about 15 pounds per square inch (psi) pushing on that glass of water from all directions.

Before you flip the glass upside down, the air pressure inside the glass and outside the glass are the same. However, during the flipping process, a tiny bit of water leaks out but no air gets in. This means the air left in the glass has a lower pressure than the air outside the glass. The outside air pushes up more than the inside air and the weight of the water push down and the water stays in the glass.

So, what keeps the card from falling off and letting the air in and the water out of the glass? The answer is surface tension and adhesion. Water has a positive end and a negative end. Because opposites attract, the water molecules line up with the opposite charges sticking together, making a sticky skin on the surface of the water. This sticky skin holds the water together. Scientists call this surface tension. The water sticks to itself but also to other stuff, such as the index card. The index card literally sticks to the surface of the water to keep air from getting in and water from getting out.

Upside-Down Glass of Water, Part 2

What if you turn your glass upside down and take off the index card?

Do It!

Supplies

Mason jar with ring, Cheesecloth (or screen), Water, Index card

1. Cut a piece of cheesecloth a bit larger than the top of the mason jar. Lay it on the jar and screw the ring on top.
2. Fill the jar halfway with water. Hold the jar with one hand and put your other hand flat over the index card. Quickly flip the jar upside down. Remove your hand from the index card. Slowly slide the index card off the glass. Does the water stay in the jar? Tap your finger against the cheesecloth. Does the water still stay in the jar?

What's Happening?

Without the index card in place, surface tension is the main force holding the water in the jar. If you look at the cheesecloth while the jar is upside down, you'll see the water bulging through each hole. The water molecules stick to each other, forming a surface tension skin on the surface of the water. This sticky surface tension keeps the water from leaking through the holes.

---

151 Balloon in a Bottle

It's like a ship in a bottle … but with a balloon!

Do It!

Supplies

Plastic bottle, Balloon, Thumbtack, Nail

1. Push a balloon into the bottle and stretch the opening over the opening of the bottle. Blow into the balloon bottle. Can you blow up the balloon?
2. Use the thumbtack to poke a hole in the bottom of the bottle. With the nail, make the hole a little bigger. Blow into the balloon bottle. Can you blow up the balloon?
3. Blow up the balloon in the bottle again, and then put your finger over the hole in the bottom. What happens?
4. To trick a friend, offer to hold the bottle while they try to blow up the balloon. Keep your finger over the hole so the balloon won't blow up. When they give up, take your finger off the hole and blow up the balloon easily.

What's Happening?

It is impossible to blow up a balloon inside a bottle if there is nowhere for the air in the bottle to go. With a hole in the bottle, you can blow up the balloon and push the rest of the air in the bottle out of the hole.

Air Pressure Chop

There are over 70 miles of air pushing down on you right now. That is a lot of weight, but is it enough to break a ruler in half?

Supplies

Wooden ruler (without metal strip) or wooden paint stir stick, Newspaper, Tabletop

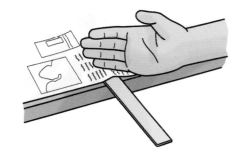

═ Do It! ═

1. Lay the ruler on the table so that a little less than half sticks out from the table. Chop the ruler hard and fast. Does the ruler move?

2. Lay the ruler on the table in the same way. Unfold two full sheets of newspaper and lay them over the ruler one on top of the other so that they completely cover the part of the ruler on the table. Smooth out the newspaper so there is no air between the paper and the table. Chop the ruler hard and fast. Does the ruler move now? Are you able to break the ruler? If not, try again and make sure the newspaper is smooth and you are striking the ruler very hard and fast.

What's Happening?

The first time you chopped the ruler without the newspaper, the ruler flipped off the table. The only force holding the ruler onto the table was gravity and the small amount of air pressure pushing on top of the ruler. Your chop easily overcame these forces. When you put the newspaper on top of the ruler, there is much more room for air pressure to push down. Air pushes down with a force of about 15 pounds for every square inch. Most newspapers are 23½ by 29½ inches. This means that, if there is no air under the paper, air pressure is pushing down on the newspaper with a force of over 10,000 pounds! However, you probably can't get all the air out from under the newspaper. When you chopped the ruler very fast, it quickly lifts the newspaper. The air does not have time to move into this space and a small vacuum is formed under the newspaper. This causes a suction effect when the high air pressure in the room pushes the newspaper back down.

What If?

What if you use just one piece of newspaper? Can you still break the ruler? What if you fold one piece in half? What is the smallest amount of paper (layers and size) you can use and still break the ruler?

153 Bernoulli Blower

Daniel Bernoulli was a Swiss mathematician and physicist in the early 1700s. He is best known for discovering that slow-moving fluids (such as air or water) have a higher pressure (push harder) than fast-moving fluids. This leads to some pretty cool phenomena, like this little toy made of string, paper, and a straw.

Supplies

Straw, Cardstock or construction paper, Hole punch, String, Tape, Scissors, Ruler, Markers (optional)

Do It!

1. Cut out a 3" x 2" rectangle from the cardstock. Roll the rectangle into a 3-inch-long tube and tape it together. Punch a hole about ½ inch from one end of the tube.

2. Cut a piece of string about 20 inches long. Thread the string through the tube and tie it so it makes a big loop. Cut off any extra string near the knot.

3. Cut a 4-inch piece of straw and stick it just up to the hole but not inside the tube. Blow hard and watch the string fly up into the air and go around through the tube. If you want, use the marker to decorate the tube and make stripes on the string so its motion is easier to see.

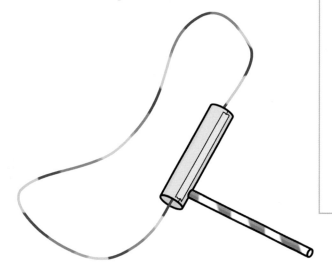

What's Happening?

According to Bernoulli's principle, fast-moving air has a lower pressure than slow-moving air. By blowing on the straw, you send fast-moving air up through the tube. The string gets carried along by the fast-moving air as it moves to the top of the tube. The slow-moving air outside of the tube pushes the string into the fast-moving stream coming out the top of the tube and lifts the string into the air. Because the string is a loop, it gets pulled back in the bottom of the tube and keeps going around.

Bernoulli's Water Gun

Daniel Bernoulli discovered that fast-moving air pushes less than slow-moving air. Little did he suspect that this discovery could be used to make a water gun!

Supplies

Straw, Glass of water, Scissors

Do It!

1. Cut the straw in half. Put one half in the glass of water and hold it so that only about an inch of straw sticks up out of the water.

2. Put the other straw in your mouth and blow hard at the top of the straw in the water. You may need to adjust the height of the straw and the angle at which you blow until a fine mist of water comes flying out of the straw in the water.

What's Happening?

Blowing across the top of the straw in the water causes low pressure above the straw. The still air in the straw and on top of the water has a higher pressure. This means the air in the straw pushes up and the air in the room pushes down on the water. All of this pushing sends water out of the straw. As soon as the water hits the fast-moving air, it breaks into tiny droplets that spray everywhere!

Bottle Crush

Flatten a water bottle using the strength of air pressure.

Do It!

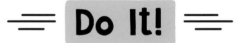

Supplies

Empty plastic water bottle, Hot water, Ice water, Large baking dish

1. Fill the baking dish with ice water.

2. Pour ¼ cup of hot tap water into the water bottle and screw the cap on. Shake the bottle for 15 seconds. Take off the cap for just a couple of seconds and then screw it back on tightly.

3. Lay the bottle in the ice water and turn it around so that the ice water covers the entire bottle. Keep turning the bottle until it starts to crush in on itself.

What's Happening?

When you shake the hot water in the bottle, you are heating up the air inside. Hot air expands and pushes out on the bottle. When you take the lid off the bottle, even just for a few seconds, the hot air pushes out of the bottle, leaving less air inside. When you put the bottle in the ice water, the air inside cools very quickly. The cold air contracts, causing less pressure inside the bottle. The higher air pressure outside pushes on the bottle, causing it to flatten!

156 Bottle Stopper

Watch as a table tennis ball appears to defy gravity!

Supplies

Table tennis ball, Plastic drink bottle, Water

== Do It! ==

1. Fill the bottle to the top with water.
2. Place the ball on top of the bottle. Slowly pick up the bottle and turn it upside down. Do NOT touch the ball while you do this. The ball and the water stay in the bottle!

What's Happening?

We hardly ever notice that air is all around us. Yet the air near the surface of the earth, where we are, is pushing on us and everything else with a force of about 15 pounds per square inch. This experiment works because of the round shape of the ball. It has a large surface area, which means that a lot more air pressure is pushing on it than a flat piece of paper of the same round size. As long as the force from air pressure on the ball is greater than the weight of the water in the bottle, it will stay in place!

157 Cups on a Balloon

Glue and tape aren't the only ways to make things stick together.

== Do It! ==

Supplies

Balloons, Disposable cups, Bowl of water, Friend

1. Dip the top of one cup into the water.
2. Blow up the balloon to the size of a tennis ball. Have your friend hold the cup under the bottom of the balloon. Continue to blow up the balloon so that some of it stays in the cup. Once the balloon is blown up all the way, let go of the cup. Does the cup stick to the balloon?
3. Try again using two cups dipped in water. When the balloon is tennis-ball size, have your friend hold the cups onto the sides of the balloon. When the balloon is fully inflated, do the cups stay on the balloon?

What's Happening?

When you stick a cup on a balloon, the balloon pushes some of the air out of the cup. As you continue to blow up the balloon, the balloon flattens and takes up less room in the cup. This means there is more room for the air that was left in the cup and causes lower pressure inside the cup. The higher-pressure air outside pushes the cup onto the balloon. Dipping the cup in the water helps prevent air from leaking into the cup.

Floating Candle

Do tea light candles float? Find out in this illuminating experiment!

ADULT NEEDED

Supplies

Tea light candle, Pie pan, Water, Food coloring, Lighter or match, Clear drinking glass

Do It!

1. Pour ½ inch of water into the pan, but not any deeper than your candle is tall. Add food coloring to make the water easier to see.
2. Place the candle in the middle of the pan and light it. Let the candle burn for a few seconds, and then place the drinking glass upside down over the candle. What happens to the flame and the water in the pan?

What's Happening?

The water level changes suddenly because of heat and air pressure. While the candle is burning, it heats the air inside the glass. The hotter air expands, pushing against the glass with a higher air pressure. When the candle uses up all the fuel in the glass and goes out, the air in the glass cools suddenly. The cooling air contracts and lowers the air pressure inside the glass. The higher air pressure in the room pushes water into the lower-pressure glass so that the pressure on both sides is equal.

Flying Cups

Levitate a cup using the power of your breath.

Do It!

Supplies

2 plastic cups

1. Place one cup inside the other.
2. Hold the cups in front of your face, level with your mouth. Take a deep breath and blow hard. What happens to the inside cup? Now blow a little more gently. Can you make one cup float inside the other?

What's Happening?

Still air pushes more than moving air. Scientists call this the Bernoulli Principle. This principle explains everything from why airplanes fly to why the shower curtain sometimes attacks you when you take a hot shower. In this experiment, it explains why the inside cup goes flying.

When you put one cup inside the other, there's a small amount of air in the bottom between the cups. This air is not moving, and neither is the air at the top of the cups. When you blow across the rims of the cups, the air moves around the top of the cup. Now the air at the top of the cups is moving and not pushing down as hard as it used to, so the air inside the outside cup pushes the top cup out.

160 Jumping Coin

Putting an empty bottle in the freezer with a coin for a lid can lead to some explosive results!

Supplies

Empty soda bottle (plastic or glass), Coin (large enough to cover the top of the bottle), Freezer, Paper towel, Water

Do It!

1. Take the top off the bottle and place it in the freezer for at least an hour until it is cold.

2. Cut out a round piece of paper towel the same size as the coin. Wet the paper towel completely. Without taking the bottle out of the freezer, place the paper towel and the coin over the top of the bottle so that the opening is completely covered. Close the freezer and wait another 30 minutes until the paper towel is completely frozen.

3. Take the bottle out of the freezer and use your hands to warm up the bottle. Make sure the opening is pointed away from you, other people, and anything that could break. After about a minute, the coin will shoot off the bottle!

What's Happening?

When you put the empty bottle in the freezer without a cover, the bottle and the air inside both get very cold. Air contracts and takes up less space when it is cold. Because the bottle is open, more air goes into the cold bottle than was in the warm bottle. Putting the wet paper towel and coin on top of the bottle seals the bottle so no air can come in or out. (The coin is too bumpy to seal it completely, so the wet paper towel ensures that the bottle is completely sealed.) When you take the bottle out of the freezer and warm it up, the air expands again and takes up more space. Because extra air went into the cold bottle, there is more air than the warm bottle can hold, and it pushes the coin off the top.

What If?

What if you use a smaller or larger bottle? What if you put the frozen bottle in hot water to warm it up even quicker? What can you change to make the coin shoot higher and more quickly?

Magnus Flyer

This simple flyer uses the same science that pitchers use to throw a curve ball.

Supplies

2 Styrofoam cups, Tape, String, Rubber band, Markers (optional)

Do It!

1. Place one cup on the table upside down and the other on top of the first right-side up so that the bottoms are together. Wrap tape around the cups to hold them together. You can decorate the cups with markers, if you like. The decorations make it easier to see the spinning motion.

2. Cut a piece of string about 30 inches long. Tie one end of the string to the rubber band to make the launcher.

3. Wrap the string around the center of the flyer, where the cups are taped together. Stretch out the rubber band at the end of the string so that it goes once around the flier, as well. Hold the flyer with one hand so that the rubber band comes out underneath the flyer. Stretch out the rubber band away from you and pull the flyer toward your face. Release the flyer. Watch it spin and glide!

What's Happening?

When you release the launcher, the cups spin in the air. If you look carefully, the flyer is moving away from you, but the cups are spinning toward you. This is called bottom spin. This bottom spin causes whirlpools of air behind the cups, which pushes the flier up and forward. Scientists call this the Magnus Effect. In baseball, the Magnus Effect is used to throw curve balls, but instead of topspin, the pitcher adds a sidespin, which causes the ball to turn or curve sideways.

What If?

What if you use smaller or larger Styrofoam cups? What size cups gives the longest and highest flight?

Does the length of the string in the launcher matter? Try using long rubber bands in a chain instead of the string. Which launcher gives the longest flight? What happens if you wrap the launcher around the flier in the other direction?

162 Cup Jump

Can you make a table tennis ball jump without touching it?

Supplies

Table tennis ball, 2 cups

Do It!

1. Place the ball in one cup and put the empty cup right behind it.
2. Gently blow across the top of the first cup and slightly down toward the far side of the ball. What does the ball do? Give a big, strong blow and watch it jump from one cup into the other. It may take some practice to get the angle and strength of the blow just right to make the ball jump directly into the other cup.

What's Happening?

When you blow across the top of the cup and down on the far side of the ball, you create low pressure in these areas. The air under the ball and closer to you is not moving and has a greater pressure, which pushes the ball up and into the other cup.

163 Floating Ball

Make a ball float with the power of science!

Do It!

1. Turn the hair dryer on its highest setting and point it straight up. Place the ball in the flow of air. What does the ball do?
2. Slowly tilt the hair dryer at an angle. How far can you tilt the hair dryer before the ball falls?
3. Gently move the hair dryer straight up and down. What does the ball do now?

Supplies

Hair dryer, Table tennis ball

What's Happening?

The fast-moving air coming out of the hair dryer has a much lower pressure than the still air in the room around it. The stream of fast-moving air pushes the ball up. Every time it starts to move out of this stream of fast air, the high pressure from the still air in the room pushes it back. Tilt the hair dryer until the weight of the ball is greater than the high pressure pushing upward, and the ball falls.

What If?

Can you float more than one ball at a time with the hair dryer? What other objects can you float? Try a balloon or an empty toilet paper tube.

Ball in the Funnel  164

Can you blow a ball out of a funnel?

Supplies

Funnel,
Table tennis ball

Do It!

1. Place the small end of the funnel in your mouth. Tilt your head back so the large end is pointed up.

2. Place the ball in the funnel. Blow as hard as you can. Does the ball come out? Try it again, but this time, while you're blowing, tilt your head forward so the large end of the funnel points down. Does the ball come out of the funnel while you are blowing?

What's Happening?

It turns out that blowing into the funnel keeps the ball inside the funnel. When you blow, the fast-moving air creates low pressure under and around the ball. The high pressure in the room pushes the ball into the funnel. The harder you blow, the more the ball sticks in the funnel!

Shoot the Breeze

The next three experiments use the power of air to create a cannon.

Basic Air Cannon 165

Use a simple cardboard box to shoot air all the way across the room!

Do It!

Supplies

Large box (at least
12 inches long and
12 inches wide),
Tape, Scissors,
Styrofoam Cups

1. If your box has any loose flaps, tape them in place so you have a sealed box. Cut a hole about 4 inches across on a small end of the box.

2. Stack a pyramid of Styrofoam cups as a target for your cannon.

3. Stand about 3 feet away from the cup pyramid. Aim the open end of the cannon at the cups. To shoot the cannon, take both hands and slam them on the sides of the box. An air cannonball will knock over the cups! Keep moving back to see how far away you can use the cannon to knock over the cups.

166 Portable Air Cannon

This air cannon is small enough to fit in your backpack.

Supplies

Plastic yogurt cup, Balloon, Scissors, Tape, Toilet paper

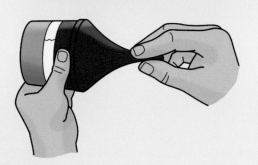

Do It!

1. Cut a small, round hole in the middle of the bottom of the yogurt container.

2. Stretch the balloon by blowing it up and letting the air back out. Cut the open end off the balloon and stretch the top over the large opening of the yogurt container. Tape the balloon in place.

3. To shoot the cannon, pull back on the balloon, and then release it so that it snaps back onto the yogurt cup. Air will shoot out of the small hole. Tape long strips of toilet paper from the top of a doorway to use as a target for your cannon. How far away can you stand and make the toilet paper move?

167 Smoke Rings

Use smoke to see just what comes out of the air cannon.

ADULT NEEDED

Do It!

Supplies

Incense stick, Lighter, Air cannon (either the basic or portable version)

1. Light the end of the incense stick and let it burn for two seconds. Blow it out and stick the smoking end inside your air cannon. Cover the opening with your hands so the smoke doesn't escape. When the cannon is full of smoke, take out the incense stick and put it aside.

2. Shoot the air cannon. Do you see the smoke rings?

3. Now that you can see the air coming out of your air cannon, you can measure its speed. Stand 6 feet away from a target and time how long it takes the smoke ring to get there. Use a calculator to divide the distance by the time to get the speed.

What's Happening?

When you shoot an air cannon, the air inside pushes out through the hole. As this air comes out, it pushes the air that was already there out of the way, creating a twisting doughnut of air called a toroidal vortex. A vortex describes the twisting of a fluid. You have probably seen a vortex when you drain the bathtub. Vortices are special because the motion is stable and doesn't need any help to keep its shape. The toroidal vortex from your air cannon is so stable, it will travel across the room before it falls apart. When you add smoke to your cannon, you see exactly how far it goes!

Big Bag Blow-up

How many breaths do you think it would take to blow up a garbage bag? Can you blow up the bag with just ONE breath?

Supplies

Large garbage bag

Do It!

1. Gather the open end of the garbage bag and blow air into it just like you would a balloon. How many breaths does it take to fill the bag with air?

2. Squeeze the air out of the bag. Hold the bag open about a foot in front of your mouth. Take a deep breath and blow as hard and long as you can into the bag. Are you able to blow up the bag with just one breath?

What's Happening?

When you hold the bag close to your mouth and blow, the only air going into the bag is the air from your lungs. It takes a LOT of breaths to fill the bag. When you hold the opening of the bag farther away and blow air out of your mouth, it moves faster than the air in the rest of the room. Still-moving air has more pressure, or pushes harder, than fast-moving air. As the fast-moving air moves into the bag, the higher-pressure still air in the room pushes into the bag and fills it quickly!

Water Fountains

Use the power of air pressure to create three amazing water fountains.

On-Off Fountain

Turn this water fountain on and off with just the tip of your finger.

Do It!

Supplies

Small water bottle, Bucket, Water, Straw, Modeling clay, Thumbtack

1. Poke a hole in the bottom of the plastic bottle. Cut the straw in half. Wrap clay around the middle of the piece of straw and stick the straw into the top of the bottle. Use the clay to seal the straw into the bottle.

2. Fill the bucket with water. Stick the bottle into the water, straw-end first, so that almost all the bottle is under water. Water should come bubbling up through the straw inside the bottle like a fountain. Put your finger over the hole in the bottom of the bottle (sticking out of the water). What happens to the fountain? Take your finger off the hole. What happens now?

What's Happening?

When you push an empty bottle full of air down under water, the water pushes on the air trapped in the bottle, causing high air pressure inside the bottle. The air pushes out of the hole as the water pushes up through the straw. When you close the hole, the water flows until the pressure in the bottle is the same as that in the water, and then the fountain stops flowing. Remove your finger and the fountain flows again.

170 Fountain Inside a Bottle

Watch as a fountain forms in a bottle!

= Do It! =

1. Depending on the size of your bottle, you might need to cut the straw. The straw should be about 3 inches shorter than your bottle. Wrap modeling clay around the straw about an inch from the end.
2. Pour hot water into the soda bottle. Hot water from the faucet will work fine, but hotter water will make the fountain rise higher. Pour cold water into the bowl, along with a couple of ice cubes and a few drops of food coloring.
3. Quickly pour the hot water out of the bottle and put the straw into the bottle. Use the modeling clay to seal the straw on the bottle with the long end inside the bottle. Immediately turn the bottle upside down in the bowl of cold colored water. Watch the fountain inside the bottle!

Supplies

Glass soda bottle, Modeling clay, Straw, Bowl, Hot water, Cold water, Ice, Food coloring

What's Happening?

The hot water in the bottle is used to heat up the bottle and the air inside of it. Hot air molecules move faster and farther apart than cool air, so there is less air inside the hot bottle than when it was cool. When you put the straw in the bottle and seal it with clay, it is difficult for the cooler air to get into the bottle. Once the bottle is upside down in the cold water, the air inside cools and contracts. This creates low pressure inside the bottle, and the cold water pushes up the straw and sprays into the bottle.

171 Fountain Outside a Bottle

Fountains don't always need to be inside bottles to work.

= Do It! =

1. Poke a hole in the middle of the side of the bottle. Push the pen through to make a round hole. Stick the straw through the hole so that the bottom of the straw is near the bottom of the bottle. The bendable part of the straw should be outside the bottle and bend upward. Use the clay to seal the hole around the straw.
2. Fill the bottle with water and place it in the tray to catch the water. Blow up the balloon and put it on the top of the bottle. Watch the fountain flow outside the bottle!

Supplies

2-liter soda bottle, Balloon, Bendable straw, Modeling clay, Pen, Tray

What's Happening?

A balloon full of air has very high air pressure. If you let go of the balloon before tying it off, it pushes out on the water so that it flows out through the straw.

At Home

Use the laboratories in your home—the kitchen and bathroom—with experiments using eggs, water, and ice.

Hot Chocolate Effect

172

This experiment is perfect for a cold morning, and you can drink it when you are done!

Food

= Do It! =

Supplies

Ceramic mug, Instant hot chocolate mix, Hot water, Metal spoon

1. Tap the rim of the empty mug with your spoon and listen to the pitch (how high or low the sound is). Does it change?
2. Pour hot water into the mug and tap again. Any change?
3. Stir the water and tap the mug while the water is swirling. Any change now?
4. Pour a packet of hot chocolate into the mug. Stir it and tap again. You'll notice that the pitch gets higher. Stir and tap again. The pitch goes down and then rises again!

What's Happening?

Air bubbles are mixed into the liquid as you stir, which slow the speed of sound in the hot chocolate. This lowers the pitch of the sound that travels through the mug when tapped. As the water spins, the bubbles rise and pop. With fewer bubbles in the hot chocolate, the speed of sound and pitch increases.

Bendable Bones

173

Can you tie these bones in a knot? Can you tie them in a bow?

= Do It! =

Supplies

Clean chicken bones, Large jar, White vinegar

1. Put the bones in the jar and cover them with vinegar. Cover the jar with a lid.
2. Leave the jar on the counter for three days.
3. After three days, take the bones out of the jar. Can you bend them in knots? If not, stick the bones back in the jar, replace the vinegar, and wait another day or two before trying again.

What's Happening?

Bones contain minerals, mostly calcium and phosphorous, that make them strong and hard. Vinegar is a weak acid that scientists call acetic acid. The vinegar pulls out the minerals in the bone. All that's left is bendy, flexible cartilage.

174 Egg in a Bottle  ADULT NEEDED

You may have seen a ship in a bottle, but have you ever put a whole egg in a bottle?

Supplies

Peeled hard-boiled egg, Glass bottle with an opening or neck smaller than the egg's diameter, Match, Sink

= Do It! =

1. The key to successfully getting the egg into the bottle is timing. Light a match and quickly drop it in the bottom of the bottle. The match should keep burning. If it goes out, drop in another lit match.

2. Count to three and put the egg on top of the bottle pointy side down so that it seals the opening.

3. Wait. After a few seconds, the egg will start to ooze down into the bottle.

What's Happening?

The burning match heats the air in the bottle, causing the air to expand. When you place the egg on top of the bottle, the match will go out as the oxygen burns up. The air cools and contracts so that the air pressure inside the bottle is much lower than the air pressure outside the bottle. The air outside of the bottle pushes the egg inside.

To get the egg out, reverse the process by making the air pressure inside the bottle greater than the air pressure outside so the air pushes the egg back out again. Here are two ways to do this:

The Easy Way

Turn the bottle downward at an angle. Shake it around a little until the egg is in the neck of the bottle and covers it completely with the pointy side pointed outward. Make sure there aren't any match bits in the way. Then bring the bottle to the sink, and let hot water run over the bottom of the bottle. This will heat the air inside the bottle so that it expands and pushes the egg out.

The Fun (Messy) Way

Try this method outdoors. Add two effervescent tablets to the bottle and ½ cup of water. Quickly turn the bottle upside down so that the egg is in the neck of the bottle with the pointy side pointed downward. As the tablets bubble in the water, they produce carbon dioxide gas, which builds up the air pressure inside the bottle very quickly and shoots the egg out.

What If?

What if you use very hot water instead of a match?

Straw Through a Potato

Here's one way to prove your superhuman strength!

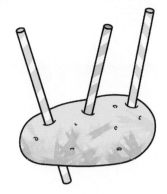

Do It!

Supplies

Straw, Potato

1. Place your thumb over the end of the straw.
2. Stab the potato, and watch the straw go right through. Just watch out that your hand isn't on the other side or the potato won't be the only thing with a hole!

What's Happening?

A plastic straw is pretty weak. If you try to jam it into the potato without covering the end of the straw, the straw will bend before it even pierces the skin. By trapping the air inside with your thumb, you strengthen the straw so that it can't bend. As the straw goes through the potato, it just gets stronger because the air inside is compressed when the other end fills up with potato!

Drink a Rainbow

Rainbows aren't just for unicorns. Try this colorful density column experiment you can drink!

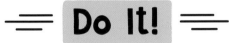

Do It!

Supplies

Tall glass, A variety of juices, Water, Blue food coloring, Measuring cup, Syringe (optional)

1. Pour a cup of water into the glass and add a few drops of blue food coloring.
2. Pour ¼ cup of one juice into the glass.
3. With a syringe or measuring cup, carefully pour in ¼ cup of another juice so it runs down the inside of the glass. If the new juice sinks below the first juice, it is denser than the first. If it floats on top, it is less dense.
4. Continue with the rest of the juices and water until you have a layered rainbow of juice.

What's Happening?

A layering of liquids like this is called a density column. Density is a measure of how much stuff (or mass) is in a set volume. In this demonstration, the volume is ¼ cup. The mass depends on the sugar and other stuff that is in the juice. The juices with a higher density sink to the bottom, and the juices with lower density float on top. The layers form when you slowly introduce the juices by pouring them on the inside of the glass, so they don't mix with each other.

Taste with Your Eyes

Can you trick your taste buds with food coloring?

Supplies

Food coloring, 4 clear cups, White grape juice, At least 6 volunteers

Do It!

1. Pour some juice into the four cups.
2. Add food coloring to three of the cups so that one is orange, one is red, one is green, and one stays clear. Don't let your volunteers see!
3. Show the first volunteer the glasses of juice. Ask them to predict each flavor, and write their answer.
4. Let the volunteer taste each of the drinks. Ask what flavor they taste, and rate them from most to least sweet. Write this down, as well.
5. Repeat with each of your volunteers. Did the predictions match what they tasted? Did anyone realize that the juices all have the same flavor?

What's Happening?

We associate color with certain flavors. With sweet food, red usually means cherry, orange color means orange flavor, and green means lime. What we see can override what we think we taste.

Taste with Your Nose

Have you smelled a meal so good you could taste it? Your sense of smell is a big part of how food tastes.

Do It!

Supplies

3 different flavor jellybeans, 3 plastic bags, Nose plug, Blind fold, At least 6 volunteers

1. Put each flavor jellybean in a plastic bag and squish them. Make sure you have twice as many jellybeans of each flavor as volunteers.
2. Have your first volunteer wear a nose plug and a blindfold.
3. Give them a jellybean to eat. Write down the answer they tell you next to the correct flavor. Repeat this for all three flavors.
4. Remove the nose plug but leave the blindfold on. Ask your volunteer to smell each bag and identify the flavor by smell.
5. Let the volunteer smell and taste the jellybeans and ask them to identify the flavor.
6. Repeat this for each volunteer.

What's Happening?

Much of the flavor of food comes from the thousands of receptors in your nose. When your sense of smell is blocked, it is more difficult to taste flavors.

Better with Butter

The best butter is the kind you make yourself.

Supplies

Measuring cup, Large cup, 3 cups of heavy whipping cream, Clean glass jar with a lid, Stopwatch, Bowl, Water, Sealable container for storing your butter

Do It!

1. Pour 1½ cups of cream into the large cup, and let it sit on the counter until it is room temperature. While you're waiting, start making butter with the cold cream.

2. Pour ½ cup of cream straight from the fridge into the glass jar. Put the lid tightly on the jar, start your stopwatch, and start shaking vigorously. You will need to shake the jar for up to 20 minutes (or more!), so it helps to have a friend who will take turns with you.

3. After 5 to 20 minutes, the solid parts of the cream will separate from the liquid parts. When you have a solid yellow lump in a jar of watery buttermilk, stop shaking (and stop the stopwatch).

4. Take the yellow butter blob out of the jar and put it in a bowl of clean water. Rinse the butter and squish as much of the liquid out as you can. Pour out the water and rinse the butter at least two more times. This will keep your butter from turning rancid before you can eat it.

5. Once your butter is well rinsed, put it in the sealable container and store it in the fridge.

6. Make six batches of butter—three using the cold butter and three using the room temperature butter. Clean the jar in between each batch. Which temperature cream made butter faster? Is there a difference in the color, texture, or taste of the butters?

What's Happening?

When you shake cream, the fat bounces around and clumps together, eventually clumping so much that the buttery fat separates completely from the liquid in the cream. Warm molecules bounce around faster because they have more energy. The molecules in the room-temperature cream are warmer and already bouncing faster than the ones in the chilled cream. This means the room-temperature fat molecules will clump together and form butter faster.

What If?

What if you put a marble in the glass jar with the cream? Does it speed up the process?

180 Ice Cream in a Bag

Do the ice cream dance!

Supplies

1 gallon freezer bag, 1 quart freezer bag, 1 cup half-and-half, 2 tablespoons sugar, 1 teaspoon vanilla extract, Ice, ½ cup rock salt, Thermometer, Gloves

What's Happening?

Plain ice both melts and re-freezes. When you add salt to the bag, more energy is needed to melt the salty ice. The salty ice pulls that energy from the warmer bag of ice cream, making it colder.

Do It!

1. Pour the half-and-half, sugar, and vanilla into the smaller freezer bag. Seal the bag so there is little extra air inside.
2. Fill the larger freezer bag half full of ice. Record the temperature of the ice in the bag.
3. Add the rock salt to the ice.
4. Place the smaller bag with the ice cream mixture in the larger bag of ice and salt. Seal the large bag.
5. Put on gloves and shake the bags for 10 to 15 minutes.
6. When the ice cream is solid, remove it from the larger bag. Measure and record the temperature of the ice left in the larger bag. What happened to the temperature of the ice as you shook the bag?

181 The Gelatin Jiggle

What fruits make a gelatin that jiggles instead of a mushy mess?

Supplies

4 packages of cherry sugar-free gelatin, 4 large bowls, 1 peach, 1 can of peaches, 1 can of pineapple, 1 pineapple, Knife, Pot, Measuring cup, Clock

ADULT NEEDED

Do It!

1. Cut the fruit into bite-sized pieces. Measure 1 cup of each of the four fruits.
2. Prepare 4 bowls of gelatin by following the directions on the box.
3. Add a different fruit to each bowl and label each of the bowls.
4. Refrigerate the bowls.
5. Every 10 minutes, touch the gelatin. When no gelatin sticks to your finger, the gelatin is set. Write down the time.
6. Which fruit took the longest to set? The fastest? Did any fruits never set?

What's Happening?

Fruits contain enzymes, chemicals that help them grow and ripen. Some fruits contain an enzyme that digests gelatin. If you add a fruit with this enzyme, the gelatin won't set. However, canning or cooking the fruit destroys this enzyme. Which fruits contain the gelatin-eating enzyme?

Make Meringue

This easy dessert requires a lot of arm power, so roll up your sleeves and give those egg whites what for.

ADULT NEEDED

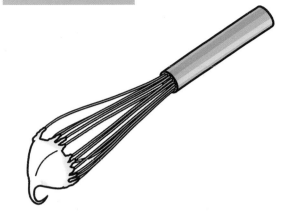

Supplies

12 room temperature eggs, 4 cups of sugar, Measuring cup, Stopwatch, Whisk, Glass bowl, Plastic bowl, Copper bowl, Spoon, Parchment paper (optional), Baking sheet, Oven

Do It!

1. Preheat your oven to 225°F.
2. Crack two of the eggs, and pour just the egg whites into the glass bowl.
3. Start your stopwatch, and begin to briskly whisk the eggs.
4. After a minute or so, the eggs will become foamy. Keep whisking while gradually adding ⅔ cup of sugar.
5. After several more minutes of whisking, the eggs should become stiff and shiny. If you lift the whisk out of the eggs, a peak should form that doesn't fall down. Stop your stopwatch when this happens and record the time.
6. Place a piece of parchment paper on your baking sheet. Scoop the egg whites onto the baking sheet with a spoon, placing them 1 inch apart.
7. Put the baking sheet in the oven and bake for 90 minutes. Remove the meringues before they turn brown, and let them cool completely before eating.
8. Repeat this two times for each bowl. Which type of bowl took the longest to whip the meringues? Were there differences in color or consistency?

What's Happening?

Egg whites are made of 90 percent water and some protein. When you first crack the egg, the egg white proteins are wrapped around the water. As you beat the egg whites with a whisk, you unwrap the proteins and add a whole lot of air bubbles. The unwrapped proteins realign to form a net that holds the air bubbles in place. As you bake the meringue, the air evaporates, leaving a tasty protein shell.

So why does it matter which bowl you use? The tiniest bit of oil or grease can keep the proteins from realigning to make big, fluffy clouds. Oil and fats stick to plastic bowls and are pretty much impossible to remove completely when cleaning. So unless your plastic bowl is brand new, odds are a tiny bit of oil got in your meringue. Copper bowls help meringues even more. A tiny bit of copper from the surface of the bowl gets mixed into the egg whites and stabilizes them, making it easier for them to hold in all those air bubbles.

183 Yeasty Beasties

Those tiny holes in a slice of bread are bubbles made by the burps of billions of tiny fungi called yeast. Harness their gas to blow up balloons.

Supplies

5 identical empty bottles, Warm water, Measuring cup, 5 packets of baker's yeast, Sugar, Sucralose, Corn syrup, Honey, 5 balloons

Do It!

1. Blow up each balloon three times. Label each bottle with a different sweetener. One bottle will not have a sweetener.
2. Pour ½ cup of warm water into each bottle, and then add a packet of yeast to each.
3. Add a tablespoon of sweetener to each bottle matching its label.
4. Swirl the bottles gently to mix the contents. Put a balloon on the top of each bottle. Wait an hour. Which balloon is the biggest? Which inflated the fastest?

What's Happening?

As the dry yeast is brought back to life by the water and eats the sugar, it releases carbon dioxide gas. The gas fills the bottle and then fills the balloon. Which of the sugars in your experiment was the best food for the yeasty beasties?

184 Gluten Goodness

Why are some breads light and fluffy, while others are dense and chewy? The magic ingredient is gluten.

Do It!

Supplies

Whole-wheat flour, Bread flour, All-purpose flour, Pastry flour, Water, 4 bowls, Measuring cup, Measuring tape

1. Pour 1 cup of whole-wheat flour in a bowl, and add ¾ cup of water.
2. Mix the flour and water until you have a soft, rubbery ball.
3. Measure the ball, and then let it rest on the counter for 10 minutes.
4. Run cold water over the ball in the sink. Squeeze it to remove the starch. You will see the white starch dissolving in the water. Stop when the water runs clear and the ball is a sticky web of gluten strands. Now the ball is pure gluten.
5. Measure your gluten ball. Has the size changed? How does it feel, stretch, look, and bounce?
6. Repeat the process with the other flours. Which flour had the biggest change in size when you removed the starch?

What's Happening?

When bread rises, the yeast in the dough makes gas. The stretchy gluten in the flour fills with gas like a balloon. More gluten means more and bigger "balloons" in the bread, making the bread more light and fluffy.

Fruity DNA Extraction

All living things have one thing in common: DNA!

Supplies

Rubbing alcohol (70% or greater), 3 strawberries, Sealable plastic bag, 2 clear glasses, Water, Dish soap, Salt, Half a banana, Kiwi, Measuring cup, Coffee filter, Skewer

Do It!

1. Put the rubbing alcohol in the freezer.
2. Pull the leaves off the strawberries, and put them in the plastic bag. Push all of the air out of the bag and seal it tight.
3. Mash the strawberries until you have a slimy mess.
4. In one of the glasses, pour 1 cup of water, 4 teaspoons of soap, and 1 teaspoon of salt. Stir the mixture gently so you don't make bubbles.
5. Open the bag of strawberries and pour 1/3 cup of the soap-salt mixture in with the fruit. Push the air out of the bag and seal it. Gently squish the bag for 30 seconds until blended. Let the bag sit for 20 minutes.
6. Put a coffee filter over the other glass so that the center is in the glass and the sides are folded over.
7. Pour the fruit mixture into the coffee filter. Squeeze out the liquid into the glass, careful not to tear the filter.
8. When you've squeezed out all the liquid you can, carefully pour the rubbing alcohol down the side of the glass. The alcohol layer on top should be as thick as the juice layer.
9. After a few seconds, you will see a white cloudy layer form between the fruit and the alcohol. This is the DNA! After 10 minutes, it will rise to the top of the alcohol layer. If you aren't that patient, poke the tip of the skewer into the middle of that layer. Gently twist the stick so that the DNA wraps around it, and pull it out of the glass.
10. Repeat the process with the kiwi and half a banana. Which fruit produced the most DNA?

What's Happening?

To take the DNA out of the cell, first you must break open the cells. When you squished up the fruit, you broke up the cells. The soap in the extraction solution destroys the rest of the cell walls and the membrane of the nucleus, letting out the DNA. The salt in the solution causes the proteins and carbohydrates that make up the rest of the cell to sink to the bottom while the DNA stays on top. Next, you filtered out most of the other plant parts so you are left with DNA dissolved in water. Adding cold rubbing alcohol to the mixture simply increases the amount of DNA you are able to separate from the rest of the cell parts. Because different plants (and animals, for that matter) have different amounts of DNA, how much you can extract from each plant should vary in the same way.

Get the Iron Out

It turns out that most cereals contain the same iron found in nails. See it with your own eyes

Supplies

3 types of cereals with different iron contents, 2 tall glasses, Measuring cup, Plastic spoon, Strong magnet (neodymium magnets work best), Clear packing tape, Plastic sandwich bag, Camera or paper and pencil

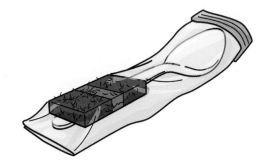

Do It!

1. Pour 1 cup of one cereal into a tall glass.
2. Fill the cup with water so that it is about an inch above the cereal.
3. Let the glass sit for at least five minutes so the cereal gets good and soggy.
4. Put the strong magnet in the corner of the plastic bag so it is tight around the magnet.
5. Tape the magnet onto the end of the handle of the spoon so some of it hangs off the end and the bag is sealed. Cut off the rest of the bag. This is your magnetic stirrer.
6. Fill the second glass with clean water.
7. Stir the cereal soup with the magnetic stirrer (the magnet should be inside in the soup) for about two minutes.
8. Gently rinse off your stirrer and take a look at the magnet. You should see black particles sticking to the magnet. This is the iron from the breakfast cereal.
9. Take a photo or make a drawing so that you can compare the amount of iron in the different cereals. Repeat this for the other two cereals. If you can, repeat more than once for each cereal. Which cereal did you remove the most and least iron from? Does this match the iron contents on the cereal labels?

What's Happening?

Your body needs iron to survive. Red blood cells use iron to carry oxygen from your lungs to the rest of your body. Because some people don't get enough iron from foods like red meat and green leafy vegetables, iron is added to foods like cereal. The iron powder used in these foods is the same iron used to make nails!

Just like with a nail, bringing a magnet near the cereal attracts the iron. In fact, if you float a single piece of cereal in a bowl of water and your magnet is strong enough, you can move the cereal around the bowl by moving the magnet in the air above it.

What If?

What if you try this experiment on other iron-fortified foods, such as baby food, energy bars, or vitamin supplements?

Drink Your Iron

When you don't have enough iron in your body, you feel tired and get sick more easily. A delicious way to get iron is through fruit juice!

Supplies

Pitcher, 3 tea bags, 6 clear glasses, 6 spoons, Measuring spoon, Masking tape and marker, Pineapple juice, White grape juice, Prune juice, Cranberry juice, Apple juice

Do It!

1. Pour a pint of hot water into the pitcher and add three tea bags. Let the pitcher sit for an hour.

2. Pour ¼ cup of each juice into a different glass. (One glass will have no juice.) Label each glass.

3. Add ¼ cup of tea to each glass and stir each with a spoon. Let it sit for 20 minutes.

4. Lift each glass and look for dark particles on the bottom.

5. Let the tea mixtures sit for another two hours, and then look for dark iron particles again. Which juice produced the most particles? Does the number of particles correspond to the iron content of the juices?

What's Happening?

Tea is full of chemicals called polyphenols, which give tea its flavor and provide health benefits. Some of those polyphenols also react with iron in foods, like fruit juice, and form solids that sink to the bottom of the glass.

Clearing Up Cola

Sometimes mixing drinks leads to deliciousness, but pouring milk in your cola leads to something surprising and a little gross.

Do It!

Supplies

Small clear bottle of cola, 2% milk

1. Remove the label from the bottle of cola so that you can see the experiment easily.

2. Open the cola and pour in some milk so that the liquid is just an inch from the top. Put the lid back on the bottle and watch. The changes may take up to an hour.

What's Happening?

After about 15 minutes, you will see dark, foamy clumps near the bottom of the bottle. The phosphoric acid in the cola is reacting with casein protein in the milk, causing it to clump with caramel coloring and other parts of the soda. After an hour, the bottom will be full of the dark, curdled milk. The clear top layer is the water, sweetener, and the rest of the proteins and fat from the milk. Let the bottle of cola sit overnight. When you wake up, it should be completely clear!

189 Ripening Fruit

When you're faced with a hard pear, ripen it with science!

= Do It! =

Supplies

4 unripe pears,
2 ripe bananas,
3 paper lunch
bags, Marker,
Masking tape

1. With the marker, label the bags: "Pear," "Pear & Banana," and "Pear & 2 Bananas."
2. Place the fruit in the bags, and seal them with tape. Leave the last pear on the counter.
3. Keep track of the date and time you put the fruit in the bags. Every 12 hours, check the pears' ripeness by pressing on the side of the pear firmly with your finger for two seconds. If the fruit stays indented after you remove your finger, then it is ripe. If you cannot see where you pressed, put the fruit back and reseal the bag. Check the pear on the counter too.
4. Note when each pear ripens. Did the pears in the bag ripen before the one on the counter? Did the bananas help the pears ripen faster?

What's Happening?

Have you ever heard the saying "one rotten apple will spoil the bunch"? Long ago, apples were stored in large barrels in cool cellars so they could be eaten year-round. An over-ripe apple in the barrel would give off a chemical called ethylene that caused the apples to ripen too quickly and rot before they were eaten. Here, the ethylene given off by the bananas caused the pears to ripen sooner. The ethylene molecule is too big to escape from the paper bag. Oxygen — which keeps the fruit from rotting — can flow freely in and out of the bag.

190 Floating Fruit

It's the citrus Olympics! Which fruit will float above the rest?

= Do It! =

Supplies

2 oranges, 2 limes,
2 lemons, Large
bowl of water

1. Peel the rind off of one orange, one lemon, and one lime. Leave the other fruits unpeeled.
2. Put all the fruit in the bowl of water and watch what happens. Which fruits float and which fruits sink? Do any hang out in the middle?

What's Happening?

Juicy fruits like oranges and lemons are mostly juice on the inside, which has a density about the same as water. But the rinds have pockets of air and act like little life jackets. Limes are different. If you cut the fruit in half, you'll see that the lime has a lot more pulp and a denser flesh than oranges and lemons. This makes the lime denser and weighs it down in the water, even with the rind on.

Mayo Emulsion

When a bottle of vinaigrette dressing sits for awhile, the oil and vinegar separate into two layers. Even if you shake the bottle as hard as you can, the oil and vinegar will always separate – that is, unless you make an emulsion!

Supplies

Vegetable oil, Water, White vinegar, 2 small bowls, Fork, Egg, Mustard powder, Sugar, Flour, Pint-sized glass jar with cover, Measuring cup, Measuring spoon, Magnifying glass

Do It!

1. Pour ¼ cup of water and ¼ cup of vegetable oil into the jar, and put the cover on tightly.
2. Shake the jar as hard as you can for one minute to mix the oil and water completely.
3. Let the jar sit for five minutes and observe what happens, using the magnifying glass to look closely as the two liquids separate.
4. Separate the egg white and yolk into the two small bowls and then use a fork to beat each of them until they are smooth.
5. Open the jar and add the egg yolk to the oil and water.
6. Shake the jar as hard as you can for three minutes so the oil and water are completely mixed.
7. Let the jar sit for five minutes and observe what happens with the magnifying glass. Do the oil and water separate this time?
8. Clean out your jar and add another ¼ cup of water and ¼ of vegetable oil, and then add the egg white to the jar, as well.
9. Shake the jar as hard as you can for three minutes until the oil and water are completely mixed.
10. Let the jar sit for five minutes and observe what happens with the magnifying glass. Do the oil and water separate this time?
11. Repeat this process three more times with a tablespoon of mustard powder, a tablespoon of sugar, and a tablespoon of flour. Which additives kept the oil and water from separating?

What's Happening?

Oil and water don't mix because the water molecules stick to each other more than they stick to the oil. The oil will float on top because it's less dense than the water. However, when you add an emulsifier to the mixture, the water and oil will stay mixed up. The emulsifier sticks equally to water and oil, so it surrounds tiny droplets of each and lets them hang out together. We call this stable mixture of oil and water an emulsion.

Apple Exposure

Can you stop the oxidation process that makes apple slices turn brown? **ADULT NEEDED**

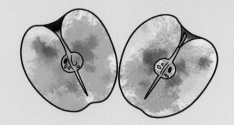

Supplies

4 apples, Knife, 6 bowls, Masking tape, Marker, Measuring cup, Water, Lemon juice, Salt, Lemon-lime soda, Honey, Carbonated water, Resealable bag

═ Do It! ═

1. Put one liquid in each of the bowls. One bowl will be empty. Label the bowls.
   - 1 cup of carbonated water
   - 1 cup of lemon-lime soda
   - 1 cup of water + 1 tablespoon of lemon juice
   - 1 cup of water + ⅛ teaspoon of salt
   - 1 cup of water + 2 tablespoons of honey
2. Cut the apples into eight slices. Put four slices in each of the bowls and four more in a resealable bag, sealing it tight.
3. After five minutes, pour out the liquids, and wait for one hour. Did any of the apple slices turn brown? How about the slices in the empty bowl? Which liquid kept the apples white longest?
4. Taste the apples. Do any taste different?

What's Happening?

When a cut apple is exposed to oxygen in the air, it reacts with the apple's enzymes to make it brown. This is called oxidation. Weak acids (lemon juice, soda, salt water, and carbonated water) slow the reaction. Honey and the resealable bag keep the air away from the apple.

193

One Plus One

Dissolve sugar into water and see how things add up... or don't!

═ Do It! ═

Supplies

Clear quart jar, Water, Measuring cup, 1 cup of sugar, Masking tape, Marker

1. Place tape on the side of the jar from top to bottom.
2. Pour 1 cup of water into the jar. Label the water line on the tape 1 cup.
3. Pour in another cup of water. Label the water line 2 cups.
4. Empty the jar and dry it.
5. Pour 1 cup of sugar into the jar, and then 1 cup of water. Mix. What is the level?
6. Add sugar ¼ cup at a time until it reaches the 2-cup level. How much sugar did you add to make 2 cups of solution?

What's Happening?

The sugar dissolves, but the air in the spaces between the sugar grains does not. When you pour the sugar into the water, the air isn't poured in. Even though you mixed 1 cup of water plus 1 cup of sugar, you still get less than 2 cups of sugar water.

Salty Science

ADULT NEEDED

Common wisdom says to add salt to water when you cook because it makes the food cook more quickly. Does a pinch of salt really make a difference? How about a whole cup of salt?

Supplies

Small sauce pan, Stove top, Measuring cup, Measuring spoon, Water, Table salt, Food thermometer

= Do It! =

1. Pour 4 cups of water into the pan and place it on the stove.
2. Turn the burner on high and wait for the water to come to a complete boil.
3. Carefully measure the water's temperature, and then turn off the burner.
4. Once the water has stopped boiling, add 1 tablespoon of water and 2 tablespoons of salt.
5. Turn the burner on high and wait for the water to come to a boil again.
6. Measure the temperature of the water, and then turn off the burner.
7. Repeat the process as you continue to add salt to the water, doubling the amount of salt in the water each time, and adding 1 tablespoon of water each time to make up for the water that has evaporated during boiling.
8. The last time you measure the boiling point, the pot will be half water and half salt. What happened to the boiling point as you added salt? How hot do you think the water would boil if you doubled the salt again? Did you notice anything about how long it took the salty water to come to a boil?

What's Happening?

When you heat water, you are giving the molecules energy so they can move around faster. If you add enough heat, the water molecules can break free of the liquid water to become a gas and the water starts boiling. The bubbles in the boiling water are those fast-moving molecules that broke free from the liquid water.

When you add salt, it takes more energy for the molecules to break free. Salt is a crystal called sodium chloride, but when you add it to water, the sodium and chlorine in the salt break apart. The water molecules stick to the sodium and the chlorine more than they stick to each other, so it takes more energy to break free of the liquid. More energy is more heat and more heat is a higher temperature! Therefore, when you add salt to water, you have to heat (or energize) the water more before it starts to boil.

How the Cookie Crumbles, Part 1

Bakers have long searched for the perfect chocolate chip cookie recipe. Take a scientific approach and investigate the effects of patience on a simple cookie recipe.

ADULT NEEDED

Supplies

Ingredients for 1 batch of chocolate chip cookies, Refrigerator, 3 bowls, Plastic wrap, Clock, 4 sealable containers, 6 taste testers, Masking tape, Marker

═ Do It! ═

1. Prepare a batch of chocolate chip cookie dough.

2. Split the dough into four equal balls. Wrap three of the balls in plastic wrap and put them in the three bowls. Put the bowls in the refrigerator.

3. Use the last ball of dough to bake cookies according to the directions in the recipe.

4. After the cookies have cooled, have your taste testers eat a cookie. Write down their observations about the cookies. Are they crunchy, crispy, or chewy? Did they spread out or rise?

5. Put the other six cookies in a container to taste again at the end of the experiment. Label the container "Fresh Dough."

6. Bake another batch of cookies after 12 hours, 24 hours, and 48 hours. Have your taste testers evaluate the cookies right after they are baked and put the rest in a container for later. Make sure you label the containers so you know when the cookies were baked.

7. After you bake the cookie dough that has been in the fridge for 48 hours, have your taste testers compare all four batches. How did the flavor, texture, and appearance change as the dough was in the fridge for longer periods of time? Does refrigerating your dough make better cookies? What length of time gives the best-tasting cookies?

What's Happening?

When you bake, you usually mix the dry ingredients, and then add the wet ingredients. When you first mix the dough, tiny bits of wet ingredients and dry ingredients are next to each other. As the dough sits in the refrigerator, the dry ingredients absorb moisture from the wet ingredients. This means the cookie dough is more uniform and will bake differently than fresh dough.

Cookie Crumbles, Pt. 2

Cookies are better with butter, but does it matter if that butter is frozen, cold, or melted?

ADULT NEEDED

Supplies

Ingredients for 4 batches of chocolate chip cookies, Microwave, 6 (or more) taste testers, 4 sealable containers, Masking tape, Marker

═ Do It! ═

1. Put two sticks of butter in the freezer, two on the countertop, and the other 4 in the fridge. Wait a couple of hours.

2. Bake 4 batches of cookies. Each batch will use butter with a different temperature: frozen, refrigerated, room temperature, and melted in the microwave. With an adult's help, bake the cookies. When cooled, put the cookies in containers, and label them according to which butter you used.

3. Have your taste testers try each of the cookies. Write down their observations. Are they crunchy, crispy, or chewy? Did they spread or rise? Which cookie is their favorite?

What's Happening?

Butter gives cookies flavor, keeps them tender, and causes cookies to spread. The butter's temperature determines how much air is in the cookie. Melted butter has no air and makes denser, chewier cookies. Cooler butter keeps air bubbles when it is mixed with the other ingredients, making lighter, firmer cookies.

Cookie Crumbles, Pt. 3

What is the difference between baking powder and baking soda, and can it help you make better cookies?

ADULT NEEDED

Supplies

Ingredients for 3 batches of chocolate chip cookies, Baking soda, 6 taste testers, 3 sealable containers, Masking tape, Marker

═ Do It! ═

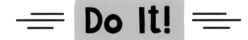

1. Make 3 batches of cookie dough:
   - For the first batch, use baking powder.
   - For the second batch, use baking soda.
   - In the last batch, use a half teaspoon baking powder and a half teaspoon baking soda.

2. Bake the cookies according to the recipe directions. When cool, put the cookies in containers labeled "soda," "powder," and "soda and powder."

3. Have your taste testers try the cookies. Write down their observations. Which cookie is their favorite?

What's Happening?

Combining baking soda and an acid will create bubbles in your food. When the food bakes, the bubbles turn into air pockets. Baking powder is a mixture of baking soda and cream of tartar. When wet, these powders make bubbles. There is no acid in the cookies baked with baking soda, so you probably got flat cookies with very few air pockets.

198 Perfect Popcorn, Part 1

Pop quiz: What kind of popcorn maximizes the number of popping kernels?

ADULT NEEDED

== **Do It!** ==

Supplies

9 brown paper lunch bags, 3 different types of popcorn, Microwave oven, Large bowl

1. Label each bag for each type of popcorn. Put ¼ cup of the corresponding popcorn in the bags. Fold the top of the bag twice, and seal it with tape.
2. Microwave one bag for four minutes, and stop the microwave when there are more than two seconds between pops. Note the time and use this same time for the rest of the experiment.
3. Dump the popcorn into the large bowl. Count the unpopped kernels. Observe the shape, size, and color of the popcorn. Pour it back into the paper bag.
4. Repeat the process for each type of popcorn. Which had the least number of unpopped kernels? Were there any other differences in size, color, or taste?

What's Happening?

Each popcorn kernel is made up of starch and water. When the kernel heats up, the water turns to steam, and the kernel expands until it explodes into a piece of popcorn. Different types of popcorn have different shapes, types of starch, and amounts of water.

199 Perfect Popcorn, Part 2

Where is the best place to keep your popcorn so it lives to pop another day?

ADULT NEEDED

== **Do It!** ==

Supplies

Popcorn kernels; 3 airtight containers; 9 brown paper lunch bags; Masking tape; Measuring cup; Access to a fridge, freezer, and cupboard; Microwave oven; Large bowl

1. Place 1 cup of popcorn in each of the three containers, and label them. Put one container each in the freezer, fridge, and cupboard for 24 hours.
2. Put ¼ cup of the freezer popcorn in a paper bag, fold the bag twice and seal with tape, and label the bag "Freezer." Put the sealed container in the freezer.
3. Microwave the bag for four minutes. Stop the microwave when you count more than two seconds between pops. Note the time, and use this same time for the rest of the experiment.
4. Pour the popcorn into the bowl. Count the unpopped kernels.
5. Repeat the process two more times for the freezer popcorn and three times each for the fridge and cupboard popcorn. Which had the fewest unpopped kernels?

What's Happening?

Popcorn gets its popping power from moisture inside the kernel. Popcorn kept in the fridge or freezer dries out faster, and the moisture in the cold kernels takes longer to heat.

Use Your Noodle

Boiling a lot of water before you put noodles in a pot takes a long time. Try some not-so-common ways of cooking noodles to see if you can save time and energy.

ADULT NEEDED

Supplies

Five 1-pound boxes of elbow macaroni, Water, Pot, Slotted spoon, Colander, Stopwatch

≡ Do It! ≡

1. Cook each of the five boxes of noodles using each method below. For each method, time how long you heat the water using the stove and the total time it takes to cook the noodles.

2. For methods 1 to 4: While the noodles cook, use a slotted spoon to take the noodles out and taste if fully cooked every minute. The noodles are fully cooked when they are soft but not crunchy and not mushy.

   • Method 1: Put 4 quarts of cold water in the pot. Turn on the stove. When the water is at a full boil, add the noodles. Turn off the stove when the noodles are cooked.

   • Method 2: Put 2 quarts of cold water in the pot. Turn on the stove. When the water is at a full boil, add the noodles. Turn off the stove when the noodles are cooked.

   • Method 3: Put 2 quarts of cold water in the pot and pour in the noodles. Turn on the stove. Turn off the stove when the noodles are cooked.

   • Method 4: Put 2 quarts of cold water in the pot and pour in the noodles. Let the noodles soak in the water until they are cooked.

   • Method 5: Put 2 quarts of cold water in the pot. Turn on the stove. When the water is at a full boil, add the noodles. Turn off the stove and cover the pot. Check the noodles every minute after 10 minutes. Only remove the lid briefly to remove a noodle to taste.

   Which method cooked the noodles the quickest? Which used the least energy (the stove was on for the shortest amount of time)? Was there any difference in the taste of the noodles?

What's Happening?

The first step in cooking dry noodles — which are made of starch and protein — is to get them wet. The starch absorbs the water until it bursts. The starch inside the noodles gradually soaks up water, making the noodle softer. The proteins also begin to cook, keeping the noodles from turning into a total starchy mush. The noodle is perfectly cooked when the starches are wet and the protein is cooked but not so much that it falls apart. Do you really need all that water, and does it need to boil to properly cook the noodles all the way through?

201 Hot Water Freeze

Hot water sometimes freezes faster than cold water, and scientists are not completely sure why. See if you can figure it out!

ADULT NEEDED

Supplies

4 identical glass cups, Large bowl for heating water, Water, Microwave, Refrigerator, Freezer, Hot mitt, Clock, 3 thermometers, Food scale, Masking tape, Marker

Do It!

1. Measure ½ cup of water into two of the cups.

2. Label one cup "Cold," and place it in the refrigerator.

3. Label the other cup "Room Temperature," and place it on the counter.

4. Wait 15 minutes for the temperature of the waters to match their location.

5. Measure ½ cup of water into the third cup, and mark the top of the water with tape. Label this cup "Hot." Pour ½ cup of water in the last cup, and put both of these cups in the microwave. Heat the water for one to two minutes or until the water is steaming.

6. Remove the water from the microwave. If the water in the third cup is below the level marked by the tape, pour in some of the extra hot water from the last cup so that it is back to the ½ cup level.

7. Place a thermometer in each cup, and record their temperatures. Place the labeled cups in the freezer. Make sure they are all on the same level and none of the cups are touching anything in the freezer.

8. Measure the temperature of the water in each container every five minutes. Keep the freezer door closed as much as possible. Once the temperature of the water reaches 32°F/0°C, stop taking temperatures. Continue to observe the water every five minutes to see which forms ice crystals first.

9. Which cup of water reached the freezing temperature first? Which actually froze first? If the hot water did not freeze first, can you change some of the conditions so that it does?

What's Happening?

Nobody can really explain what happens here. Some scientists observe that the hot water freezes before the cold water, and others do not. All agree that sometimes the hot water does freeze fast, but no one is sure of the conditions that allow this to happen or why it happens. Now known as the Mpemba Effect — named after a high school student in Tanzania who was the first to scientifically study the effect — hot water freezing more quickly than cold water was observed as far back as Aristotle and has been written about by several scientists since then.

Upside-down Toast

When you drop your buttered toast, why does it land butter-side down?

Supplies

Toast,
Aluminum foil,
Measuring
tape, Low
table, Books

Do It!

1. Wrap one side of the toast with foil. This simulates the weight of butter.
2. Measure the height of your table, and then slide your toast off the table edge.
3. Record what side your toast landed on. If the toast flipped when it landed, it landed on an edge. Repeat six times.
4. Place a book on the edge of your table so that the surface is at least 4 inches taller. Drop your toast six times from this new height.
5. Continuing adding height and dropping the toast until you reach 48 inches. At which heights did your toast land butter-side down? How about butter-side up?

What's Happening?

As the toast slides off the edge, one side starts to fall before the rest, causing the toast to spin. If the table is high enough, the toast will rotate completely and land butter-side up. If the table is too low, there will not be enough time for the toast to spin all the way around and it will land butter-side down.

Potatosmosis

203

Spuds and salt come together for this fascinating experiment.

Do It!

1. Pour 1 cup of water in the first bowl. In the second bowl, mix 1 cup of water and 1 tablespoon of salt. In the third bowl, mix 1 cup of water and 4 tablespoons of salt. Leave the last bowl empty. Label each bowl.
2. Peel the potatoes, and cut them into 12 1-inch squares.
3. Weigh the pieces three at a time on the scale, and write down their weights. Put three pieces in each bowl.
4. Let the potatoes soak for 30 minutes.
5. Weigh the pieces. Compare the before and after weights. Which solutions caused the potatoes to gain or lose weight?

Supplies

4 small bowls,
Measuring cup,
Measuring spoon,
Salt, Masking tape,
Marker, 2 large
potatoes, Peeler,
Knife, Kitchen scale

What's Happening?

When water moves in and out of a plant cell wall, we call that osmosis. Osmosis is a type of diffusion, which is the movement from high to low concentration. Here, the water moves from high concentration in the potato to low concentration in the salt water, causing the potato to lose weight.

204 Curds & Whey

I'm not entirely sure what a tuffet is or why Miss Muffet was sitting on one, but in this experiment, you can make your own curds and whey. Just keep an eye out for spiders.

ADULT NEEDED

Supplies

Jar or small bowl, Cheesecloth, Rubber band, 1 cup skim milk, 1 tablespoon lemon juice, Measuring spoon, Measuring cup, Metal saucepan, Stove or hot plate, Kitchen scale, Whole milk, Half-and-half

⹀ Do It! ⹀

1. Create a strainer by placing three layers of cheesecloth over a jar or small bowl and securing it with a rubber band.

2. Pour 1 cup of skim milk into the saucepan.

3. Heat the milk on the stove until you see steam rising off the top. Be careful not to boil the milk.

4. Stir in 1 tablespoon of lemon juice.

5. Heat the milk until you see solids separate from the liquid. The solids are curds and the liquid is whey.

6. Turn off the heat, and carefully pour your curds and whey through the strainer to separate them. Let the curds drain for at least two minutes.

7. Take the cheesecloth off the strainer, and squeeze out the rest of the whey.

8. Observe the curds. What color are they? How wet are they? What is the texture when you squeeze the curds in your hand?

9. Use the kitchen scale to weigh the curds made from skim milk. Then you can even taste the curds and whey (a little salt might help).

10. Clean up your supplies, and repeat the process for the whole milk and half-and-half. Which kind of milk made the most curds? How did the curds' color, texture, and taste compare?

What's Happening?

A glass of milk is mostly made of water. In the water are tiny bits of proteins, lactose, and fat mixed so smoothly that you can't see them. In this experiment, you separated the curds (solids) from the whey (liquids). This happens because of a protein in milk called casein.

Casein carries minerals like calcium and phosphorus to the cells in your body. In a regular glass of milk, the casein proteins repel each other. But when you add an acid like lemon juice, they change shape and stick together, gathering lactose and fats along the way in solid chunks called curds. The water and the rest of the proteins and fats are left behind in the whey.

Cook an Egg

You don't actually need a stove to cook an egg. Just don't try to eat these!

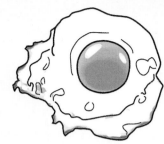

Supplies

Raw egg, Bowl, Rubbing alcohol

*Wash your hands with soap after handling raw eggs

Do It!

1. Pour rubbing alcohol into the bowl.
2. Crack the egg into the bowl of rubbing alcohol. What happens to the egg?
3. Check on the egg every 10 minutes. How does it change? After about one hour, the egg should be completely "cooked."

What's Happening?

When you cook an egg with heat, the proteins in the egg white become denatured. This means it loses its regular shape and gets tangled up with other proteins in the egg. This causes the egg whites to change from a clear liquid to a white solid. Alcohol does pretty much the same thing to the proteins in the egg white, using a chemical reaction instead of heat.

Spinning Eggs

Have you ever wondered how to tell a raw egg from a hardboiled egg without breaking the shell? Just give the eggs a spin!

Do It!

Supplies

Raw egg, Hardboiled egg

1. Let both eggs sit out on the counter for 15 minutes so they are room temperature.
2. Spin the eggs on their side one at a time. Do the eggs spin in the same way?

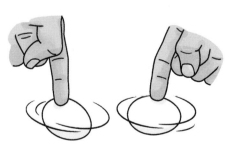

What's Happening?

The insides of raw egg are liquid, but a hardboiled egg is solid. When you spin a raw egg, its center of gravity changes as the liquid inside the egg moves around, causing a wobbly spin. When you spin a hardboiled egg, the solid center has a fixed center of gravity, giving a smooth, balanced spin.

207 Egg Toss

Throw eggs at a target – all in the name of science!

Supplies

Raw eggs, 2 sheets, 2 friends

* Be sure to wash your hands with soap after handling raw eggs to prevent the spread of bacterial diseases like salmonella.

Do It!

1. Have your two friends hold the sheet up flat against a wall (preferably outside, in case you miss!).

2. Stand back about 3 feet from the wall and throw an egg as hard as you can at the sheet.

   What happens when the egg hits the wall?

3. Now have your two friends hold the other sheet up in an open area outside.

4. Have them hold the top of the sheet up high and the bottom of the sheet up and out a bit so the sheet hangs loosely and the bottom makes a curve, like the letter "J."

5. Stand back about 3 feet and throw an egg as hard as you can at the sheet. What happens when the egg hits the sheet?

What's Happening?

When you throw an egg at a wall, it smashes into a mess! But when you throw an egg at the curved sheet, the egg doesn't even crack. The difference in these two cases is the change in momentum, called impulse.

Momentum is mass multiplied by speed. Because the mass of the eggs is about the same, what matters is the speed. The change in momentum for the egg is about the same in both cases: it goes from moving very fast to stopping completely.

But the time it takes to stop in each case is totally different. Impulse, or change in momentum, is the force the egg feels, multiplied by the amount of time it feels that force.

When the egg hits the wall, the time to stop is very small. This means the force is very large — large enough to smash the egg! But when you throw the egg against the sheet, the time to stop is much longer, so the force is much smaller, and the egg is unbroken.

What If?

What if you stand closer to or farther from the sheet? What if your friends hold the sheet very tightly?

Floating Eggs

Do eggs float or sink? In this experiment, they do both at the same time!

Supplies

Tall clear glass, Raw egg, Water, Salt, Measuring spoon, Stirring spoon

Do It!

1. Fill the glass with enough water to cover the egg. Put the egg in the glass. Does it float?
2. Add 1 tablespoon of salt to the water, and give it a gentle stir. Does the egg float now?
3. Keep adding salt, 1 tablespoon at a time. How much salt causes the egg to start floating? How much salt causes the egg to float to the top of the water?
4. Once the egg floats at the top, pour in fresh water. Where does the egg float now?

What's Happening?

An egg is denser than water, so it sinks to the bottom of the glass. Adding salt increases the water's density. When the egg lifts off the bottom of the glass, the density of the egg and salt water are about the same. When the egg floats at the top, the salt water is much denser than the egg. The salt water is so dense that the fresh water you add to the glass just floats on the salty water. The egg is floating on the salt water and sinking in the fresh water at the same time!

Naked Egg

Turn a raw egg into a "naked" egg with this overnight trick!

Supplies

Egg, Vinegar, Cup, Spoon

*Use your naked egg for the experiment on page 148!

Do It!

1. Put the egg in the cup, and pour vinegar into the cup until the egg is completely covered.
2. Wait 24 hours, and then carefully pour the vinegar out and add fresh vinegar to cover the egg again. Wait another 24 hours or until the eggshell is completely dissolved.
3. Rinse off the egg. You now have a naked, bouncy egg! Be careful: The egg membrane will break if you bounce the egg too hard.

What's Happening?

The shell of an egg is mostly made of calcium carbonate. Vinegar reacts with the calcium carbonate to make water, calcium acetate, and carbon dioxide gas. Did you notice all those carbon dioxide gas bubbles on the shell as it dissolved? Under the shell is a flexible membrane that keeps the egg together.

The Incredible Shrinking Egg

Now you'll take that naked egg and make it shrink and grow again!

Supplies

Naked egg, Corn syrup, Cup, Spoon, Water, Food coloring

*To make a naked egg, try the "Naked Egg" experiment on page 147.

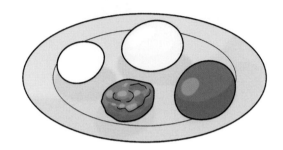

Do It!

1. Put the egg into the cup and pour in enough corn syrup to completely cover the egg.

2. Place a spoon in the cup so it holds the egg down under the corn syrup.

3. Leave the egg in the corn syrup for at least 24 hours.

4. Pull the egg out and rinse it off in water. How has the size of the egg changed?

5. Rinse out the corn syrup from the cup and fill it with water. Add a few drops of food coloring.

6. Put the shrunken egg into the water and leave it for another 24 hours.

7. Pull the egg out of the colored water and rinse it off. How has the size of the egg changed now? What color is the egg?

What's Happening?

The membrane or skin of an egg is semi-permeable. This means that certain molecules, such as oxygen and water, can pass back and forth through the membrane but others, such as corn syrup, cannot.

When you put the egg in the corn syrup, the two liquids try to move so that there are equal amounts or concentrations on both sides of the membrane. However, because the corn syrup can't get into the egg, most of the water moves out of the egg, leaving a shrunken egg behind.

When you put that shrunken egg into a glass of colored water, the water moves back through the membrane and carries the coloring with it. Soon you have a very large egg colored on the inside!

What If?

What if you let the egg sit in other liquids, such as milk and oil? Do these liquids travel through the membrane?

Foldable Egg

Did you ever imagine you could fold up an egg and put it in your pocket? You can with this experiment!

Supplies

Raw egg, Pushpin, Bamboo skewer, Straw, Vinegar, Cup, Baby powder (optional)

*Be sure to wash your hands with soap after handling raw eggs to prevent the spread of bacterial diseases like salmonella.

Do It!

1. Use the pushpin to poke a small hole on one end of the egg.

2. Turn the egg over and make a larger hole in the other end of the egg.

3. Now poke several small holes near the larger hole and gently break away the shell between them.

4. Push the bamboo skewer through the larger hole and wiggle it around to scramble the egg in side.

5. Holding the egg over the sink, place the straw over the small hole and blow hard, pushing the egg out of the larger hole and into the sink.

6. Keep blowing until no more egg will come out.

7. Pour a little water into the egg and slosh it around, and then use the straw to blow everything out of the egg again.

8. Place the egg in the cup and pour vinegar into the egg and the cup until the egg is completely covered and stays under the vinegar.

9. Leave the egg for 24 hours.

10. Empty the cup and pour fresh vinegar over the egg. Repeat this process every 24 hours until the shell of the egg is dissolved and you are left with just the membrane.

11. Gently rinse the membrane, inside and out, with water.

12. Carefully squeeze the water out of the membrane, and then blow into one end of the egg to inflate it again. Now you can fold up the egg membrane and then bounce it around in your hand as the air fills up the egg again! You can also sprinkle baby powder on the outside and inside of the egg membrane to keep it from drying out, so it will last

What's Happening?

Unlike the calcium carbonate in the hard eggshell, the egg membrane does not dissolve in vinegar (acetic acid). The membrane is designed to protect the baby chick while it is inside the egg, so it is very flexible and strong. Egg membranes are made of keratin, a protein that makes your own skin strong and flexible, as well!

What If?

What if you use brown or organic eggs? Is there a difference in their membranes or how long it takes for the shell to dissolve?

Egg Strength

Do you think you can crush an egg with just your hand? It might be harder than you think!

Supplies

Raw eggs, Bowl

* Be sure to wash your hands with soap after handling raw eggs to prevent the spread of bacterial diseases like salmonella.

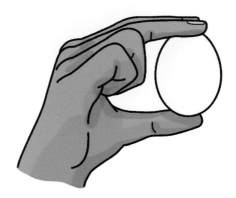

= Do It! =

1. Take off any rings from your fingers and wrap your whole hand around an egg.

2. Hold the egg over the bowl and squeeze as hard as you can — and then squeeze even harder. Can you break the egg?

3. Hold the egg by its ends, placing your thumb on one end and your index and middle fingers on the other end.

4. Hold the egg over the bowl and squeeze the egg as hard as you can between your fingers. Can you break the egg?

5. Hold the egg in your palm over the bowl, pressing down as hard as you can with just your thumb. Can you break the egg?

What's Happening?

Eggshells alone are very fragile, but the shape of the egg gives it strength. The curved form of the egg spreads the pressure evenly around the egg so even squeezing as hard as you can, you won't break the shell.

The ends of the egg are like arches, making them the strongest parts of the egg. Squeezing the ends of the shell won't break the egg, either. But if you apply a sharp force at a single point, like with your thumb, you will be able to break the eggshell. This is why a hen can sit on the egg without hurting it but the baby chick can peck its way out with a sharp beak.

Balance an Egg

There's a myth that eggs can only be balanced on end during the spring and fall equinoxes because of a stronger gravitational pull from the sun. In fact, an egg can be balanced any day of the year!

Do It!

Supplies

Raw egg, Flat tabletop, Salt

1. Hold the egg so it is standing on end, using just your hands to carefully balance it.

2. If you can't balance it, make a small pile of salt on the table and place the egg on end in the pile of salt. Now can you balance the egg on end?

3. Gently blow the salt out from under the egg to leave the egg standing on end all by itself!

What's Happening?

Throughout the year, weather and day length varies as the Earth's tilt toward the sun changes. However, all year long, the gravitational pull of the sun doesn't change and you are just as likely to balance an egg no matter how many hours of daylight you get.

Walking on Eggshells

Can you literally walk on eggshells without breaking them? Give it a try!

Do It!

Supplies

6 dozen (or more) raw eggs in their cartons, Garbage bag, Friend or a chair

1. Inspect all the eggs and remove any that are cracked.
2. Place all the eggs in the carton, pointy-side down.
3. Lay out the bag and line up the open cartons in two long rows on top of the bag.
4. Place the cartons next to each other with the lids on the outside.
5. Lean on a friend or a chair and gently place your feet on the first two cartons of eggs, keeping your feet completely flat.
6. Walk with flat feet down the eggs to the end. Can you do it without breaking any eggs?

What's Happening?

Eggs are designed to be incredibly strong. The ends of the eggs have an arched shape that allows them to withstand a lot of force. By standing on the eggs with a flat foot, you are probably covering five eggs with each foot. So, if you weigh 100 pounds, each egg only has to support 10 pounds of weight.

Water Filter

ADULT NEEDED

Most of us don't have to worry about finding clean water to drink. We can just turn on the tap or open a bottle. But in some parts of the world, water comes from wells, lakes, and rivers that may not be clean enough to drink. Water filters, like this one, are used to clean the water for drinking.

DO NOT DRINK the filtered water. This water filter removes visible dirt but not the invisible pathogens that could make you sick.

Supplies

2-liter bottle, Scissors, Coffee filter, Sand, Gravel, Muddy water, Bowl, 3 clear glasses

Do It!

1. Ask an adult to help you use the scissors to cut the bottle in half.

2. Take the lid off the bottle, and put the top part upside down, like a funnel, in the bottom part.

3. Put the coffee filter in the bottom of the funnel. (You may need to cut the filter or fold it so that it fits.) You can also wet the filter with clean water so that it sticks to the bottle and stays in place. You want at least one layer of coffee filter covering the opening in the bottom of the funnel.

4. Pour a cup of sand into a bowl of clean water to rinse out any dust.

5. Pour out the clean water and scoop the sand into the funnel so that it sits on top of the coffee filter.

6. Rinse the gravel in the same way and put it on top of the sand.

7. The water filter is now assembled! Pour some of the muddy water into the top of the funnel so that it goes through your filter and drains into the bottom of the bottle.

8. Pour the filtered water into one glass, muddy water into another glass, and clean water from the tap into the last glass. How do the three waters compare? Does the filtered water appear as clear as the tap water?

What's Happening?

As the muddy water flows through your filter, it runs into physical barriers that catch the dirt particles in the water. First the gravel catches the largest pieces of dirt. The sand catches the smaller parts, and the coffee filter catches the tiny bits of dirt you can hardly see.

What If?

What if you add other barriers to your water filter? Try cotton balls, crushed charcoal, and anything else you can think of.

Straw Sprinkler

This simple pump pulls water from a bowl of water and sprays it all around. Make sure to do this experiment outdoors or somewhere you can make a watery mess!

Do It!

Supplies

Straw, Bamboo skewer, Scissors, Tape, Bowl of water

1. Twist and push the pointy end of the skewer through the center of the straw.
2. About an inch on both sides of the skewer, cut part way through the straw so that it can bend open but is still attached.
3. Bend down the two outside pieces of straw to make a triangle with the skewer through the middle.
4. Tape the ends or the straw near the bottom of the skewer to hold them in place. Make sure the bottoms of the straw ends are open.
5. Place the sprinkler into the bowl of water. The bottom of the straw triangle should be in the water but the top should be out of the water.
6. Use your hands to spin the skewer very quickly and watch the water fly!

What's Happening?

When you spin the sprinkler, the water inside the straw spins too. The sides of the spinning straw push the water inwards to make it turn in a circle. Scientists call this centripetal force. Newton's third law of motion says that every force has an equal and opposite re-force, so the water also pushes outward on the straw. Because the straw is sloped, the re-force pushes water up the straw until it flies out the open end at the top.

Ice Cube Rescue

For those times when you need to pull an ice cube out of your drink, but you don't want to get your hands wet and cold!

Do It!

Supplies

Glass of water, Ice cube, Thread, Salt

1. Place the ice cube in the glass of water. Can you use the thread (no hands!) to grab the ice cube and pull it out of the water?
2. Lay the thread on the ice with the ends outside the glass.
3. Sprinkle a little salt on the ice and thread.
4. Wait 15 seconds. Grab the thread and pull out the ice!

What's Happening?

Adding salt to water lowers the temperature at which it melts and freezes. When you put salt on the ice cube, it started to melt, but as the water and ice cooled the melted ice, it froze again—with the thread now inside the ice cube.

218 Solar Still

If you're ever stranded on a desert island with nothing but salt water to drink, this solar still will come in quite handy!

Do It!

Supplies

Bowl, Plastic cups 1" shorter than the height of bowl (can be cut to size), Clear plastic wrap, Tape, Small rock, Ruler, Measuring spoon, Measuring cup, Water, Salt

1. Pour 2 inches of water into a bowl and mix in 2 tablespoons of salt until it dissolves.
2. Place a plastic cup in the center of the bowl.
3. Stretch plastic wrap over the top of the bowl and seal it with tape.
4. Place small rocks on the center of the plastic wrap above the cup.
5. Press down slightly on the plastic wrap so it stretches and sags down above the cup.
6. You've made a solar still! Place it in bright sunlight.
7. After four hours in the sun, remove the plastic wrap from the bowl and measure the amount of distilled water in the cup. How does the distilled water look and taste?

What's Happening?

The sun heats up the salt water until it evaporates from a liquid to a gas and rises into the air. When the gas hits the cooler plastic wrap, it condenses back into liquid water droplets. Gravity pulls the droplets down the plastic toward the rock, where they drip down into the cup.

219 Ice Cube Island

You may have seen ice cubes float in a drink, but does cold water float too?

Do It!

Supplies

Water balloons, Bucket, Water

1. Fill a bucket halfway with cold water.
2. Fill a water balloon with cold water.
3. Put the bucket and balloon in the freezer for 10 minutes to get it really cold.
4. Fill the other bucket halfway with hot tap water.
5. Fill a water balloon with hot water too.
6. Put the hot and cold balloon in the bucket of hot water. Do they sink or float?
7. Then put the hot and cold balloon in the bucket of cold water. Do they sink or float?

What's Happening?

Water molecules move around faster in the hot water balloon than in the cold balloon. The hot water has more space between the molecules and is therefore less dense. That's why the hot water balloon floats and the cold water balloon sinks!

Hot + Cold Water

What do you get when you mix hot water with cold? You'll be surprised!

Supplies

2 identical, small glass jars; Red and blue food coloring;
Spoons; Water; Baking pan; 2 index cards
(larger than the tops of your jars)

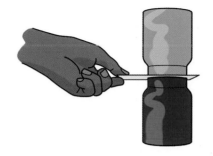

Do It!

1. Fill one jar to the top with water.
2. Add blue food coloring and stir the water so it is completely blue.
3. Put the jar in the freezer for 10 minutes until it gets very cold, but does not freeze.
4. Fill the other jar to the top with hot water; you can use hot water from the tap or heat the water in the microwave.
5. Add red food coloring and stir the water so it is completely red.
6. Put both jars in the baking pan (to catch any spilled water).
7. Put the index card on top of the blue jar.
8. While holding the index card on top of the jar, quickly and carefully pick up the jar and turn it over. (When the jar is upside down, the card will stay on by itself.)
9. Place the upside-down blue jar on top of the red jar.
10. Look carefully at all sides of the jars to make sure they are lined up exactly on top of each other. Then, carefully pull out the index card. You might want a helper to hold the jars in place while you do this. What happens to the hot red and cold blue water when you remove the index card?
11. Repeat the experiment, but this time, put the cold blue water on the bottom and hot red water on top.

What's Happening?

When you heat water, the molecules move around faster. The quicker hot water molecules are more spread out than the slower-moving cold water molecules. And if the molecules are more spread out, the water is also less dense.

When the denser, cold blue water is on top, it quickly sinks into the less dense, hot red water. The hot red water also rises to the top, causing the two temperatures and colors to mix.

But when the less dense, hot red water is on top, it stays there. The colors don't mix because the less dense liquid is already on top and the denser liquid is on the bottom. If you left the jars until the bottom warmed up and the top cooled down, you would see the colors gradually mix.

Leaky Bottle

How can a water bottle have holes, but no water leaks out?

Supplies

Disposable water bottle full of water,
Tack or safety pin, Sink

 ## Do It!

1. Make sure the bottle is filled completely to the top and the cap is screwed on tightly. Keep the bottle in or next to the sink for the rest of this experiment.

2. Hold the top of the bottle (not the sides) while you use a tack or safety pin to poke a hole in the center of the bottle. Does the water come out?

3. Squeeze the bottle. Does the water come out now?

4. Take the lid off the bottle. What's happening?

5. Refill the bottle and put the cap on tightly.

6. Make two more holes, one near the top of the bottle and another near the bottom.

7. Take off the lid and watch how the water comes out of the three holes.

What's Happening?

The key to this experiment is pressure. The air is pressing in on the outside of the bottle and the water is pressing out on the inside of the bottle.

When you make a hole in the bottle with the cap on, the pressure outside and inside are the same and water does not flow out of the hole.

When you take the cover off the bottle, the pressure inside is greater than the pressure outside because the air is also pushing down on the water and water flows out of the hole.

With three holes in the bottle, you can see the difference in pressure. The water flowing out of the bottom hole goes out much farther than the water flowing out of the top hole. The bottom hole has more pressure because it has more water (and air) above it pushing down. This higher pressure pushes the water out faster!

What If?

What if you trick your friends with this experiment? Start by poking holes all around the bottle. Ask if they want a drink and hand them the bottle while holding it by the cap. When they grab the bottle with their hand, the pressure will cause the bottle to leak all over!

Oil Spill Cleanup

You may have heard of oil accidentally spilling into the ocean. This experiment will give you an idea of how you can clean up spilled oil on a smaller scale.

= Do It! =

Supplies

Large baking dish, Water, Vegetable oil, Blue food coloring, Paper towel, Cotton balls, Nylon dish scrubber, Dish soap

1. Fill the baking dish with 2 inches of water. Mix in a couple drops of blue food coloring.

2. Pour 2 tablespoons of oil onto the water to simulate an oil spill in the ocean. Place the paper towel on the oil spill.

3. Wait 30 seconds, and then lift the paper towel. How much of the oil did it soak up?

4. Pour two more oil spills into your blue water and use the cotton balls to clean up one, and the dish scrubber to clean up the other. How much oil did these soak up?

5. Pour one more oil spill into the baking dish ocean.

6. Put 2 drops of dish soap in the middle of the oil and then use your finger to stir the water and oil. What happens to the oil spill?

What's Happening?

The paper towel and cotton balls absorb the oil. You can also add a dispersant like soap or detergent to break up the oil into smaller pieces so that the ocean waves disperse the oil spill. This way it will have a smaller impact on the environment and make it easier for bacteria in the water to break down the oil.

Ketchup Diver

Send a ketchup packet on a deep-sea adventure!

= Do It! =

Supplies

Empty 2-liter bottle, Ketchup packets, Water, Tall glass

1. Fill the glass almost full of water.

2. Put the ketchup packets in the glass one at a time. Do they float?

3. Find a packet that floats at the top of the glass, but just under the water level. Keep this packet and put away the rest.

4. Remove the label from the 2-liter bottle and fill it with water.

5. Put the ketchup packet in the bottle, fill it all the way to the top with water and put the cap on tightly.

6. Place both hands on the bottle and squeeze. What happens to the ketchup packet in the bottle?

What's Happening?

The ketchup packet floats because it has air inside. When you squeeze the bottle, you also squeeze the ketchup packet and compress the air just enough that it becomes more dense and sinks. When you let go of the bottle, the air expands again, and the ketchup diver returns to the top.

224 Floating Ball

Will a table tennis ball float in the center of a cup of water?

Supplies

Cup, Table tennis ball, Water

Do It!

1. Fill the cup almost full of water.
2. Put the ball in the water; notice that it floats to the side.
3. Move the ball to the center and let it go. Can you get the ball to stay in the center? Can you get it to stay on the side?
4. Take the ball out and pour more water into the cup to the very top.
5. Put the ball back on the water. Where does it float now? Can you get the ball to stay in the middle? Can you get it to stay on the side?

What's Happening?

Water sticks to itself and forms a skin over the surface. The force that holds the skin together is called surface tension. When the skin touches the edge of the cup, it curves. In a partially full cup, the edge of the water curves up. When you place the ball on the water, it also curves up where it touches the ball and the surface tension pulls on the ball. Unless the ball is exactly in the center of the cup, the ball is pulled by the surface tension to the edge. In an overfull cup of water, the edge curves downward. Now the surface tension pushes on all sides of the ball and keeps it in the center.

225 Surface Tension Shimmy

Watch water and rubbing alcohol shimmy and shake as their surface tensions battle it out!

Do It!

Supplies

Glass or ceramic plate, 2 cups, Water, Rubbing alcohol, Food coloring, Dropper

1. Pour some water into the cup and mix in a few drops of food coloring.
2. Pour a little of the colored water into the center of the plate so it makes a small puddle of water, about 2 inches across.
3. In another cup, mix some rubbing alcohol with a few drops of a different food coloring.
4. Pour a couple drops of the colored rubbing alcohol into the middle of the colored water puddle. What do you see?

What's Happening?

Water has a much higher surface tension than rubbing alcohol. This means the water sticks to itself much more strongly than it does to the rubbing alcohol. When you drop the rubbing alcohol into the water, the water pulls away, leaving a rubbing alcohol crater. Along the edges, you will see the rubbing alcohol and water shake and shimmy as they eventually mix together.

Water Wheel

Using just the power of water, a water wheel can lift heavy objects!

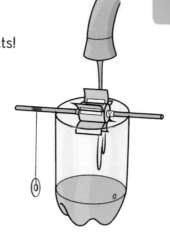

Supplies

Empty thread spool, Plastic disposable cup, 2-liter bottle, Masking or duct tape, Scissors, Straw, Thread or dental floss, Metal washer

Do It!

1. For the water wheel, cut six identical rectangles from the plastic cup. They should be as long as the spool and about 1 inch wide.

2. Tape the rectangular blades to the spool so they are evenly spaced and curve in the same direction.

3. Put the straw through the hole in the spool.

4. Tape the spool in place in the center of the straw.

5. To make the water wheel holder, ask an adult to help you cut the top off of the 2-liter bottle, and cut two V-shaped notches on opposite sides of the bottle.

6. Poke a couple of holes in the bottom of the bottle for the water to drain out.

7. Cut a piece of thread about 12 inches long and tape one end to the end of the straw.

8. Tie the other end of the string to the metal washer.

9. Put your water wheel holder in the sink, placing the water wheel on the holder so the straw rests in the V-shaped notches and the spool part of the water wheel is right under the faucet.

10. Turn on the water. Does the water wheel spin? If not, adjust the position of the wheel and flow of the water.

What's Happening?

Water wheels are used to lift or turn objects. The motion energy of the falling water is transferred to the wheel, causing it to turn. Anything connected to the wheel will turn, as well.

In this experiment, the straw turns and winds up the string to lift a metal washer. In hydroelectric plants, the wheel turns a giant magnet surrounded by wires. The spinning magnet causes electric current in the wires that can be sent out to power homes with electricity.

What If?

What if you use larger blades? Does it matter how many blades are on the spool? Does the size or number of blades affect how fast your water wheel spins or how much weight it can lift?

Ice Cubes or Oil Cubes?

You know that ice cubes float in water, but what about in oil? And do frozen oil cubes float in oil, or in water?

Supplies

Ice cube tray or 4 small cups, 2 large clear glasses, Vegetable oil, Water, Freezer, Food coloring (optional)

Do It!

1. Fill at least two wells of the ice cube tray all the way to the top with water and at least two with oil.

2. If you like, put a drop or two of different color food coloring in the water ones.

3. Put the tray in the freezer for at least two hours, or until the water and oil cubes are both frozen. Look at the cubes in the ice cube tray. How do the sizes of the ice and oil cubes compare to the size of the water and oil you poured into the tray?

4. Pour water into one glass and oil into the other.

5. Drop one ice cube and one oil cube in each glass. Which cubes float in water and which sink? Which cubes float in oil and which sink?

6. Let the glasses sit out for a couple of minutes until the cubes start to melt. What happens to the water in the oil cup as the ice cube melts? What happens to the oil in the water cup as the oil cube melts?

What's Happening?

Water is the most important liquid on Earth. Humans, plants, and animals could not survive without it. But water is also the most unusual liquid on Earth.

Most liquids, like oil, expand when they are heated, and shrink when they are cooled. You should have noticed that the level of the frozen oil cube was lower than the liquid oil that you poured in the ice tray. The oil shrinks or takes up less space as it freezes. The frozen oil cube also sinks in the liquid oil.

Water is completely different! Like other liquids, water expands when it is heated and shrinks when it is cooled *until* it reaches about 39°F (4°C). Below 39°F, water begins to expand again! Its mass stays the same, but its volume increases. This means that really cold water (below 39°F) and ice float. The frozen ice cube will be larger than the liquid you poured in the ice tray, and the ice cube floats in both the water and the liquid oil.

Super Cool Water

This water is so cool, you can turn it instantly into ice!

Do It!

Supplies

2 unopened bottles of purified water, Ice, Rock salt, Water, Bucket, Thermometer, Bowl, Flavored sugar syrup (optional)

1. Put the bottles in the bucket and cover them with ice.
2. Pour ½ cup of salt over the ice. If you have a large bucket, use more salt.
3. Fill the rest of the bucket with water.
4. Place the thermometer in the bucket, and wait until the temperature reaches 17°F (-8°C).
5. Pull one of the bottles out of the bucket, taking care not to bump the bottle.
6. Hold it by the lid and bang it on the counter. What happens to the water inside the bottle?
7. Place a couple of ice cubes in the bowl.
8. Carefully pull the other bottle out of the bucket.
9. Unscrew the top and slowly pour the water onto the ice cubes. What happens to the water as you pour? If you have flavored sugar syrup or juice, pour it in the bowl for an instant snow cone!

What's Happening?

Water freezes at 0°C or 32°F, but it needs to be a crystal or seed to start the process. In water from your tap, there are minerals and other chemicals in the water that make this happen. Because purified water is "pure," it can be cooled below freezing or super cooled without forming ice. Once the water is super cooled, a small bubble or piece of ice can start the freezing process.

Ice Cube on a Wire

An ice cube on a wire would make a very COOL necklace on a hot day!

Do It!

Supplies

18-inch piece of thin wire, 2 pencils, Sturdy plastic cup, Ice cube

1. Wrap each end of the wire around a pencil several times, until you have about 8 inches of wire stretched between the pencils.
2. Turn the cup upside down and place the ice cube on top.
3. Hold the pencils like handles and place the top of the wire across the toothpick.
4. Pull down hard on the pencils for a few minutes. What happens to the wire?
5. Stop pulling when the wire is all the way inside the ice cube. You have an ice cube on a wire!

What's Happening?

Pressure melts ice. Scientists call this regelation. For instance, the pressure from an ice skate melts the top layer of ice, so a skater glides on a thin layer of water. When the pressure is removed, the water refreezes. It appears as if the wire was frozen in the ice cube!

Walking Water

Watch water defy gravity!

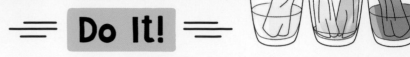

Do It!

Supplies

Paper towel, Scissors, 3 clear glasses, Water, Food coloring

1. Cut the paper towel in half lengthways, and then fold it in half lengthways twice, so you have a long strip that is four layers thick.
2. Pour water into two of the glasses so they are almost full.
3. Put two colors of food coloring in each glass.
4. Place the three glasses in a row with the empty glass in the middle.
5. Put one end of a strip in the empty glass, and the other in one of the glasses of colored water.
6. Do the same with the other strip, but put one end in the other glass of colored water.
7. If the middle of the strips stick up in the air, slide the glasses apart a bit so they stay flat on top.
8. Wait 15 minutes, and then check on the glasses. What do you see?
9. Check again after 30 minutes. Has anything changed?

What's Happening?

The water moves along the paper towel using capillary action. The water sticks to itself (called cohesion) but it sticks to the paper towel (called adhesion) more. The water crawls up the tiny gaps in the fibers of the paper towel. This is the same method plants use to get water from their roots to the tips of their leaves.

---

231 Soap-powered Boat

Sail the soapy seas with this simple ship!

Do It!

Supplies

Foam egg carton, Scissors, Bowl of water, Dish soap, Toothpick

1. Cut out a boat from the flat top of the egg carton, about 2 inches long and 1 inch wide.
2. Cut a point at the top of the boat so it's shaped like a house.
3. Cut a small, upside-down-triangle-shaped hole from the bottom of the boat.
4. Place your boat in the center of the water.
5. Dip the tip of the toothpick into the dish soap and then dip it into the hole at the bottom of the boat. Watch your boat zoom around!

What's Happening?

The water in the bowl sticks together, especially on the top of the water. This stickiness is called surface tension and forms a skin on top of the water that is hard to break. This is one reason your boat floats on top of the water instead of sinking to the bottom. The soap has a much smaller surface tension. The surface tension skin on top of the water pulls away from the soap like a balloon popping. This sends your boat zooming.

Most water contains tiny amounts of minerals that give it a unique taste and affects how it makes bubbles.

Supplies

3 different sources of water, 3 clear 20-oz. soda bottles, Ruler, Ivory dish soap, Measuring cup, Stopwatch or clock

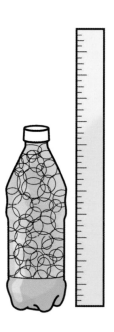

Do It!

Before you begin, find water from at least three different places where you want to measure the water hardness. For example, the faucet at your house, bottled water from the store, your best friend's house, your school, or the water fountain at the playground. The farther away these places are from each other, the better.

1. Use the measuring cup to pour exactly 1 cup of water into a soda bottle for each place from which you are collecting water.

2. Label the bottles.

3. Place two drops of soap into the first bottle and screw the top on very tight.

4. Shake the bottle as hard as you can for a full 60 seconds.

5. As soon as you are done shaking the bottle, use the ruler to measure the total height of the bubbles in the bottle. If the water is very soft, the whole bottle may be filled with bubbles. If the water is very hard, you may not have any bubbles at all! Most places will be somewhere in between.

6. Repeat the process for the other bottles of water. How does the amount of bubbles from each place compare?

What's Happening?

Water hardness is a measure of the minerals in water. Hard water has more minerals than soft water. If you live near an ocean, you probably have soft water because removing salt from water also takes out the minerals that make water hard.

If you get your water from a river, your water is probably hard. The flowing water from rivers takes minerals out of the rocks in the riverbeds. Well water is usually hard too. Wells pull up water that is in between layers of rock underground. This water dissolves minerals from the rocks.

233 Hero's Engine

Hero was a Greek engineer who lived in Alexandria about 2,000 years ago. He invented the first steam engine using the same science as the engine you can make here with a cup, straws, and water!

Supplies

Large foam cup, Pen or sharp pencil, String, Scissors, 2 bendy straws, Water, Sink or large bowl

Do It!

1. Use the pen to poke two small holes near the top of the cup on opposite sides.

2. Thread a piece of string through the holes and tie a knot a couple of inches above the top of the cup so that there is extra string above the knot.

3. Cut both straws so there is about 1 inch of straight straw on either side of the bendy parts.

4. Use the pen again to poke two slightly larger holes about ½ inch from the bottom on opposite sides of the cup. The holes should be just large enough for the straws to fit snuggly.

5. Slide a straw into each hole so that the bendy part is on the outside of the cup.

6. Straighten the straws so they both stick directly out from the cup.

7. Hold the cup by the extra string over the sink or a large bowl and pour water into the cup. Does water come out of the straws? Does the cup move?

8. Bend the straws so they both point clockwise.

9. Fill the cup with water and hold it over the sink again. Does water come out of the straws? Does the cup move now?

What's Happening?

Air pressure pushes the water out of the cup and through the bent straws. But Newton's third law tells us that every force has an equal and opposite re-force.

This means the water also pushes back on the straws, causing the cup to spin around. The cup spins in the opposite direction that the water moves and with the same force that pushes the water out of the straws.

In Hero's original steam engine, called an *aeolipile*, the curved straws would be at the top of a sealed metal cup. Fire is used to heat the water in the cup and it turns to steam. As the steam rushes out of the straws, the cup turns. This turning motion could be used to pull a rope and move heavy objects or turn wheels to grind up grain.

Moving Molecules

What makes hot water hot and cold water cold?

Supplies

3 clear jars, Water, Food coloring

Do It!

1. Fill one jar with water and leave it on the counter for 30 minutes.
2. Fill another jar and put it in the freezer for 10 minutes to get very cold but not freeze.
3. Fill the third jar with hot tap water. You may need to work on the timing so that you have a jar of room temperature water, a jar of cold water, and a jar of hot water at the same time.
4. Add three drops of food coloring to each jar. What happens to the food coloring in the different temperatures?

What's Happening?

Heating water adds energy. This energy causes the water molecules to move around faster. Cooling water removes energy and the water molecules slow down. When you add food coloring to the jars with different temperatures of water, you can see the water molecules moving!

In the jar of hot water, the fast-moving molecules mix the color into the water. In the jar of cold water, the color sinks to the bottom of the slow-moving water. The water at room temperature is somewhere in between.

Pepper Scatter

This experiment is so simple and dramatic, you might even think it's magic!

Supplies

Bowl, Water, Ground pepper, Liquid soap

Do It!

1. Fill the bowl with water. Sprinkle pepper over the water.
2. Stick your finger in the middle of the bowl. What's happening?
3. Put a tiny amount of liquid soap on the tip of your finger. Stick your finger in the middle of the bowl again. What happens now?

What's Happening?

First, pepper is hydrophobic. This means it is not attracted to water. This helps to keep it dry and on top of the water.

Second, water is attracted to itself and sticks together. This causes a skin of water on the surface that is hard to break called surface tension. The pepper sits on top of the surface tension skin. When you add soap to the water, the skin breaks. The soap gets between the water molecules so they can't stick together. The skin pops like a balloon when you touch it with soap and carries the pepper out to the edge of the bowl.

236 Bottle Pour

What's the quickest way to empty water from a bottle?

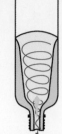

 **Do It!**

Supplies

3 identical bottles of water, Stopwatch, Friend, Sink

1. Have your friend time how long it takes to pour the water from a bottle into the sink using each of these methods.

Method 1: Turn the bottle completely upside down.

Method 2: Turn the bottle sideways, at an angle, so the water comes out smoothly.

Method 3: Turn the bottle completely upside down and swirl it continuously so the water moves around the inside of the bottle like a tornado. Which method emptied the bottle quickest?

What's Happening?

With each method, gravity pulls the water out of the bottles. However, to get water out of a bottle, air needs to get in to fill up the empty space where the water used to be.

When you held the bottle upside down, air bubbles went up through the bottle. This is not the quickest way to let water out and air in. When you turn the bottle sideways, there is plenty of room for the air to come in, but the water comes out slowly because the bottle is sideways. When you hold the bottle upside down and swirl it, you provide a hole in the middle for air to come in as gravity pulls the water out of the bottle.

237 Penny Drop

How many drops of water fit on top of a penny? You might be surprised!

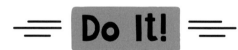 **Do It!**

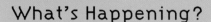 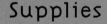

Supplies

Clean penny, Dropper, Water, Rubbing alcohol, Vegetable oil, Dish soap, Paper towel

1. Lay a paper towel on a flat surface and place the penny in the middle.
2. Fill the dropper with water. Hold the dropper close to the penny and place a drop of water on it.
3. Slowly add drops until the penny overflows and spills onto the paper towel.
4. Repeat with alcohol, oil, and dish soap, making sure you clean the penny before adding drops of liquid. How many drops of each liquid can you fit on the penny?

What's Happening?

Most liquids stick to each other. This stickiness forms a skin over the surface of the liquid. The skin holds a drop together, which is why a drop appears rounded. The force that holds this skin together is called surface tension. Liquids with the strongest surface tension skins, such as water, can fit the most drops on the coin. Eventually, you will add so much liquid that the skin can't hold it all in and it pops.

Down the Drain

Do toilets flush one way in the Southern Hemisphere and another way in the Northern Hemisphere?

Supplies

Sinks, Toilets

= Do It! =

Sink Test

1. Fill the sink halfway with water, and then turn the water off. Wait at least three minutes until the water is completely still. Make sure no one walks near the sink or disturbs the water in any way. You want to be sure that no other factors affect the direction in which the water drains.

2. Slowly and carefully remove the plug and watch the water drain down the sink.

3. Write down the direction in which the water spins. Does the direction change while the water drains?

4. Test each sink at least three times.

Toilet Test

5. Find a clean toilet and, just like with the sink, make sure the water is very still.

6. Flush the toilet. Write down the direction in which the water spins. Does the water pouring back into the toilet affect the direction in which the water drains?

7. Test the same toilet at least three more times. Test as many sinks and toilets as you can. Did the water always drain the same way? What factors do you think might affect the direction in which water drains?

What's Happening?

The Coriolis force is caused by the rotation of the Earth. Everything on the planet rotates with the Earth. If you could look down on the North Pole of the spinning Earth, you would see that it turns counterclockwise. If you then look at the South Pole, you would see it spins clockwise. Check this out on a globe!

But because the Earth rotates relatively slowly — about once every day — this force is extremely small. For large amounts of slow-moving fluids, such as the atmosphere, it has a larger, lasting effect. Hurricanes in the Northern Hemisphere spin counterclockwise, and in the Southern Hemisphere they spin clockwise — just like the Earth. Also like the Earth, hurricanes turn relatively slowly and the direction of the spin is controlled by the direction in which the Earth spins.

For smaller amounts of a fluid, such as the water in your toilet, this force is easily overcome by even the tiniest disturbances and design flaws in the sink. These factors are more likely than the Coriolis force to influence the direction in which the water drains.

Plunger Tower

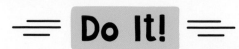

A plunger is a useful tool when the toilet backs up – and to demonstrate of the power of air pressure!

Supplies

Toilet plunger, Petroleum jelly, Hardcover books, Rubber bands

Do It!

1. Rub petroleum jelly along the outer edge of the plunger.
2. Hold one of the books closed with rubber bands.
3. Lay the book on the floor and push the plunger forcefully onto the book (not the rubber bands), so that it squishes and pushes the air out. Lift the plunger straight up. Can you lift the book?
4. Attach more books with rubber bands. How many books can you lift?

What's Happening?

Plungers get their power from air pressure. When you squish a plunger on a flat surface and push the air out, you are creating a vacuum. That means there is very little air inside the plunger. However, outside of the plunger, there is a lot of air pushing very hard. Almost 15 pounds of force pushes on every square inch from the weight of the air! This is the force that holds the books onto the plunger.

240 Oil + Water = ?

Oil and water don't mix...or do they?

Do It!

Supplies

Clear cup, Water, Vegetable oil, Bar of soap, 3 toothpicks

1. Fill the cup half full of water. Use a toothpick to place a few drops of oil into the water.
2. Use a clean toothpick to try to break up the oil drops. What happens?
3. Rub the the third toothpick on the bar of soap and try to break up the oil drops. What happens now?

What's Happening?

Oil and water don't mix. Water molecules stick to each other stronger than they stick to oil. Because oil molecules are not packed together as tightly as water molecules, oil is less dense and floats on top of water.

However, when you add soap, something changes. Soap molecules, or surfactants, have two ends: one that is attracted to water and another that is attracted to oil. The soap surrounds the oil molecules with the end that is attracted to oil so that they can break up and move around the water. There is even a special word for an oil molecule surrounded by soap: micelle. By adding soap to the oil, you create tiny micelles on top of the water!

Mirror, Mirror in the Steam

Have you ever stepped out of a hot shower and saw a steamed-up mirror? Why does that happen?

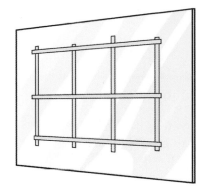

Supplies

Large mirror, Shower (in the same room as the mirror), Shaving cream, Bar of soap, Liquid hand soap, Dishwashing soap, Potato, Paper towels, Glass cleaner, Masking tape, Pen

Do It!

1. Clean the mirror well with glass cleaner. Use the masking tape to divide your mirror into six 6-inch squares.

2. On the tape, label the squares with the name of each item you will be testing, leaving one square blank. You will compare the other squares to this one and use it to make sure the mirror really fogs up.

3. Cut the potato in half and rub the inside of the potato over the square labeled "Potato." Use a dry paper towel to rub the mirror until it is shiny again.

4. In the square labeled "Bar of Soap," rub the dry bar of soap over the mirror in the square. Then use a dry paper towel to rub the mirror until it's shiny again.

5. Do the same thing in the other squares with the liquid hand soap, shaving cream, and dishwashing soap.

6. Now it's time to get clean! Take a long, hot shower. Which squares got steamy and which stayed steam-free? Leave the squares on the mirror for a week and look every time someone in the house takes a shower to see which squares stayed steam-free.

What's Happening?

When you take a hot shower, you might notice clouds of steam in the air. The water is so hot that it changes from water (a liquid) to steam (a gas). This is called evaporation. When this steam hits your cold mirror, it turns back into water and sticks to the mirror. This is called condensation. If you look close at the steamed-up mirror, you will see tiny drops of water all over the mirror.

One way to keep your mirror from steaming is to warm up the mirror so the steam doesn't condense back to water. Or you can put something on the mirror so that the water doesn't bead up into tiny drops when it condenses. Certain chemicals, such as glycerin, mix well with water and are called hydrophilic. This causes the water to spread out over the mirror so that you can see yourself.

242 Floating Bowling Balls

Can you float a bowling ball in the bathtub?
The results are striking!

Supplies

Bathtub, Bowling ball (12 pounds or less), Bowling ball (heavier than 12 pounds), 6 cups of salt

⹀ Do It! ⹀

1. Fill your bathtub almost full of water, leaving a few inches at the top.
2. Gently place the bowling balls in the bathtub. What happens?
3. Pour salt into the tub and mix it around. Does anything change?

What's Happening?

All bowling balls, no matter their weight, are the same size or volume, with a circumference of 27 inches. Because they have the same volume, this means that heavier bowling balls are denser, while lighter bowling balls are less dense. When you put the bowling balls in the tub, the ball that is 12 pounds or less floats! Anything heavier than 12 pounds will sink to the bottom. When you add salt to the water, you make it denser, so that even a 16-pound bowling ball will float. You should have seen both bowling balls in the tub float after you added the salt.

243 Soap Clouds

ADULT NEEDED

What happens when you microwave soap?

Supplies

4 bars of soap, including Ivory, Bowl of water; Microwave oven; 4 paper plates

⹀ Do It! ⹀

1. Place the bars in a bowl of water. Which soaps float? Which sink? Remove the bars and dry them off.
2. Place each soap on its own plate and put one plate of soap in the microwave. Cook the soap on high for one minute.
3. Remove the soap and wait two minutes for it to cool. How is it different from before it was cooked? Does it look or feel different?
4. Cook each of the soaps, one at a time, for one minute in the microwave and observe any changes.

What's Happening?

Ivory soap is the only soap that floats. Look carefully at it, and you'll notice tiny bubbles all over its surface. This is because Ivory soap has air bubbles whipped into it, unlike other soaps. When you cook Ivory soap in the microwave, the soap becomes soft and the air and moisture trapped in those bubbles heats up and expands, making a foam. The other bars of soap melt.

Oily Water Mix-up

Water and oil don't mix – unless they get a little help!

Supplies

Clean bottle with a lid, Water, Vegetable oil, Shampoo, Measuring cup

Do It!

1. Pour ½ cup of water into the jar. Pour ¼ cup of vegetable oil down the inside of the jar.
2. Cover the jar and shake it hard for 30 seconds. Do the liquids look mixed together? Let the jar sit for five minutes. The water and oil should separate into two layers.
3. Squeeze some shampoo into the jar and watch what happens.
4. Cover the jar and shake it hard for 30 seconds. Are the oil and water mixed up? Let the jar sit for five minutes. Do the water and oil separate into two layers?

What's Happening?

Oil and water don't mix because they stick to themselves and not to each other. Soap, on the other hand, sticks to just about everything. Scientists call soap a surfactant. These stick to the oil and water, allowing the oil and water to stick to each other. With soap around, oil and water DO mix!

Toilet Paper Inertia

What's the most efficient way to remove toilet paper from the roll?

Supplies

Full roll of toilet paper hanging on a holder

Do It!

1. Unroll the toilet paper on the holder. Can you get enough paper on the floor so that it rolls on its own?
2. Roll the paper back up. Hold the end of the paper (near the roll) with both hands and yank it. The paper should rip right off.

What's Happening?

The key to controlling how the toilet paper rolls is inertia. The concept comes from Newton's first law: "An object at rest remains at rest and an object in motion remains in motion unless acted on by a force." Inertia is this tendency to remain at rest or motion and depends on the mass of the object. In our case, the object is a roll of toilet paper. In the first part of the experiment, your force was just large enough to get the paper rolling and keep it rolling. But in the second part, the inertia of the "massive" paper roll kept it at rest while the less massive piece ripped off.

246 Wrinkly Fingers

Have you ever taken a bath or spent hours in the pool and then your fingers and toes are all wrinkly? For a long time, people thought that skin absorbing water caused the wrinkles. But if that's the case, why doesn't your whole body get wrinkly?

Supplies

3 large bowls, 10 marbles, 5 or more volunteers, Stopwatch

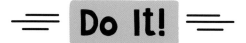

Do It!

1. Fill one large bowl with warm water. Have a volunteer hold both hands in the water for 20 to 30 minutes, until their fingertips are completely wrinkly.

2. Place 10 marbles in one of the bowls, and then place the bowl of marbles on one side of your volunteer and an empty bowl on the other side.

3. Ask the volunteer to move the dry marbles, one at a time, from one bowl to the other, transferring each marble from one hand to another on the way. Time how long it takes them to move all the marbles.

4. Pour water into the bowl with the marbles and have your volunteer soak their hands for a few more minutes to keep them wrinkly.

5. Again, time how long it takes your volunteer to move the wet marbles from one bowl to the other in the same way.

6. Let your volunteer take a break so their fingers dry out and become un-wrinkly again.

7. Repeat the experiment with smooth fingertips, and wet and dry marbles.

8. Use several volunteers (at least five) to do the same experiment, mixing up whether they start with wet or dry hands. Average the times for each of the four situations. Under which conditions did your volunteers move the marbles the quickest?

What's Happening?

Since the 1930s, scientists knew that finger wrinkling was controlled by your body's autonomic nervous system, the system that also controls your breathing, heart rate, and perspiration. They noticed that people with nerve damage do not get wrinkly fingers in the water and realized that finger wrinkling is caused by blood vessels constricting below the skin.

One theory about the reason our fingers wrinkle when they get wet is that, like the treads on a tire, the wrinkles increase your grip on wet objects. Scientists have performed experiments like this one and gotten mixed results as to whether wrinkled fingers really do make it easier to hold on to wet objects. What do you think?

Elephant Toothpaste

This foam explosion creates what looks like toothpaste that's big enough for an elephant!

Supplies

20-oz. soda bottle, Funnel, Hydrogen peroxide, Dish soap, Yeast, Small bowl, Measuring spoon, Measuring cup, Safety glasses and clothes, Plastic wash basin

Do It!

1. In the small bowl, mix 2 teaspoons of yeast in 2 tablespoons of warm water.
2. Funnel ½ cup of hydrogen peroxide into the bottle. Add three drops of dish soap and swish the bottle around to mix.
3. Place the bottle in the basin. Pour the yeast solution into the bottle, quickly remove the funnel, and get out of the way!

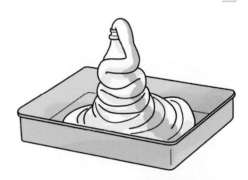

What's Happening?

Hydrogen peroxide is water with an extra oxygen atom — H_2O_2. It's not very stable, and slowly decomposes into water and oxygen. The yeast speeds up, or catalyzes, the process so that all the oxygen gas is released quickly. The gas gets trapped in the soap, creating LOTS of bubbles, resembling toothpaste for an elephant. When the experiment is over, you're left with water, soap, and a little yeast.

Bubble Snakes

Why bother with one bubble when you can have a giant snake of bubbles?

Supplies

6-inch square of the following fabrics: Cotton, Jersey, Terry cloth, and Nylon; Empty 16-oz. soda bottle; Scissors; Rubber band; Bowl; Liquid dish soap; Outdoor space

Do It!

1. Cut the bottom off the bottle. Stretch one piece of fabric over the large end. Secure it with a rubber band.
2. Mix 1 cup of water and ¼ cup of liquid soap in the bowl.
3. Put the cloth end of the bottle into the bowl so the fabric soaks up the soap.
4. Take the bottle out and blow into the small end of the bottle as hard as you can. A snake of bubbles should grow out of the fabric.
5. Repeat the process with the other fabrics. Which fabric made the longest snake? Which fabric was easiest to blow through?

What's Happening?

When you blow through your bubble snake maker, you are creating hundreds of tiny bubbles that stick together. The number and size of the bubbles depend on the holes in the fabric. Bigger holes mean bigger bubbles!

Bomb Your Bath

These bath bombs combine the fun of bubbles with soothing bath salts.

ADULT NEEDED

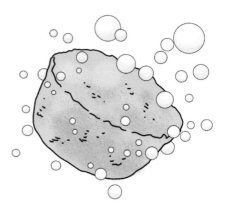

Supplies

Mini muffin pan, Large bowl, Small bowl, Masking tape, Marker, Water, Vegetable oil, Citric acid, Baking soda, Cornstarch, Epsom salt, Dropper, Measuring spoon, Spoons for mixing, Thermometer, Stopwatch, Oven

Do It!

1. In the large bowl, mix together 2 tablespoons of citric acid, 4 tablespoons of baking soda, 3 tablespoons of cornstarch and 1 tablespoon of Epsom salt.

2. In the small bowl, mix together 2 teaspoons of water and 2 teaspoons of vegetable oil.

The next few steps are tricky, so read ahead to be ready!

3. Have a clean spoon ready. Add two drops of the oil mixture to the dry mixture. Use the back of the spoon to pat down the fizzing, mixing in the damp part with the dry mixture.

4. Repeat this until all the oil mixture has been added to the dry mixture. It should be damp enough to hold its shape.

5. Place a drop of vegetable oil in each muffin tray well. Spread the oil over each well with your finger. Spoon the mixture into the pan and push down to pack the mixture tight.

6. Preheat the oven to 170°F. Place the pan in the oven, and then turn the oven off. Leave the pan in the oven with the door closed for one hour. While the bath bombs are drying, clean out the big bowl.

7. Remove the bath bombs from the tray. If they are crumbly, try again with more liquid.

8. Fill the large bowl with hot water. Drop the bath bomb in the water and time how long it takes to stop fizzing.

What's Happening?

The fizz of the bath bomb comes from the citric acid and baking soda. Baking soda is a base and citric acid is — surprise! — an acid. When you mix these together, they produce a salt and carbon dioxide gas. This gas is what makes that fun fizz.

The longevity of the fizz depends on the amount of baking soda and citric acid in the bath bomb AND how easily they can get together. If there is a lot of cornstarch, it takes longer to dissolve, and you get a longer fizz time. This also means you will have a less impressive fizz, because it's spread out over a longer time.

Mother Nature is your lab partner with these experiments about all-things outdoors, including weather, plants, and bugs.

Microbe Mud

Microscopic, single-cell microbes are EVERYWHERE: in your stomach, on your skin, in the air, and in the dirt. Most microbes don't bother us, many are helpful, and a few can make you sick. In this experiment, you will make a Winogradsky column to study the microbes in mud.

Do It!

Supplies

Clear tennis ball bottle; Bucket; Trowel; Mixing bowl; Spoon; Hard-boiled egg yolk; Newspaper; Scissors; Water; Access to a pond, lake, creek, or other natural source of water and mud

1. Go to the water's edge and fill your bucket with wet mud. Remove any rocks, leaves, or sticks. Add water from your water source until the mud is the consistency of a milkshake.

2. Cut the newspaper into small pieces.

3. Put one-fourth of the mud into the mixing bowl. Add the egg yolk and newspaper. Mix everything, and then put it in the bottle. Tap the bottle hard on the ground to remove any air bubbles.

4. Fill the bottle with mud, leaving 2 inches at the top. Tap the bottle periodically to remove air bubbles. Add an inch of water on top, leaving another inch of air. Cover the bottle with the lid or with plastic wrap secured with a rubber band.

5. Keep your bottle out of direct sunlight, and check it every day for about eight weeks. Over time, you will start to see layers form.

What's Happening?

You are growing a microbe zoo! Microbes need water and food to live and grow. There is plenty of water in the mud; the newspaper and egg yolk provide most of the food. Near the bottom of the bottle there is less oxygen and more sulfur from the egg yolk. You should see green, black, and purple bacteria that eat sulfur. In the middle, you should see white, red, orange, brown, or purple bacteria. The white bacteria oxidize sulfur. The rest feed on the carbon in the newspaper. You might even see some bubbles here from carbon dioxide released by the bacteria. In the water and thin mud at the top, you should see green and brown algae and cyanobacteria. They get their food from nutrients in the mud and convert it to energy using sunlight. This also produces oxygen, which you might see as bubbles.

251 Bird Smart

This experiment works best during the winter.

Do It!

Supplies

Sunflower seed birdseed (black oil and striped work best); 2 pie pans

1. Sort the sunflower seeds so that you have an equal amount of empty and filled shells.
2. Place the full shells in one pan, and the empty shells in the other. Put the pans outside about 3 feet apart.
3. Sit several yards away from the pans or go inside where you can watch without disturbing the birds. Keep track of how many birds visit each pan. Did more birds visit the pan of empty seeds or full seeds? Are you able to see how the birds figured out the difference?

What's Happening?

Sunflower seeds attract the widest variety of birds. Black oil seeds have thinner shells that are easy to open for any seed-eating bird. Birds will often pick out the largest seeds to eat, but it is hard to tell what is inside a sunflower shell. Some birds pick up the shells before opening them, perhaps to decide if they are worth the effort. Others may open several empty shells before giving up. What do you observe?

252 Aquascope

Get a close look at underwater critters without getting your face wet!

Do It!

Supplies

Plastic bottle (1 liter or larger); Scissors; Plastic wrap; Rubber band; A pond, creek, or river

1. Cut off the top and bottom of the container so you have a long tube.
2. Place plastic wrap over one end and secure it with a rubber band. Make sure the plastic wrap is not completely tight so that it will stretch inward just a bit in the water.
3. Push the plastic wrap end of the aquascope under water and look through the open end. You should be able to see clearly underwater.

What's Happening?

When you place the aquascope in the water, the plastic wrap will stretch inward a little, creating a magnifying glass at the end of your tube. The curved surface will bend the light so that the image you see under the water is slightly larger than real life.

Save the Bees!

Mason bees pollinate hundreds of flowers each day. They make their homes in tree holes or anywhere they can find them. Make a mason bee house for these active pollinators.

Supplies

Metal soup can, Electrical tape, Hammer, Nail, String, Paper, Pencil, Masking tape, Acrylic paint, Tape, Stickers (optional)

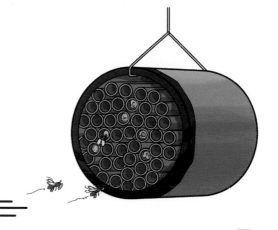

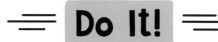 **Do It!**

1. Fold electrical tape around the top edge of the can to cover any sharp edges.

2. Make a hole near the edge of the bottom of the can. Thread the string through the can and tie a knot. You will use this to hang the bee house on a tree or fence.

3. If you want, decorate your house with tape, stickers, and acrylic paint that won't wash off in the rain.

4. Cut the paper 1 inch shorter than the length of the can, and 5 inches wide. Wrap the paper around the pencil and tape it to keep it from unraveling. Slide the tube off the pencil and place it in the can. Make enough tubes to fill the can.

5. Hang your mason bee house outside, 3 to 5 feet from the ground on a tree or fence. Face it east to get the morning sun.

6. In the early spring, you should see residents in your mason bee house. You will notice mud, leaves, or bits of fluff in the holes as the bees prepare their new nest for eggs.

What's Happening?

Mason bees lay their eggs in small holes instead of building a hive. They don't work in groups, but will raise their eggs near each other. A mason bee house is the perfect way to protect these amazing pollinators.

Don't worry about getting stung by mason bees. The males don't have stingers and the females only sting if they are trapped or squeezed.

Look for these mason bee activities:

- When there is enough food in the hole, the female will come out of her nest, turn around, and then back herself in to lay another egg.

- If a mason bee accidentally goes into another bee's hole, the intruder will back out and find the correct nest. Mason bees use smelly chemicals called pheromones to help them identify their own hole.

- Using a flashlight at night or in the early morning, you can see the bees at rest in their holes, with their eyes looking out at you.

254 Soda Bottle Bird Feeder

Do birds have a favorite color? This experiment is best done in the winter.

═ Do It! ═

Supplies

5 clear, plastic soda bottles; Scissors; 5 12-inch-long sticks; String; Birdseed; Yellow, blue, red, and white construction paper; Tape

1. Make five bird feeders:
   - Cut two small holes 3 inches from the bottom on opposite sides of the bottles. Slide the stick through so that it sticks out on both sides.
   - Cut a large hole in the side of the soda bottle just above the stick.
2. Cover the outside of four feeders with construction paper. Each feeder should be a different color. Leave one clear.
3. Fill each bottle with birdseed. Tie a string around the neck of each bottle and hang them from tree branches in the same area.
4. Watch the feeders. What kinds of birds visit each feeder? Do all the birds prefer one color feeder? Did they avoid any of the feeders?

What's Happening?

Different birds are attracted to different colors. Some birds are attracted to colors that match their feathers, and others may see a certain color as a good source of food. For example, blue jays are more attracted to blue, while goldfinches prefer yellow. Almost all birds avoid the color white, as this is a warning color.

255 Tempachirp
Can you tell the temperature from a cricket's chirping?

═ Do It! ═

Supplies

5 crickets, 5 shoeboxes, Thermometer, Stopwatch

1. Put each cricket in a separate shoebox. In the morning, take your crickets outside. Wait 10 minutes for them to get used to the temperature. Measure the temperature while you wait.
2. Time 15 seconds and count the number of chirps from one of the crickets. Repeat for each cricket.
3. Later in the day, when it is warmer outside, measure the temperature and count the chirps again. Do this four times during the day at different temperatures.
4. Average the number of chirps for each temperature. Do the number of chirps increase or decrease with the temperature?

What's Happening?

Crickets cannot regulate their body temperature like we can. They depend on the motion of their legs and wings (which causes the chirping sound) to keep their bodies warm when it is cold, or cool when it is warm. As the temperature rises, the rate of chirping increases.

Termite Tracks

Termites have a bad reputation, but they are interesting insects that just want to find food.

Supplies

Termites*, Cardboard, Spray bottle with water, Plastic container with lid, Baking pan, Paper, Pencil, Black permanent marker, Papermate® black ballpoint pen, Bic® black ballpoint pen, Black crayon, Brush

*Find termites under logs and mulch, or contact a termite exterminator. Do NOT take the queen. Without a queen, you don't need to worry about a termite or two getting loose.

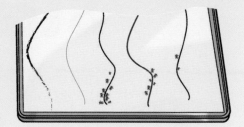

Do It!

1. Place the cardboard in the container. Spray it until it is damp but not soaking. Keep your termites in the container for several weeks with the lid on tight.
2. Draw long, parallel lines on the paper with the pencil, marker, crayon, and pens. Put the paper in the bottom of the pan.
3. Place three termites on the paper in the pan. Watch where they go. Do they follow any of the lines?

What's Happening?

Termites live underground and use smell to communicate. They give off chemicals called pheromones to give direction. In this experiment, a chemical in one of the writing utensils is like the pheromone left as a trail to food sources. The termites follow the ink because they think it will lead to a meal.

Magni-bucket

Take this magnifying bucket outdoors to get a close-up look at nature.

Supplies

Plastic ice cream bucket, Scissors, Ruler, Masking tape, Plastic wrap, Large rubber band, Water

Do It!

1. Measure 1 inch up from the bottom of the bucket and cut a hole big enough to fit your hand. Cover the cut edges with tape.
2. Cover the top with plastic wrap and secure it with the rubber band. Leave the plastic wrap a little loose.
3. Pour water on the plastic wrap so that it sags a little.
4. Slide an object that you want to inspect closely through the hole in the bucket. It should appear much larger.

What's Happening?

The weight of the water pushes down on the plastic wrap, making a small bowl on the top of your magni-bucket. The water is rounded and thicker in the middle, just like the lens of a magnifying glass, so objects close to the lens appear larger.

Star Bright, Star Light

How many stars can you see from where you live? Before we started lighting up the outdoors, you could see as many as 3,000 stars in a clear night sky. Unless you live far from modern civilization, that number is probably much lower where you live. In this experiment, you will count all the stars in your night sky.

= Do It! =

1. Cover the top of the flashlight with red cellophane. The red light will make it easier to see the stars and record data.

2. Go outside after dark near your house on a clear night with no moon. Look through the toilet paper tube at a random spot in the sky and count how many stars you can see through the tube. Write down this number.

3. Count the stars you can see through the tube in nine other locations. Average the number of stars you saw through the tube. Multiply this number by 104 to get the total number of stars in the sky. How does your sky compare to an ideal sky where 3,000 stars are visible?

4. Count stars under a streetlight and compare the number of stars to a less well-lit area. How does your location affect the number of stars visible in the sky?

Supplies

Toilet paper tube (with or without toilet paper), Flashlight, Red cellophane, Paper and pencil

What's Happening?

If you live in a big city, there are not many stars visible at night. In these areas, only the moon and the brightest stars and planets can be seen because of light pollution. Light pollution is caused by all the light from our cars, houses, stores, and streetlights. All this light makes it hard to see stars in the sky.

There are different types of light pollution based on what causes the light and where it shines. If your neighbor's porch light shines into your bedroom window, this is called "light trespass." Really bright lights that make it harder to see can cause glare. The biggest problem is often just sky glow, when all the lights from a city or sports arena reflect off buildings, the ground, and clouds to make the sky much brighter than it should be.

Cloud in a Jar

Clouds aren't just in the sky. Now you can create one for yourself!

Supplies

Glass jar with a lid, Hot water, Ice, Aerosol hairspray

Do It!

1. Fill the jar about one-fourth full of hot tap water.
2. Swirl the water around the jar to coat it.
3. Place the lid upside down on top of the jar and fill the lid with ice. Quickly lift the lid, spray hairspray into the jar, and then replace the lid. Watch a cloud form! Once the cloud fills the jar, lift the lid and watch it escape.

What's Happening?

Hot water vapor evaporates from the water and rises in the jar. As the vapor rises, it hits the cool air at the top and loses energy. It then condenses back into liquid water. Tiny drops of hairspray act like cloud seeds, which the vapor clings to as it rises to the top of the jar. Those tiny drops of condensed water make up the cloud. Scientists call these cloud seeds "cloud condensation nuclei." In nature, cloud seeds can be dust, ash, or even pollution.

Measure Air Pressure

Under pressure? You'll know for sure after you make your own barometer.

Do It!

Supplies

Straight-neck glass soda bottle, Glass jar, Water, Food coloring, Permanent marker, Ruler

1. Fill the jar about one-third full of water.
2. Place the bottle upside down in the jar. The water should come about halfway up the neck. Add or remove water if needed. Add a few drops of food coloring to make it easier to see.
3. Mark the bottle in inches from top to bottom. This will help you compare the air pressure each day.
4. Replace the upside-down bottle back onto the jar.
5. Place the barometer outdoors, out of direct sunlight, where it won't get knocked over. Check on the barometer each day. The water inside the bottle will rise and fall with the air pressure. If the water rises, the pressure is high. If the water level is low, the pressure is low.

What's Happening?

Air pressure changes depending on the air speed, temperature, and other factors. Fast-moving air has a lower pressure than still air. When the pressure is high, the air pushes the water inside the barometer and it rises. When a storm is coming, the pressure lowers and the water falls back down.

Measure Humidity

Make a hygrometer with a single strand of hair.

Supplies

Strand of hair (at least 10 inches long), Rubbing alcohol, Water, Small bowl, Measuring spoon, Cotton swab, Heavy cardboard (at least 4 inches longer than the hair and about 12 inches wide), Cardstock, Tape, Pushpin, Scissors, Ruler, Marker, Hair dryer, Steamy bathroom

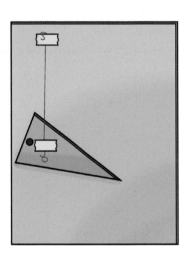

═ Do It! ═

1. Mix 1 teaspoon of rubbing alcohol with 3 teaspoons of water in the small bowl. Dip a cotton swab into the solution and wipe down the strand of hair.

2. Tape one end of the hair to the top of the cardboard about 2 inches from the left side.

3. Cut a 10" x 1" arrow out of the cardstock. Use a pushpin to attach the flat end of the arrow on the left side of the cardboard near the bottom of the strand of hair. Tape the hair to the arrow about an inch to the right of the pushpin. The hair should be pulled tight but not stretched straight down from the top of the cardboard to where it is attached to the arrow.

4. Use a hair dryer to dry the hair completely. You will know the hair is dry when the arrow doesn't move. Mark the end of the arrow and label this 0.

5. Take the hygrometer into the bathroom when someone takes a hot shower and steams up the bathroom. Mark the location of the arrow after it has been in the steamy bathroom for a while and stops moving. Label this mark 100.

6. Make three marks equally spaced between the 0 and 100. Label these in order: 25, 50, and 75. Your hygrometer is now ready to measure humidity. What is the humidity right before a rain storm, during the storm, and afterwards? What is the humidity on a clear, sunny day?

What's Happening?

Have you ever noticed that your hair is longer and frizzier when the weather is hot and humid, and shorter and straighter in cool, dry weather? The coil-shaped proteins in your hair, called keratin, cause this change. The coils in keratin are held together by a chemical bond that breaks around the water in damp, humid air. This makes the hair stretch longer and pushes the arrow down. When the hair dries, these bonds reform and the hair shrinks back, pulling the arrow up.

Measure Rainfall

Do you know how much rain falls where you live?

Supplies

Plastic bottle, Scissors, Sand, Ruler, Permanent marker, Water

Do It!

1. Cut the top off the bottle just below the straight sides.
2. Pour 1 inch of sand into the bottom of the bottle. This will keep the bottle from falling over.
3. Pour just enough water into the bottle to cover the sand. Mark the water level in the bottle and label it 0. Label each inch above the 0 mark up to the top.
4. Place the top of the bottle upside down inside the bottle.
5. Place your rain gauge outside. After it rains, look at the side of the bottle to see how much rain fell.

What's Happening?

Rain falls into the upside-down bottle top, which acts like a funnel and directs the water into the bottle. Make sure you bring your eyes down level with the bottle to read the water level accurately.

Measure Temperature

Is it hot or cold? Make a thermometer to find out.

Do It!

Supplies

Small bottle (plastic or glass), Rubbing alcohol, Water, Food coloring, 2 clear straws, Clay, Bowl, Ice

1. Fill the bottle one-fourth of the way with water and one-fourth with alcohol. Add two drops of food coloring.
2. Place a straw into the bottle 2 inches into the liquid. Use clay to hold the straw in place. Seal it onto the top of the bottle.
3. Use the second straw as an eyedropper. Place the straw into the alcohol and seal it with your finger. Drip the alcohol into the other straw until the level of liquid in the straw is an inch above the clay. Swirl the bottle to mix.
4. Add hot tap water to the bowl and set the thermometer inside. Watch the liquid in the straw. What happens?
5. Now add ice water to the bowl with the thermometer. What happens now?

What's Happening?

When water and alcohol are heated, the molecules move faster and take up more space. Because your thermometer is sealed, the only place for the warm liquid to go is up the straw. When the liquid is cold, the molecules move slower, take up less space, and the liquid goes down. Use the change in volume to measure the temperature. When the liquid is higher in the straw, it is warmer than when the liquid is lower.

An anemometer is used to measure wind speed. Watching this anemometer spin around might make you a bit dizzy!

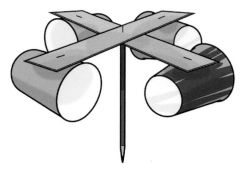

Supplies

Cardboard, Scissors, Ruler, 4 paper cups, Stapler, Tape, Thumbtack, Straight pin, Pencil with an eraser, Marker, Fan (optional), Stopwatch

Do It!

1. Cut out two strips of cardboard about 12 inches long and 1 inch wide. Use the ruler to make sure they are the same length. Mark the center of each strip.

2. Staple the side of a cup to the end of each cardboard strip. Make sure the cups are facing in opposite directions. Color one side of one of the cups so that it's different from the other three cups.

3. Tape the cardboard strips together to make an X. They should cross exactly at the center. The top of each cup should be pointed at the bottom of the next cup all the way around.

4. Use the thumbtack to make a hole right in the middle of the X. Poke the hole and wiggle the thumbtack around to widen the hole slightly. Then push the straight pin through the hole and straight into the pencil eraser. The anemometer should spin freely around the pin.

5. Hold the anemometer by the pencil and take it outside on a windy day, or hold it in front of a fan. Watch the cups spin around. Use the stopwatch to count how many times the marked cup spins around the anemometer in 15 seconds. Multiply this by 4 to get the number of spins per minute. How does the wind speed in spins per minute vary from day to day, or from morning to evening? What is the highest number of spins per minute you can measure?

What's Happening?

Even though we move easily through the air, air still has mass. When you feel the breeze on your face and in your hair, you feel the air molecules pushing on you. Faster-moving air pushes harder than slower-moving air. We call the moving air "wind." When the wind hits the cups, the push from the air molecules causes them to spin around the pin. The faster-moving air pushes harder on the cups than slower-moving air, and causes them to spin faster. The speed at which the cups spin changes depending on how hard the air pushes or how fast the wind is blowing.

Tornado in a Bottle

No need to head for cover – this tornado is safely stuck inside a bottle.

Supplies

2 2-liter soda bottles, Metal washer, Duct tape, Water, Food coloring or glitter (optional)

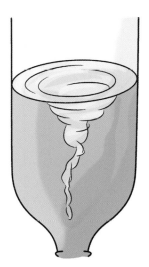

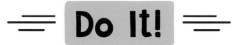 **Do It!**

1. Fill one bottle about two-thirds full of water. Add food coloring or glitter if you want.

2. Place the washer on top of the bottle and the other bottle upside down on top of the washer. Make sure the openings in the bottle and hole in the washer all line up. Secure the bottles and washer in place with duct tape. Use enough tape to ensure the water will not leak out of the bottles.

3. Flip the bottles upside down so that the bottle with water is on top. Does the water go down into the bottom bottle? If not, tilt and swirl the top bottle. You will see a mini tornado form in the top bottle as water pours down into the bottom bottle. Flip the bottle over and try it again!

What's Happening?

A vortex is a spinning mass of air or water. Many storms — such as tornadoes, hurricanes, and typhoons — are examples of air vortexes. To create a vortex in your bottle, you first need to give the top bottle a swirl to start the spinning motion. As the water spins faster, it pushes toward the outside of the bottle, leaving a small hole in the middle. Air from the bottom bottle comes up the middle, and water from the top drains down through the hole between the bottles. The vortex in your bottle is made of water instead of air, so although it looks like a tornado, it is actually a whirlpool.

What If?

What if you use larger or smaller bottles, or more or less water? Try adding something to the water, such as a squirt of dish soap or some small toys.

Bottle Ecosystem

Make your own little world of interacting organisms.

Plants

Supplies

2 clear 2-liter bottles; Scissors; Gravel or small pebbles; Soil; Small plants; Worms, pill bugs, or other insects; Water

Do It!

1. Cut the top off one bottle right where the sides start to curve. Cut the bottom off the other bottle, also where the sides start to curve at the bottom. Recycle the smaller pieces and slide the top a couple of inches over the bottom to make a very large bottle.

2. Remove the top and place 1 to 2 inches of gravel or pebbles in the bottom of the bottle. Cover this with 4 to 6 inches of soil. Add a couple of worms, pill bugs, or other insects. Mix in a handful of dead leaves or mulch so they have food. Make a hole and place the small plants in the soil. Pat the soil firmly around the plants. Water the plants so that the soil is moist but there is no standing water in the bottle.

3. Place the top back on the bottle and make sure the cap is on top. Set the bottle ecosystem in a sunny window or outside. Observe the bottle every day. Does the plant grow? Does the water condense and cause it to rain inside the bottle? Can you see the worms and insects?

What's Happening?

An ecosystem is a group of plants, animals, and their environment. The ecosystem in the bottle includes the plants, soil, and insects all interacting together. The insects produce carbon dioxide when they eat the leaves and mulch in the soil. The plants use the carbon dioxide to create energy and release oxygen that the insects breathe. The water cycles through the soil, into the plant, out to the air where it condenses on the bottle and rains back down into the soil. Can you think of anything else that the plants, insects, and soil share?

What If?

What if you make several ecosystems and change one of the variables? Try different plants or types of soil. Use different amounts of water or add different insects.

Flower Power

Why do you put freshly cut flowers in water? Where does all the water go?
Find out by adding food coloring to the water so you can see how it travels.

Supplies

4 white flowers (carnations and daisies work well), 4 cups or vases, Water, Food coloring, Scissors

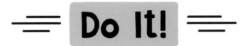

Do It!

1. Fill four cups or vases with water. Add at least 1 teaspoon of food coloring to three of the cups so that the color is very dark. Use a different color in each cup.

2. Cut about 4 inches off the bottom of the stem of each flower. Cut the stem at an angle instead of straight across.

3. Put a flower in each cup. Check on the flowers every couple of hours for at least a day. Do the flowers change color? What parts of the flowers are colored and which parts stay the same? Compare the flowers to the one without food coloring in the water.

What's Happening?

Plants, including flowers, need sunlight, soil, air, and water to grow. When you water plants, you pour the water on the ground so that the roots can suck it up and send it to the rest of the plant. When you cut the flower off a plant, the stem is basically a pipe for pulling up water using a process called transpiration. Transpiration starts when water evaporates out of tiny openings in the leaves called stomata. This causes a low pressure at the top of the plant so water is pulled up from the bottom where the pressure is higher — kind of like drinking from a straw. Trees can transpire gallons of water each day. Keep track of the water level in the cups to see how much water your flowers transpire each day.

What If?

What if you use different types of flowers, such as roses or flowers that are not white? What if you move the flower from one color to another? Do the colors mix?

Many of the vegetables you buy at the grocery store or farmers market come with the roots still attached or contain seeds. These are usually tossed in the trash or compost, but they can be used to grow new food!

268 Celery

Celery is the easiest food to grow from leftover scraps.

= Do It! =

1. Cut the bottom off the celery.
2. Pour about an inch of water into the bowl and place the celery, bottom down, in the water. The water should just cover the bottom inch of the celery.
3. Place the bowl in a sunny window. After about a week, you will see roots. Then it is ready to transplant into the ground or a pot with just the leaves above the soil. In a few weeks, the celery will sprout a new head, and soon you will be ready to harvest.

Supplies

Celery, Knife, Bowl, Water, Garden or pot with soil

What If?

What if you try other plants like celery, such as bok choy, romaine lettuce, or cabbage?

269 Garlic

A single garlic bulb contains many cloves, and a single clove can grow a whole new bulb!

= Do It! =

1. Remove the clove of garlic from the bulb and peel off the papery skin. One end of the clove is pointy and the other is flat. The flat end contains the roots, and the pointy end is where the leaves will come out.
2. Find a sunny spot and push the clove, roots first, down into the soil so that the tip is even with the top of the soil. Water the soil regularly. In a few months, you will have a new garlic bulb!

Supplies

Garlic clove, Garden or pot with soil

What If?

The garlic bulb is the root of the plant. What if you plant other edible roots, such as ginger and onions? Can you grow a new root to eat?

Potatoes

Do you have an old potato in the back of the pantry with "eyes"?
These are the start of a new plant!

Supplies

White potato with eyes, Garden or pot with soil and compost, Knife

Do It!

1. Cut the potato into 2-inch pieces. Each piece should have at least two eyes on it. Leave them out overnight to dry out a little. This keeps them from molding underground.

2. Plant the potato pieces in a sunny spot about 4 inches into the soil with the eyes facing up. As you see more roots, add more rich soil on top until the original potato pieces are about 8 inches deep. Make sure the soil is mixed with compost, because potatoes need lots of nutrients to grow. In a couple of weeks, you will see a stem and leaves. In about four months, you should be able to pick some potatoes.

Pineapple

You don't have to live in the tropics to grow a pineapple plant at home.

Supplies

Pineapple, Knife, Glass, Water, Toothpicks, Garden or pot with soil

Do It!

1. Cut the top off the pineapple so that all the yellow fruit is removed. Pull off a few leaves from the bottom so that you can see the stem. You should see tiny scales — the start of roots. Turn the pineapple top upside down and let it dry for a week.

2. Fill a glass with water. Poke four toothpicks into the stem on opposite sides. Place the pineapple top in the glass of water so that the toothpicks hold it near the top. The water should just cover the bottom of the stem.

3. Place the plant in a sunny window — the sunnier, the better. Change the water every week. Soon, you will see roots form. When they are about 3 inches long, plant the pineapple in soil. Unless you live somewhere that is warm all year round, use a pot so that you can bring the plant inside during winter. It takes a year or two before the plant produces a baby pineapple.

What's Happening?

All the foods used here are still alive when purchased from the store. All it takes is a little water on the roots and a lot of sunshine on the leaves to start the plants growing again.

Leaf Chromatography

Most leaves change color in the fall. Where does that color come from?

Supplies

Leaves (at least 10 from different types of trees), Scissors, Tall glasses (one for each type of leaf), Rubbing alcohol, Wooden spoon, Coffee filters, Tape, Pencils (one for each type of leaf), Dishpan (optional), Hot water (optional), Strainer or colander (optional)

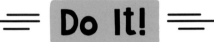

Do It!

1. Separate the leaves into piles by type of tree.

2. Cut the leaves into small pieces. Put the pieces from each type of tree into separate glasses. Pour just enough rubbing alcohol into the glasses to cover the pieces. Grind up the leaf pieces in each glass with the spoon. The rubbing alcohol should turn the color of the leaf pieces. To speed up the process, place the glasses into a dishpan and pour hot water into the pan (but not into the glasses). This will heat up the mixture and break it down quicker. Let the leaf pieces soak up the alcohol for 30 minutes.

3. Cut strips from the coffee filter a bit shorter than the glasses. Tape a strip to the middle of each pencil. Place a pencil on each glass with the strip hanging down into the alcohol, but not touching the glass. The strip will soak up the alcohol and carry the leaf pigments with it.

4. After five minutes, the alcohol will reach the top of the strip. Pull it out of the glass. What colors do you see on the strip? How are the different types of trees similar? How are they different?

What's Happening?

Leaves get their green color from chlorophyll, a pigment that converts sunlight into energy. Plants use chlorophyll to turn water and carbon dioxide into sugar. But leaves have other pigments too. Xanthophyll and carotenoids give leaves yellow and orange colors. In the spring and summer, chlorophyll covers up the other colors. But in the fall, when there is less sunlight, the chlorophyll breaks down and the other colors emerge. In the fall, leaves make anthocyanin, which gives them a red color.

Depending on when you picked your leaves, you will likely see a green band of color on the strips for the chlorophyll, along with yellow and orange bands for the xanthophyll and carotenoid. If you picked your leaves in the fall, you might also see red bands for the anthocyanin, as well.

Transpiration

When people get hot, they sweat or perspire, and when they breathe, they respire.
Plants do a bit of both at the same time – they transpire!

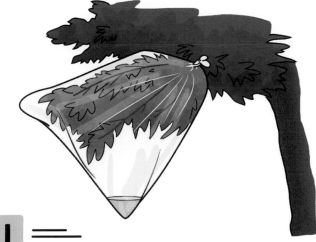

Supplies

Leafy bush or plant; Large clear
plastic bag; String; Measuring
cup; A warm, sunny day

== Do It! ==

1. In the morning, put as many leaves and branches as you can into the plastic bag without removing them from the bush or plant. Tie the opening of the bag closed around the branch. Wait about 12 hours until evening.

2. Remove the bag and pour the water into a measuring cup. How much water is in the bag? Dry out the bag and put it back on the same branch and leave it on overnight. Check the bag in the morning and measure how much water was collected. How did the amount of water the plant transpired during the day compare to the amount transpired overnight?

What's Happening?

Plants drink in water from their roots and send it out to the stems and leaves. This helps make energy out of sunlight, in much the same way our body uses oxygen to make energy out of the food you eat. Plants also let some of the water evaporate out of the leaves to cool down the plant when it is hot, just like how people sweat or perspire to cool down. In plants, this process of pulling water up through the roots and evaporating out of the leaves is called transpiration. In this experiment, you collect the water that evaporates out of the leaves. You probably discovered that the plants use much more water during the day than they use during the night.

What If?

What if you compare transpiration in different types of plants?

274 Mold Terrarium

The fungus is among us, as you'll see in this moldy experiment.

Supplies

Clear plastic container with a lid, Tape, Small pieces of fruits and vegetables, Water

Do It!

1. Dip the food in water, and then place it inside the container. Close the lid tightly and tape it shut so that no one can open it. Label the container "Do Not Open."

2. Observe your mold terrarium every day. After a few days, you will start to see fuzzy stuff growing on the food. Which fruits and vegetables did the mold grow on first? After a while, the mold will spread and look really disgusting. How many different types of mold do you see? When you are done with the experiment, DO NOT OPEN THE TERRARIUM! Put it directly in the trash. Mold can make you sick if you breathe in the spores.

What's Happening?

Unlike plants, molds do not grow from seeds. Instead, they grow from tiny spores that are floating in the air around you right now. When the spores fall onto something damp, they grow into mold. Instead of making their own food, molds just eat whatever they are growing on.

275 Potato Maze

Animals can find their way through mazes, but how about a potato?

Do It!

Supplies

Sprouting potato with eyes, Shoebox, Scissors, Cardboard, Tape

1. Cut a 1-inch square hole in the short end of the shoebox. Use the cardboard, scissors, and tape to make a maze inside the shoebox. Make sure there are holes or gaps big enough for the potato vines to get through.

2. Place the potato in the shoebox on the opposite side of the hole. Put the lid on. Place the shoebox in a sunny place. Make sure sun shines through the hole in the box. Check on the potato every few days. How long does it take for the potato sprouts to find the light?

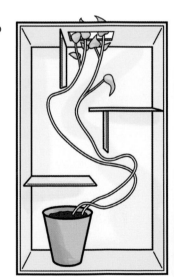

What's Happening?

Potatoes, like most plants, are heliotropic. This means they point their leaves toward the sun to get the most light. Pigments in the potato called phytochromes react to the sunlight, causing the plant to bend and grow toward the light. The potato can sense where the light is shining into the shoebox through the little hole and grows toward it. Eventually, you will see leaves poking out of the hole.

Poinsettia Acid/ Base Indicator

Poinsettias are beautiful holiday plants. When the holidays are over, the leaves make an excellent acid/base indicator!

Supplies

Red poinsettia plant, Hot water, Scissors, Measuring cup, 2 bowls, Strainer or colander, Coffee filters, Acids (vinegar, lemon juice, coffee, milk), Bases (baking soda mixed in water, ammonia, detergent)

Do It!

1. Pull several red leaves off the poinsettia plant. Cut the leaves into small pieces and place them in the measuring cup. When you have 1 cup of cut-up leaves, put them in the bowl.

2. Cover the leaves completely with hot water. Let them sit for one hour.

3. Pour the water and leaves through the strainer and into the second bowl. This bowl should now just contain a dark-pink liquid. Put two coffee filters into the liquid and let them soak up the pink liquid.

4. Lay the filters out flat to dry. Once they are dry, cut them into strips. You now have poinsettia acid/base indicator strips! The pink papers will change color when placed in different liquids. Dip a strip into ammonia. What color is the strip? Dip another strip into vinegar. What color is the strip now? Try all the other acids and bases, plus any other liquids you want to test.

What's Happening?

Scientists describe how acidic or basic a liquid is by using pH. The term "pH" stands for "power of Hydrogen." It is a measure of how many charged hydrogen atoms, or ions, are in a liquid. Acids have a lot of hydrogen ions, and bases have very few. The scale runs from 1 (extremely acidic) to 14 (extremely basic), with water in the middle near 7 or neutral.

Poinsettia leaves contain a chemical called anthocyanin. Anthocyanin gives the leaves a bright red color, but also changes color when exposed to acids or bases. In this experiment, the anthocyanin from the poinsettia leaves turns dark pink in the presence of acids, and greenish brown in the presence of bases.

Upside-down Plants

How do plants know which way is up?

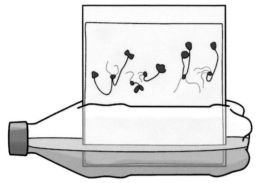

Supplies

Clear plastic water bottle, Radish seeds, CD case, Hot glue gun or strong tape, Scissors, Ruler, Paper towel, Permanent marker

Do It!

1. Cut a 5"x ½" hole on the long end of the empty bottle.

2. Remove the black insert from the CD case. Glue or tape the bottle to the insert, with the hole of the bottle facing up.

3. Cut the paper towel so that it fits inside the CD case. Place it flat inside the bigger side of the case.

4. Fill the bottle with 2 inches of water. Place the case into the bottle, hinged end first. The bottom of the paper towel should touch the water. Mark a line across the case 1 inch above the hole.

5. When the paper towel is soaked with water, remove the case from the bottle. Place 10 seeds on the paper towel along the line you drew. Press the seeds into the paper towel so they will not fall off. Close the case and place it back into the bottle.

6. Place the seed germinator in a sunny window. Observe your seeds at the same time every day. Do you notice any changes? What direction are the stem and roots growing?

7. Once the roots are an inch long, remove the case from the bottle. Take half of the seedlings off the paper towel and turn them upside down with the roots pointing up. Some of the roots may have grown into the paper towel, so be careful and keep as much of the root attached to the plant as possible. How do the upside-down seedlings compare to those that are still right-side up?

8. When the plants have grown to the top of the case, plant them in a pot or garden.

What's Happening?

Plants usually have a stem that grows up and roots that grow down. Plants use gravitropism, or the ability to detect gravity, to survive. The stem and leaves need to grow up toward the sun to get energy from light. The roots need to grow down into the soil to get water and minerals. Plants detect gravity by heavy particles in their cells called amyloplasts. Because the amyloplasts are heavy, they sink to the bottom of the cells and let the plants know which way is down.

Leaves a Light

Sunlight contains all the colors of a rainbow, but does a plant need all those colors?

Supplies

House plant with lots of green leaves; Red, green, and blue cellophane sheets OR 3 clear transparency sheets colored red, green, and blue with a marker; Black construction paper; Clear tape; Scissors

Do It!

1. Cut six rectangles from each color of cellophane and the paper. The rectangles should be slightly larger than the leaves.

2. Tape two pieces of cellophane together on three sides to create three envelopes. Slide the envelopes onto the leaves and tape down the fourth side. Place the envelopes all around the plant.

3. Place the plant in a sunny window for a week. Turn the plant each day so that all sides get plenty of sunlight. After a week, remove the envelopes. How do the leaves in the envelopes compare to the leaves that were not covered, or the ones covered in black?

What's Happening?

Leaves appear green because they reflect green light and absorb all other colors. Chemicals in the leaves, such as chlorophyll, use different colors of light to make nutrients for the plant. The leaves that received no light are wilted, while the leaves in the red envelopes are healthy.

Light vs. Dark

Plants need water, soil, air, and sunlight to grow. What happens to a seed if it's left in the dark?

Do It!

Supplies

2 egg cartons, Potting soil, Radish seeds, Water, Sunny window

1. Fill each carton with soil. Plant a seed into each of the 12 wells an inch into the soil. Water each carton until the soil is moist but not soaked.

2. Place the cartons in a sunny window. Leave one carton open and close the other. Check on the seeds each day. Water if needed to keep the soil moist. After a week, tiny seedlings will emerge from the soil. Do the seeds in the closed carton sprout and grow? If so, what do they look like?

What's Happening?

Plants have light receptors on their leaves. When they don't see light, they tell the plant stem to grow long and thin to help them find the light. The plants also don't produce chlorophyll until they sense a light source. This means the plants grown in the light are short and dark green, while the plants grown in the dark are tall and pale yellow.

Tree Direction

Stars, compasses, and GPS are all used to tell direction. Have you ever considered using the moss on trees to figure out which way is north?

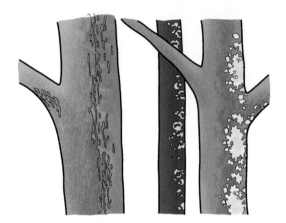

Supplies

Several trees, Compass, Wire coat hanger, Measuring tape, Masking tape

Do It!

1. Find at least three trees of the same type in the same area. Make sure that the lowest branches are higher than you can reach. Try to find trees that are out in the open, separate from other trees, and have moss growing on their trunks.

2. Bend your coat hanger into a square. Use the compass to figure out which part of the trunk faces north. Tape the wire square to the tree 3 feet up the north-facing side of the tree. Carefully observe the lichens, algae, and moss inside the square. Lichens look like crust, small leaves, or shrubs in all different colors. Algae look like a bright green, powdery covering. Mosses look like tiny green plants. Estimate the percentage of the square covered with lichen, algae, and moss.

3. Repeat the process on the other sides of the tree trunk and on the other trees. What types of organisms did you find growing on the tree bark? What percentage of the tree bark was covered on each side of the trees? Did any organisms grow on only certain sides of the tree?

What's Happening?

Tree bark protects the inside of the tree, and it also provides a home for other organisms, such as moss, lichen, and algae. However, tree bark is not the easiest place to grow. There is little water, and it dries out quickly in bright sunlight. That is why the organisms usually grow on the parts of the tree that receive the least amount of sunlight. In the northern hemisphere, this is the north side of the tree. In the southern hemisphere, it is the south side of the tree.

Moths to a Flame

Moths are so attracted to light that they often meet their death when they get too close. You can use this fatal attraction to draw moths to a screen where they can be easily observed. This experiment is best done in late spring and summer.

Supplies

White sheet, Rope and/or duct tape, Lamp, Flashlight, Extension cord (optional), Camera (optional)

Do It!

1. Use the rope and duct tape to hang your white sheet. You can use a rope to hang it between two trees, or duct tape it to the side of your house or a shed. Be creative to figure out a way to hang your sheet screen.

2. Set up a lamp so that it shines on your sheet screen. You may need an extension cord to make sure the light is shining directly on the sheet.

3. When it is completely dark, turn on the light and wait. In a few minutes, you should see moths fly around the light and land on the sheet. Count how many moths are attracted to the light in 15 minutes. How many different types of moths do you see? You can use the camera to take pictures and identify the moths later.

What's Happening?

Why do you think moths are attracted to light? Scientists are not completely sure, but they agree that it probably has something to do with how moths use the moon to navigate, or figure out, where they are going. Man-made lights confuse moths because they are brighter and closer than the moon. One theory suggests that when a moth gets near the light source, where it is bright all around, they think the sun has come out. Because moths are nocturnal, this means it is time for bed, so they settle down and go to sleep.

The number of moths you observe will depend a lot on where you live. Scientists have found that in urban areas, where there is more light pollution, moths are evolving to be less attracted to light. Moths that are more attracted to light fly into the lights to their death before they can lay eggs, while more cautious moths live to lay eggs another day. This means that if you live in an area with lots of light pollution, fewer moths may be attracted to your light trap.

282 Bug Trap

Bugs can be a cinch to catch if you know how to nab them.

Supplies

Trowel, 2 plastic cups, Lid larger than the cups, Rocks, White paper plate, Magnifying glass

═ Do It! ═

1. Find a quiet, shady spot to set your trap. Dig a hole slightly larger than your cup. Put the cups inside each other and place them in the hole. Replace the dirt evenly with the top of the cups.
2. Set four small rocks around the container and lay the plastic lid on top to create a roof. Place another rock on top.
3. Check your trap daily to see what has fallen in. Remove the inside cup and shake the insects onto the plate to inspect them with the magnifying glass. What kind of bugs did you find?

What's Happening?

Scientists use pitfall traps to keep track of the numbers and types of insects that are on the ground. It is important to keep track of harmful insects, such as ticks that carry Lyme disease, as well as beneficial insects, such as pollinators.

283 Bugs Below

Build a funnel to capture creepy crawlies.

Supplies

Plastic milk jug, Large jar, Ruler, ¼-inch window screen in a 6-inch square, Scissors, Masking tape, Rubbing alcohol, Bucket, Gooseneck lamp, White Styrofoam plate, Magnifying glass

═ Do It! ═

1. Cut the bottom of the jug and turn it upside down over the jar to make a funnel.
2. Tape the ruler to the handle so it's just long enough to reach the outside bottom of the jar.
3. Cut several 1-inch slits in the screen, bend the corners, and place it snugly in the bottom of the funnel.
4. Fill the bucket with leaves and dirt.
5. Pour an inch of rubbing alcohol in the bottom jar.
6. Place handfuls of leaves and dirt on top of the screen. Set the funnel on top of the jar and tape the ruler to the jar so it won't tip over. Place the funnel in a warm spot with the lamp shining on it.
7. As the leaves dry over several days, insects will fall into the alcohol.
8. Pour the alcohol and insects onto the plate. Study the insects with a magnifying glass.

What's Happening?

Bugs prefer dark, cool, wet soil. As the hot, bright leaves dry, insects move down through the screen into the alcohol, where they die and become preserved.

Butterfly Feeder

Even if you don't live in the middle of a wildflower meadow, you can still attract butterflies to your yard with this easy feeder.

Supplies

Empty ketchup or salad dressing bottle (with a small hole in the lid); Sponge; Ruler; String; Scissors; Sugar; Bowl; Measuring cup; Plastic flowers, colored paper, paint, stickers (optional)

Do It!

1. Cut a long, 1-inch wide strip from the sponge. Stick it through the hole in the lid so that only about ½ inch is sticking out. The sponge should fit tightly so that your butterfly food won't leak.

2. Tie a string tightly around the mouth of the bottle. Cut two more lengths of string about 30 inches long. Tie one end to the string around the mouth of the bottle. Attach the other end to the string on the opposite side of the bottle to make a loop. Tie the second length of string in the same way to make a second loop on the other sides. Use one more piece of string to tie the tops of the loops together. Now turn the bottle upside down to make sure it hangs steadily.

3. If you like, decorate the bottle with colored paper, stickers, paint, or artificial flowers.

4. In a bowl, mix 1 cup of warm water and ¼ cup of sugar. Stir the mixture until the sugar is completely dissolved. Pour the butterfly food into the bottle. Put the lid tightly on the bottle and turn it upside down. The sponge should soak up the sugar water without leaking. If the bottle leaks, use a bigger piece of sponge.

5. Hang your butterfly feeder outside in a sunny location and watch for butterflies. It may take a while for the butterflies to find your feeder. You can attach some real flowers that butterflies like, such as lilacs or butterfly bush, to help draw their attention. What types of butterflies do you see? At what time of day do they eat? Are other insects or animals attracted to your feeder?

What's Happening?

Butterflies cannot eat, they can only drink. They use their long, straw-like tongue, called a proboscis, to slurp up anything that is dissolved in water. Butterflies mostly eat nectar from flowers, but will also eat tree sap and juice from rotting fruit. The sugar solution in your feeder is like the sweet nectar found in flowers.

285 Ant Blocker

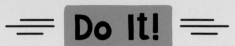

Protect your next picnic from ants with these repellents.

Supplies

Honey; Paper plates; Cotton swabs; Ant blockers, such as

- Cinnamon powder
- Chili powder
- Baking soda
- Chalk
- Lemon juice
- Vinegar

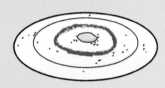

═ Do It! ═

1. Turn one plate upside down and dab honey in the center. Set the plate on the ground in an area with lots of ants.

2. Once there are several ants on the plate, make a circle around the honey using one ant blocker. There should be some ants in the circle and some out. Count how many ants are on the plate and how many cross the ant blocker circle.

3. Repeat for each ant blocker. For the liquid blockers, use a cotton swab. Which blocker would be most useful at keeping ants away from a picnic?

What's Happening?

Ants communicate using chemical signals. They release different smells to let other ants know where to go for food or areas to avoid. Smells that bring more ants are called attractants. Those that keep ants away are called repellents. To keep ants away from the honey, you want to cover the attractant so the ants don't know where to go, or copy a repellent so they avoid it.

286 Pill Bug Choices

What kind of habitat do pill bugs prefer?

═ Do It! ═

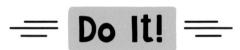

1. Cut the top off each carton to make two open boxes. Cut a ½-inch slit down one side of each of the cartons, ½ inch from the bottom. Tape the cartons together at the slits to allow the pill bugs to travel from one carton to the other.

2. Collect 10 pill bugs. Search outside in dark, damp areas, such as under rocks.

3. Place folded paper towels on the bottom of each carton. Pour water in one carton to slightly dampen the towel.

4. Place half the pill bugs on the dry side, and half on the wet side. Do they prefer one side over the other? Do they all end up on one side, or do they move back and forth? Do you think that pill bugs prefer a dry habitat or a damp one? Place your pill bugs outside when you are done experimenting.

Supplies

2 milk cartons, Scissors, Masking tape, Paper towels, Pill bugs, Cup

What's Happening?

Pill bugs are not insects. Instead, they are crustaceans, like crabs. This means they breathe through gills like underwater creatures, and they typically need moisture to breathe.

Worm Hotel

Almost everyone likes to watch worms wiggle and squirm!

Supplies

3-liter soda bottle, Scissors, 16-oz. soda bottle, Sand, Soil (not potting soil), Trowel, Spray bottle with water, Food waste (vegetables and fruits only), Cloth, Rubber band, Dark construction paper, Tape

Do It!

1. Find some worms, either near the top of the soil if it just rained, or by digging after dark. You can also buy worms at fishing or convenience stores.

2. Cut the top off the 3-liter bottle. Pour about 1 inch of sand in the bottom.

3. Fill the 16-ounce bottle with water, put the cap on, and put it inside the 3-liter bottle. This will keep your worms near the outside where you can see them.

4. Place 3 inches of soil around the inner bottle. Spray the soil with water and add a couple of worms.

5. Add a layer of sand about 1 inch deep on top of the soil. On top of this, add some food scraps (worm food) and dampen the sand and food with water.

6. Cover the food with a 3-inch layer of soil, and then alternate sand and soil until you are 2 inches from the top of the bottle. Spray each layer with water as you go, and add a worm to each soil layer.

7. Place the cloth over the top of the jar and hold it in place with the rubber band. This will keep the worms from escaping but still allow them to breathe.

8. Make a cover for your worm hotel by taping the paper into a tube to slide on and off for observation.

9. Put the worm hotel in a dark, cool spot. After three days, observe what the worms have been up to. Are there tunnels? Has anything changed in the layers? Keep your earthworms happy by spraying the top soil with water every day and adding food scraps each week.

What's Happening?

Worms are busy critters. They are eating machines, chewing up dead leaves and other organic matter in and on the soil. When the chewed-up leaves come out the other end of the worm, they are full of nutrients to help plants grow.

Worms travel underground by contracting and stretching their bodies, and grabbing onto the soil with tiny claw-like bristles. An adult male can push with 10 times its own body weight.

288 Square-foot Survey

How many plants and animals live in just one square foot of land?

Supplies

5 feet of string, 4 plastic knives, Ruler, Magnifying glass, Trowel, Paper and pencil, Field guide or the Internet

Do It!

1. Choose an outdoor area for your survey. Measure a square and push a knife into the ground at each corner. Wrap the string around the knives to outline the square.
2. Observe inside your square. Make a list of the plants, insects, and fungi you find. Sketch pictures of those you don't know to look up online or in a field guide.
3. Loosen the surface dirt. What is hiding? What does the soil look like? Is it the same in all parts of your square?

What's Happening?

When scientists survey a section of land, they take an inventory by listing all the plants and animals in that area. Scientists use this information to learn about the biodiversity of an area. This helps them make decisions about protecting plants and animals, and how to manage wildlife in the area.

289 Sugaring for Moths

For best results, try this experiment during the spring or summer.

Supplies

Brown sugar, Molasses, Ripe banana, Vinegar, Measuring spoon, Measuring cup, Fork, Bowl, Paint brush, Trees, Flashlight

Do It!

1. Place 2 cups of brown sugar into a bowl. Add just enough vinegar to dissolve the sugar. Add 2 tablespoons of molasses and the ripe banana. Use the fork to mash and mix the moth bait to the thickness of a milkshake. Cover the bowl and let it ferment at room temperature for three days.
2. At sundown, paint a large square of bait on three trees at eye height. When it's dark outside, shine a flashlight near the spot you painted on the tree, not directly at the moths. How many moths are there? Are there different types?
3. Check your spots every 30 minutes until bedtime. Did you see different moths at different times? When is the best time to see them?

What's Happening?

Though they don't have noses, moths have an excellent sense of smell. They use their antennae to sense smells up to seven miles away! This means your smelly, sweet moth bait is hard for moths to miss. You should also see a large variety of moths. In North America, there are more moth species than all bird and mammal species combined.

Making Prints

290

How can you tell who has been at the scene of the crime? Fingerprints, of course!

Do It!

Supplies

Inkpad, White or light-colored balloon

1. Roll your thumb on the inkpad so that the pad of your thumb is covered with ink.
2. Flatten the balloon. Carefully roll your thumb across the balloon to make a clean fingerprint.
3. Blow up the balloon and tie it off. Your fingerprint should be enlarged so that you can clearly see the details. Be careful not to touch or smudge your fingerprint until it is dry.
4. Inspect your fingerprint. What patterns and shapes do you see?

What's Happening?

Blowing up the balloon stretches the ink fingerprint so that you can inspect its details. You should see one or more of the main fingerprint patterns: whorl, loop, and arch. You might also see some of the tiny details that let crime solvers tell one fingerprint from another. For example, a delta is where three lines or valleys come together and bifurcation is where a line or ridge splits in two. The tiny white dots are sweat pores.

Become a Secret Agent

Dusting for Prints

291

Need to remove fingerprints from a crime scene?
Just dust for prints using a fine powder.

Do It!

Supplies

Soft makeup brush (new works best); Cocoa powder; White paper; Scotch tape; Smooth, hard objects (a mug or tabletop) to collect prints

1. Rub your index finger across your forehead, through your hair, or down the side of your nose to collect as much oil as you can onto your finger.
2. Press your finger firmly on a mug, table, or another smooth, hard surface.
3. Dip the brush into the powder so it is coated all over.
4. Gently brush back and forth across the print so the powder sticks to the fingerprint.
5. Sweep away any extra powder.
6. Carefully and firmly lay a piece of tape down over the fingerprint so there are no bubbles.
7. Pull up the tape and stick it onto the white paper. Are you able to clearly see the fingerprint?

What's Happening?

The fingerprint you left on the mug, like any fingerprint at a crime scene, is made of the oil, sweat, and dust on your finger. Greasy fingers leave the best prints. The cocoa powder sticks to the oil and grease, which then sticks to the tape, so you are able to transfer the fingerprint on to the paper.

292 Lifting Prints

This chemical reaction solidifies your fingerprints permanently.

Supplies

Clean wide-mouth jar with a lid (pasta sauce or pickle jars work well); Bottle cap; Super glue; Small, smooth, hard item to collect prints (such as a bottle cap or playing card)

Do It!

1. Rub your index finger across your forehead, through your hair, or down the side of your nose to collect as much oil as you can onto your finger.

2. Press your finger firmly on the object you are using to collect prints. You can also make a fingerprint on the inside of the glass jar.

3. Lay the jar on its side and gently place the object in the jar. Make sure each print is facing up and is not covered.

4. Carefully add just enough glue into the bottle cap to cover the bottom of the cap.

5. Place the bottle cap into the jar with the objects and put the lid tightly on the jar.

6. Let the jar sit for one hour under a lamp or in some other warm place. If you don't want to wait, you can heat the jar with a hair dryer on high for ten minutes.

7. Take the jar outside and remove the lid so the glue fumes can escape. Be careful not to tip the jar so the objects and bottle cap of glue don't fall on each other.

8. Remove each of the objects and inspect the fingerprints. Don't forget the fingerprint you left inside the jar!

What's Happening?

This method of collecting fingerprints is called *cyanoacrylate fuming,* after the chemical found in super glue. When the cyanoacrylate heats up, it evaporates into the air inside the jar. When the chemical comes in contact with the sweat and oil in the fingerprint, it reacts to form a hard, white substance that you can see. This method was first used in Japan in 1978 and is now used widely around the world because it's cheap, easy, and reliable—and not as messy as dusting!

What If?

What if you try this same method on other materials? Try plastic, wood, metal, Styrofoam, and cloth and see which material works best.

Hot Invisible Ink

Every secret agent needs a way to send messages that won't be discovered by the enemy! This ink needs a heat source to be revealed.

ADULT NEEDED

Supplies

Vinegar, Paper, Cotton swabs, Heat source (lamp, oven, iron, or hair dryer)

Do It!

1. Dip a cotton swab into the vinegar and write a message on a clean piece of paper. Let the paper dry completely.
2. Heat up your paper to reveal the message. Choose one of these methods:
   - Hold the paper close to, but not touching, a lamp until the message appears.
   - With an adult's help, heat the oven to 300°F. Put the paper on a cookie sheet and bake for 10 minutes.
   - With an adult's help, heat the iron on the "Cotton" setting, and iron your paper until the message appears.
   - Set a hair dryer on high and move it back and forth a couple of inches from the paper until the message appears.

What's Happening?

Vinegar is a mild acid and weakens the paper wherever you wrote your message. The acid also stays on the paper after the invisible ink has dried. When you heat the paper, the acidic message burns or turns brown before the rest of the paper.

What If?

What if you use milk, sugar water, lemon juice, or any other fruit drinks instead of vinegar?

Acid Ink

It takes a chemical reaction to create this secret ink!

Supplies

Paper, Baking soda, Water, Small bowl, Measuring spoon, Cotton swabs, Grape juice

Do It!

1. Mix 2 tablespoons of baking soda with 2 tablespoons of water in the small bowl.
2. Dip a cotton swab into the baking soda mixture and write your message on a clean piece of paper. Let the paper dry completely.
3. Use another cotton swab to paint grape juice over the paper and reveal the message.

What's Happening?

The baking soda, a base, reacts with the grape juice, an acid, to produce a different color on the paper.

295 Wax Resist Ink

This simple method of messaging will result in a colorful message!

Supplies

White crayon, Paper, Watercolor paints, Paintbrush, Water

Do It!

1. Write a message on the paper with the white crayon.
2. Use the paintbrush, water, and watercolors to paint all over the paper. Darker colors, such as blue, green, and red, are best.

What's Happening?

Wax repels water! In this experiment, the watercolor paints will not stick to the white crayon message, so your message is revealed.

What If?

What if you try sending a message on wax paper or other kinds of paper?

296 Glowing Ink

You can only see messages written in this ink with a black light. How revealing!

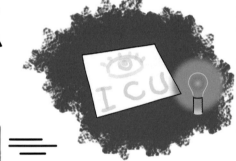

Supplies

Paper, Clear or white liquid laundry detergent, Cotton swab, Black light

Do It!

1. Dip a cotton swab into the detergent and write your message on a clean piece of paper. Let it dry.
2. To reveal the message, simply dim or turn off the lights and shine the black light onto the paper.

What's Happening?

Laundry detergent contains a type of chemical called "phosphors." Phosphors fluoresce or glow in the ultraviolet light given off by the sun (and black lights) and make your clothes look bright. To see the phosphors in your clothes, go into a dark room and shine the black light. The phosphors in your secret message also fluoresce when the black light shines on your paper.

What If?

What if you write a message with other fluorescent materials, such as petroleum jelly or tonic water?

Milky Ink

Be sure to come up with a mooo-ving secret message for this milky ink!

Supplies

Paper, Whole milk, Cotton swab, 2 sharpened pencils

 **Do It!**

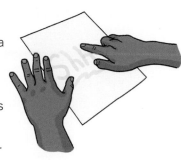

1. Dip a cotton swab into the milk and write a message on a clean piece of paper. Let it dry.
2. Take two sharpened pencils, and rub the graphite (the black parts that write) together so that graphite dust falls on the paper.
3. Use your finger to gently rub the graphite into the paper and reveal the message.

What's Happening?

It is very important to use whole milk for this experiment, because whole milk has a lot of fat. When your message dries on the paper, most of the milk evaporates but the fat stays on the paper. Graphite sticks to the fat more than the paper, allowing your invisible message to be revealed.

What If?

What if you use a different kind of milk with less fat, such as 1% or 2%?

Triple Pen Inspection

Chromatography is a scientific way of figuring out if two writing samples came from the same pen. This is a very handy tool for secret-agent scientists!

Supplies

Paper coffee filter, Scissors, 4 pencils, 4 large clear glasses, Ruler, 3 ballpoint pens that have the same color ink but different brands, Rubbing alcohol, Vinegar, Ammonia, Water, Ultraviolet lamp (optional)

 **Do It!**

1. Cut the coffee filter into four strips at least 2 inches wide.
2. Wrap one end of each of the coffee filter strips around a pencil.
3. Tape it in place so when the pencil rests across the top of the glass, the strip hangs into the glass without touching the sides and just barely touching the bottom.
4. Use a pencil to draw a line across the strip, exactly ½ inch from the bottom.

(Continued on page 208)

(Continued from page 207)

5. With each of the pens, make a pea-sized dot, ½ inch away from the line you drew on the bottom of the strip.

6. Use the pencil to label which dot came from each pen below each dot.

7. At the top of the strip, label which liquid the strip will be placed into (alcohol, vinegar, ammonia, or water).

8. Remove the filter strips from the glasses.

9. Pour a small amount of each liquid into a glass, just filling the bottom.

10. Replace the pencils across the top of the glasses so that the bottom of the filter strip touches the liquid, but the ink dot does not. You may need to adjust the amount of liquid in the glass. (Take the filter strip out of the glass before you do this; if you splash liquid directly on the ink, you'll have to redo the experiment!)

11. Wait until the liquid spreads up the filter through the ink dot and reaches the pencil.

12. Take the strips off the pencils and lay them flat to dry.

Once they're dry, inspect the strips carefully. You'll see spots or smears of color between the original ink mark. These spots or smears are the ingredients of the ink. If the spots are not obvious, try holding the paper under an ultraviolet lamp (black light). Some compounds can be seen better this way.

How many different spots did each of the inks produce? How many different colors do you see?

What's Happening?

Scientists use chromatography to figure out the ingredients in mixtures such as ink. When the mixture or ink is dissolved in a solvent, it separates into its different ingredients.

In this experiment, we used four solvents: water, ammonia, alcohol, and vinegar. As the solvent moves up the coffee filter, it separates out the ingredients.

Similar ingredients will travel up the paper the same distance, so scientists are able to identify exactly what the ingredients are. The pattern that is created is like a fingerprint for identifying the ink.

Compare the dots for the different pens. Do any have dots or smears of color at the same distance? If so, this means the inks in those pens have similar ingredients.

What If?

What if you try analyzing other mixtures with chromatography, such as lipstick, markers, or other types or colors of pens?

Liquid Magnifier

Magnifying glasses come in handy for all sorts of secret agent investigations. But what can you do when you don't have one? Make your own, of course!

Supplies

Clear 2-liter soda bottle, Marker, Scissors, Water

Do It!

1. Draw a circle about 3 inches in diameter on the soda bottle, near the top where the bottle curves the most.
2. Use the scissors to cut out the circle. It should be curved, like a small bowl.
3. Pour water into the bowl so that it's about half full.
4. Hold the magnifying bowl over whatever you need to enlarge.

What's Happening?

Magnifying lenses are convex or thicker in the middle. This shape bends the light rays so that objects close to the lens appear larger. The water in your curved soda bottle bowl is also thicker in the middle and bends light in the same way, making a liquid magnifying glass!

Straw Magnifier

This little magnifier is easy to carry and even hide in the palm of your hand. Just add a couple drops of water and anything tiny will become large!

Do It!

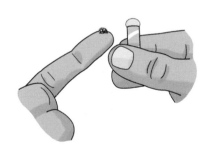

1. Cut off a piece of straw about ¼ inch long.
2. Cover one end of the straw piece with a small piece of packing tape.
3. Fill the straw to the top with water, so that a big drop sits above the level of the straw.
4. Hold your straw magnifier over something tiny and look into the straw to see it get instantly bigger!

Supplies

Straw, Scissors, Ruler, Clear packing tape, Water

What's Happening?

Water is sticky, especially on top of a cup (or straw) full of water where it meets the air. Scientists call this *surface tension*. The water on top of the straw bulges up because the sticky surface tension is holding the water together. This shape bends the light rays, so objects under the straw appear larger.

Build a Periscope

With a periscope, a secret agent can see over walls and around corners without being seen!

 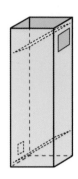

Supplies

Clean quart-sized milk or juice carton, Scissors, 2 mirrors about 2½" x 3½" in size, Tape

Do It!

1. Cut the top off of the carton.

2. Cut a small square about ¼ inch from the bottom of the carton for the eyehole.

3. Cut a large square, about twice the size of your eyehole, ¼ inch from the top of the carton on the opposite side from the eyehole. This will be the view hole where light comes into the front of the periscope.

4. Tape the short end of a mirror to the bottom of the eyehole so that it's facing up.

5. Tape the other end of the mirror to the front of the periscope. When you look through the eyehole, you should be able to see straight up to the ceiling.

6. Tape the short end of the other mirror to the very top of the carton, above the view hole, so that it's facing down.

7. Tape the bottom of the mirror to the back of the carton.

When you look through the eyehole, you should be able to see straight through the view hole! Use your periscope to look over a table and around a corner.

What's Happening?

You see things when light bounces or reflects off an object to your eye. The mirrors in the periscope reflect the light that comes in from the view hole. The top mirror reflects the light down to the bottom mirror, and the bottom mirror reflects the light into your eye.

When you look through the eyehole, it seems like you're seeing something directly in front of you, at eye level. But you're actually seeing something much higher!

To test this out, while looking through the periscope, put your hand on the carton where you think the view hole is. Did you find it right away? It's harder than you think!

What If?

What if you have a longer periscope? How will the image you see change? Try taping two cartons together to make a super long periscope.

Carnival Bottles

Ever try to win a stuffed animal by knocking over all the bottles in a carnival game? It's a lot easier if you stack the odds – and the bottles – in your favor.

Magic

Supplies

3 water bottles, Tennis balls, Measuring tape, Water, Table, Masking tape or chalk

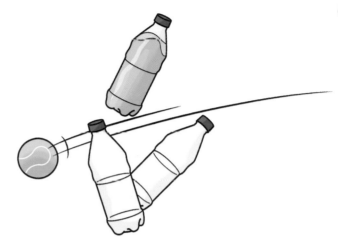

Do It!

1. Set up the table outdoors or somewhere you can throw balls without getting in trouble.

2. Fill all three bottles with water and set them on the table in a pyramid with two bottles on the bottom and one on top. Measure a distance 6 feet from the bottles and mark it with masking tape or chalk. This is where you will stand to throw balls at the bottles.

3. Throw a tennis ball at the bottles at least 12 times. Keep track of how many times you knock over one bottle, two bottles, and all three bottles.

4. Repeat the experiment with an empty bottle on top and two full bottles on the bottom, and again with a full bottle on top and two empty bottles on the bottom. In which setup were you able to knock over all the bottles the most? How about just one or two bottles?

What's Happening?

The key to this trick is center of gravity. Center of gravity is the balance point, or where the mass of an object is centered. To knock over all the bottles, the ball needs to hit at the center of gravity or lower.

When all three bottles are full of water, the center of gravity is somewhere near the top of the bottom bottles — almost in the center of the pyramid.

When only the top bottle has water, the center of gravity is in the middle of the top bottle. So, if you hit the bottom bottles, or the bottom of the top bottle, all the bottles will fall over. However, when the top bottle is empty and the bottom bottles are full, you need to hit the bottom half of the bottom bottles to knock over all three bottles, and that is very hard to do.

303 Arrow Switcheroo

The arrow points one way, and then the other. Which way do you go?

Supplies

Index card, Marker, Clear glass, Water

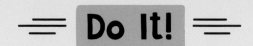

Do It!

1. Draw an arrow on the index card with a marker. Hold the arrow behind the empty glass. Which way does it point?
2. Fill the glass with water. Again, hold the arrow behind the glass. Which way does it point now?

What's Happening?

Light bends when it travels from one substance, such as air, into another, such as glass or water. Scientists call the bending of light "refraction." Light from the arrow bends when it hits the glass of water, and then again when it comes back out into the air before it hits your eyeball. The curved glass also acts as a lens, bending the light even more. The light bends so much that the arrow appears to change direction completely.

304 Bed of Tacks

This bed is too small for you, but it's just right for tired balloons.

Supplies

Cereal box, 226 flat-head tacks, 2 balloons, Ruler, Pencil, Scissors

Do It!

1. Cut an 8-inch square from the cereal box. Create a grid with the ruler by drawing a line every ½ inch from top to bottom, and again from side to side.
2. Push 225 tacks straight through the square where the lines intersect. Turn the board over with the pointy sides of the tacks facing up.
3. Blow up both balloons and tie them. Place the extra tack on the table, pointy side up. Press a balloon on top of it and push down. What happens? Push the other balloon on top of the bed of tacks. What happens to this balloon? Can you push hard enough to pop the balloon?

What's Happening?

When you push a balloon onto one tack, it pops because all the force is on that one point. With many tacks, that force is spread out, and there isn't enough force to pop the balloon. Force spread out over an area is called pressure. When a large force has a small area, the pressure is high, like the balloon pushed on one tack. When that same force is spread over a large area, the pressure is lower. That's why magicians can lie on a bed of nails. Standing on one nail would make a hole in your foot, but lying down on nails is quite comfortable!

Card Drop

Dropping a card is not as simple as it looks!

Do It!

Supplies

Deck of cards, Audience

1. Pull two cards from the deck. Hold one flat (parallel to the ground) and the other straight up (perpendicular to the ground) at same height.
2. Ask your audience which card they think will hit the ground first, and then drop the cards. Which card hit the ground first?

What's Happening?

As the flat card falls, it stays flat as gravity pulls it down. If the card starts to tilt one way or the other, it creates lift that brings the card flat again. Because you cannot hold the card straight up, and the air in the room probably is not perfectly still, the perpendicular card will spin as you drop it. The spinning motion produces lift, which causes the card to glide sideways. The gliding means this card takes a couple seconds longer to reach the ground.

Diaper Deception

Actually, there is no real deception here - just science!

Do It!

Supplies

Diaper, Scissors, Large resealable plastic bag, Measuring cup, 3 cups that you cannot see through

1. To prepare, cut open the diaper and seal it inside the bag. Shake it until you see powder come out. When you see about a tablespoon of powder, take out the diaper and pour the powder into a cup.
2. In front of your audience, pour ¼ cup of water into one of the empty cups. Tell the audience to follow the cup with the water as you move the cups around.
3. Pour the water into the other empty cup and move the cups around again.
4. Finally, pour the water into the cup with the white powder. Move the cups around again, but make sure the cup with the water and powder is on your right. Ask the audience which cup has the water. Start on your left and turn each cup over. No water will pour out of any of the cups!

What's Happening?

Diapers are absorbent because of a powder called sodium polyacrylate. Water sticks to this long molecule, which grows longer to hold more water until it is saturated. Scientists call materials that absorb water "hygroscopic." Sodium polyacrylate can hold many times its weight in water, which is why nothing comes out of the cup!

Mind Control Motion

Move objects with only your mind – and a little help from a few electrons.

Supplies

Plastic bottle cap, Straw, Balloon, Empty soda can, Head of hair or wool sweater

 **Do It!**

Can Control

1. Lay the can on a flat surface on its side so that it's able to roll easily.

2. Blow up the balloon and tie it off. Rub the balloon on your hair or a wool sweater. Bring the balloon near the can and move it slowly away from the can. Does the can move? Make sure the can does not touch the balloon. Move the balloon to the other side of the can. Does its motion change?

Spinning Straw

1. Rub the straw on your hair or the wool sweater. Lay the straw across the top of the bottle cap so that it balances in the middle.

2. Slowly move your finger toward one end of the straw. Does the straw move? What happens if you move your finger toward other parts of the straw?

What's Happening?

Rubbing a straw or balloon on your hair (or a wool sweater) removes electrons from the hair and wool and puts them on the straw and balloon so that they are negatively charged. Opposite charges attract and like charges repel. When you bring the charged balloon near the soda can, the negative electrons on the balloon repel the negative electrons in the can. Some of those electrons move to the other side of the can. This makes the side of the can next to the balloon slightly positive so that it is attracted to the balloon and rolls toward it.

The same thing happens with the straw on the bottle cap. Here, the straw has extra electrons and repels the electrons in your finger. Your finger becomes just the tiniest bit positive, which is enough to attract the end of the straw and make it spin around the bottle cap.

Dollar Bill Drop

Offer a dollar bill to your volunteer, on the condition that they can catch it.

Supplies

Dollar bill,
Volunteer, Table

= Do It! =

1. Have your volunteer rest their arm on the table with their hand hanging over the edge. Have them stick out their middle and index fingers. Hold the dollar bill long ways so that the very bottom of the bill is just between their fingers.

2. Tell the volunteer that you will drop the dollar bill and if they can catch it between their two fingers, they can keep it. Without warning your volunteer, drop the bill. Do they catch it? If not, try again.

What's Happening?

The human reaction time is about 0.2 seconds. This is the amount of time it takes your eyes to send a signal through your brain to your fingers to grab the bill. However, a dollar bill is about 6 inches long and it takes 0.18 seconds for gravity to pull the bill down 6 inches and out of your volunteer's reach. Very few people will be able to catch the dollar bill. By using the middle and index fingers, you guarantee they cannot because these are the slowest-moving fingers.

Now do the same experiment, except this time use a ruler to measure the reaction time. Use the distance in centimeters (d) that the ruler falls before you catch it to calculate your reaction time (t) using this equation: $t = (\sqrt{d})/22.1$

Toothpick Star

This trick is fun to do at the dinner table because all you need are toothpicks and water.

= Do It! =

Supplies

Toothpicks,
Plate, Water

1. Bend five wooden toothpicks in half so that they snap but do not come apart completely. Arrange them on a plate, as shown.

2. Pour a spoonful of water in the very center and watch as the toothpicks move. What shape do they make now?

What's Happening?

Wood is made of fibers that are good at absorbing water. When you add water to the center of the toothpicks where they are broken, the fibers in the wood absorb the water and expand. The expanding wood pushes the toothpicks back to a straight shape until they bump into each other to make the star shape.

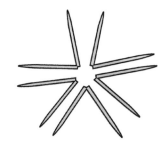

Tablecloth Tug

Add some drama to dinner by yanking the tablecloth out from under the dishes.

=== Do It! ===

Supplies

Small tablecloth or piece of fabric with no hem or stitching on the edges; Table; Rug (optional); Plate, glass of water, and silverware*

*Make sure your grown-ups know there is a very small chance that they could break

1. Lay the tablecloth on the table so that there is just enough room for one place setting and at least several inches hang down over the front edge of the table. Make sure the tablecloth is completely smooth with no wrinkles or bumps.

2. Start with just the plate in the center of the tablecloth. You might also want to place a rug under the table just in case the plate falls on your first try.

3. The secret to this trick is confidence. Do not hesitate or all will be lost. With both hands, grab the part of the tablecloth that hangs down in front. Firmly and quickly yank the tablecloth straight down until it is all the way off the table. What happens to the plate?

4. Practice a few times with just the plate, and then add the silverware and empty glass. When you feel confident enough, pour some water in the glass.

What's Happening?

Isaac Newton's first law of motion is just as much about motion as it is about staying put. He said that an object will stay right where it is unless a force acts on it. Scientists call this tendency to stay put "inertia." If you apply the force to the tablecloth and not to the dishes, they will stay right where they are.

Heavier or more massive objects have more inertia. You may have noticed that the lighter objects with less inertia, such as the silverware, move a little bit while the heavier plate and glass stay put. That's because there is a very small force acting on the dishes: friction. Friction affects the motion of two things that are sliding against each other, like the silverware and tablecloth. You can reduce the friction by using a tablecloth that is very smooth.

Invisible Extinguisher

Why blow out a candle when you can use "magic"?

311

Supplies

Tall glass, Baking soda, Vinegar, Spoon, Votive candle, Lighter or matches

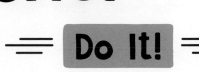 **Do It!**

1. Add two spoonfuls of baking soda to the glass. Pour in enough vinegar to more than cover the baking soda. While you wait for the bubbles in the glass to die down, light the candle.

2. After the bubbles stop, gently pour the gas that is in the glass (NOT the actual baking soda and vinegar) over the candle. What happens to the candle flame?

What's Happening?

Mixing baking soda and vinegar creates a chemical reaction that produces a large amount of carbon dioxide gas. This gas is heavier than air, so it stays in the bottom of the glass. The burning candle needs oxygen from the air to stay lit. The candle flame comes from a chemical reaction called combustion between the wax and oxygen in the air. When you pour the carbon dioxide from the glass onto the candle, oxygen cannot reach the flame and the candle goes out.

Marble Pick-up

312

Defy gravity by lifting a marble in a cup with no bottom!

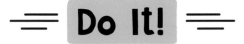 **Do It!**

Supplies

Paper cup, Marble, Scissors

1. Cut the bottom out of the paper cup. Make sure the edges are smooth.

2. Place the marble on a smooth surface, such as a tabletop, and place the cup on top of the marble.

3. Place your hand over the cup and hold it by the edges. Use your wrist to move the cup in a circular motion on the table so that the marble rolls along the bottom edge of the cup. Spin the cup faster and faster until the marble rolls up the sides of the cup. Continue to spin the cup as you lift it off the table. The marble will continue rolling around inside the cup!

What's Happening?

Isaac Newton created several laws to describe how things move. The first law says that an object will keep moving in a straight line unless a force pushes or pulls on it. The marble rolls in a straight line, but the sides of the cup push it into a circle with a centripetal force. The sides of the cup slope just slightly outward, so the marble moves upward as it pushes out. If you keep the marble moving, it will stay inside the cup.

May Centripetal Force Be with You

This spinning coin trick defies the force of gravity!

Supplies

Metal coat hanger, Quarter

= Do It! =

1. Pull the bottom of the coat hanger out so that it changes from a triangle shape to a diamond shape. Hang the diamond on your finger so that the hanger is upside down. Bend the curved part of the handle so that the end is now straight up and flat on top.

2. Carefully balance the quarter on the end of the handle. This might take a couple of tries. With your finger through the top part of the diamond and the quarter balanced on the handle, gently swing the hanger back and forth. Do not make any sudden or jerky movements. Keep the motion smooth. Slowly increase the swings until you can swing the hanger all the way around. The quarter will stay on the end of the hanger handle!

What's Happening?

According to Isaac Newton, objects — such as quarters — keep moving in a straight line unless a force acts on them. In this case, the quarter is moving in a straight line and the coat hanger keeps pushing it in a circle. That force between the quarter and hanger, called centripetal force, is just enough to beat gravity if the coat hanger is moving. If you stop the hanger when the quarter is at the top of its swing, you will see it fall straight down.

What If?

What if you use a different coin? Try a dime, penny, and nickel. Do these coins work as well as the quarter?

Falling Mug

Do you trust physics? The fate of a coffee mug is in the balance!

Supplies

Coffee mug (one your grown-ups won't mind if it breaks), 30-inch piece of string, Metal teaspoon, Pencil, Pillows

= Do It! =

1. Tie one end of the string to the spoon and the other end to the handle of the mug.
2. Hold the pencil straight out in one hand and put the string over the pencil so that the mug hangs just under the pencil.
3. Hold the spoon in the other hand and stretch it straight out across the pencil and away from the mug. When you are ready, let go of the spoon. Does the mug crash to the floor? Where does the spoon end up? The first time you do this trick, put some pillows on the floor just in case the mug hits the ground. After you get the hang of it, you can remove the pillows.

What's Happening?

If all goes as it should, the spoon will spin around the pencil and stop the mug from hitting the ground. When you let go of the spoon, gravity pulls it down and the string pulls it sideways. This causes the spoon to swing downward in an arc around the pencil. As the mug falls, it makes the string shorter. The shorter string causes the spoon to spin around the pencil faster and faster, just like when an ice skater brings their arms inward to spin faster. Eventually, the spoon wraps the string around the pencil and stops the mug from falling.

What If?

What if you use a longer string? You could use a string that is several feet long and stand on a ladder. How close does the mug get to the ground? Does the weight of the mug or the spoon matter? You can use washers, nuts, or other small objects instead of the mug and spoon to find the perfect set of light and heavy weights to make this trick work.

Balloon-kabob

Every great magician knows how to push a needle through a balloon. Now you can too!

Do It!

Supplies

Balloon (helium quality works best), Bamboo skewer, Petroleum jelly

1. Blow up the balloon and tie it off. Make sure the balloon is smaller than the bamboo skewer.

2. Rub a little petroleum jelly over the bamboo skewer. Take the pointy end of the skewer and hold it near the knot of the balloon where the balloon is just starting to stretch out. Push and twist the point of the skewer through the balloon. As soon as you break through the balloon, push the skewer in. If you hear a hissing sound, rub a little petroleum jelly around the skewer to seal the hole.

3. Turn the balloon over and find the dimple at the very top where the rubber is a little darker and not as stretched out. Again, twist and push the pointy end of the skewer until it comes out the other side of the balloon. You now have a balloon on a stick —or a balloon-kabob!

What's Happening?

Balloons are made of polymers, or chains of molecules. When you blow up the balloon, the polymer chains stretch and pull on each other but hold together. The key to getting a skewer through a balloon is to poke it between the polymer chains where they are not quite as stretched out — near the knot and on the top. Try poking the skewer through the side of the balloon where the polymer chains are stretched the most. The chains break and the balloon pops.

What If?

What if you could hold the polymer chains together? Place a piece of clear tape on the side of the balloon and try to poke a pin through it. What happens?

Camera Obscura: Pinhole

Before modern photography, artists experimented with projecting images on a screen. In Latin, *camera obscura* means "dark chamber." The camera obscura you will make is portable, but the earliest examples were rooms that were blacked out entirely, or chambers with a tiny hole through which an image of the outside world was projected on the walls.

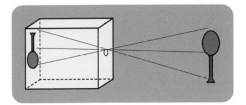

Supplies

Empty cereal box (including the bag inside), Ruler, Marker, Scissors, Duct tape (or black electrical tape), Safety pin or thumbtack, Dark room with a small lamp, Aluminum foil (optional)

Do It!

1. Fold the box so it's flat. Measure 2 inches from the bottom with the ruler and mark a straight line across the bottom. Cut the bottom off the box using the guideline. Then, refold the boxes so they are box-shaped again. Tape up the bottom of the short box so that no light can get through.

2. Cut the cereal bag in half and use one piece to cover the top of the short box. Stretch the bag tightly over the box and use duct tape secure it.

3. Put the tall box back on top of the short box and tape them back together. Be careful to cover the seam with tape so no light can get in. If you want to be extra careful, cover the whole box with aluminum foil.

4. Use the safety pin or thumbtack to make a tiny hole in the center of the bottom of the box.

5. Turn off all lights in the room except for the small lamp and put the open end of the cereal box on your face. Point the pinhole at the lamp. What do you see?

What's Happening?

When you look into your camera obscura box, you should see an upside image of the lamp projected on the screen. Because light has to travel through a straight line and through the tiny pinhole, the image you see is flipped in both directions, as shown above.

What If?

Try changing the size of your pinhole. What happens to the size of the image if you use a larger hole? How about the sharpness of the image?

Adjust the distance between the pinhole and the screen. What happens to the size and sharpness of the image when your screen is closer or farther from the pinhole? You could use a smaller box inside of a large box to have an adjustable screen.

Camera Obscura: Lens

A more advanced camera obscura uses a lens instead of a pinhole. This means you can use your viewer outside in the daylight, but now you'll need to focus your camera to see the image clearly.

Supplies

Large shoebox, Cereal box (or other source of thin cardboard), Scissors, Marker or pen, Aluminum foil, Wax paper, Magnifying glass or lens from reading glasses (you can find these at drug stores or dollar stores), Duct tape (or black electrical tape)

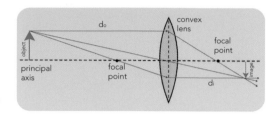

Do It!

1. Cut a round hole on the short end of the shoebox, slightly smaller than your lens or magnifying glass. Tape the lens to the outside of your box over the hole.

2. Cut a rectangular hole on the opposite end of the shoebox that is large enough to look through with both of your eyes.

3. Cut a rectangle from the extra cardboard that fits exactly inside the box. Cut out the center of this rectangle, leaving a 1-inch border. Cover the hole with a piece of wax paper and tape it into place so that it is stretched tight. This will be the screen for your image.

4. Place the screen inside the box between the eyeholes and the lens. Point the lens end of the box at a window or other bright light. Slide the screen back and forth until you see a bright, focused image. Tape the screen in place.

5. Put the cover on your shoebox and tape it in place so no extra light gets in. Look through the eyeholes at the window. What do you see? How does the image compare to the pinhole camera obscura?

6. Take your camera obscura outside and look around. You can even use duct tape to attach the box to the bill of a baseball hat so that it's wearable!

What's Happening?

A camera obscura with a lens is one step closer to our modern cameras. The lens allows you to have a larger hole, which lets more light through and creates images that are bigger and brighter.

With a lens, light is no longer simply traveling in a straight line to create an image (as in the pinhole camera obscura). Instead, the light bends as it travels through the glass to a focal point that depends on the shape and size of the glass lens. Magnifying glasses (and reading glasses) are thicker in the middle. This type of lens is called a convex lens and produces images that can be projected on a screen, unlike a concave lens that is thinner in the middle.

Colorful Cones

Use a little chemistry to create a crazily colorful campfire!

ADULT NEEDED

Supplies

Pinecones (4 or more), Bucket or large bowl, Measuring cup, Large spoon, Paper towels, Coloring chemicals (at least one of these, but you can use some or all)

- **Table salt (sodium chloride)**
- **Borax (sodium borate)**
- **Plaster of Paris (calcium sulfate)**
- **Epsom salt (magnesium sulfate)**
- **Salt substitute* (potassium chloride)**
- **Pool algaecide* (copper sulfate)**
- **De-icer* (calcium chloride)**

*Check the labels to make sure that the product you have includes the chemical listed here.

Do It!

1. Pour 8 cups of hot tap water into the bucket or bowl. With an adult's help, add 1 cup of just one of the coloring chemicals to the water and mix it in with the large spoon until the chemical is completely dissolved. Only use one chemical at a time.

2. Put four pinecones in the bucket and let them soak for eight hours or overnight.

3. Take out the pinecones and put them on a paper towel to dry. It may take a couple of days for them to dry completely.

4. Make as many pinecones as you like with the other coloring chemicals on the list. Just do a separate batch for each chemical.

5. The next time your family lights up the fireplace, or has a campfire or barbecue, have an adult add the pinecones and observe the colors of the flames. (But don't put the pinecones in the fire while you're cooking food.)

What's Happening?

The chemicals create different colors when they burn because of their atoms. All atoms have a nucleus, made of protons and electrons, around which electrons spin and move very fast. The electrons in different atoms have different (but very specific) energy levels that scientists like to describe as steps on a staircase. When an electron gains energy from heat or light (like when you burn chemicals), it gains energy and jumps up to a higher step. Eventually the electrons will fall back down to their original energy level and give up that extra energy in the form of light. The color of the light depends on how far down the staircase it had to jump. Red, orange, and yellow light have less energy and correspond to smaller steps than green, blue, and violet. The size of the steps and the color of the light given off depend on the type of atom. In this experiment, chemicals with copper give off a green or blue light, while those with calcium give off an orange light.

What If?

What if you try to identify which chemical was used on a pinecone just by looking at its flame?

What if you add more than one of the chemicals to the pinecone at a time? (The chemicals we use here are all salts and will not react with each other.)

319 Glow Stick!

Glow sticks use chemicals to produce light in all sorts of different colors. Can you make your glow stick glow all night long?

Supplies

A dark room, 3 glow sticks (all the same color), 2 tall cups, Hot (but not boiling) water, Ice water, Thermometer, Clock

Do It!

1. Label the cups "hot" and "cold." Pour hot water and ice water into the appropriate cups. Make sure the water is deep enough to cover most of the glow stick.
2. Check the temperature of the cups and the room. The temperatures should be at least 20°F apart. Add ice or hot water to the cups if they aren't.
3. Following the directions on the glow stick package, activate each glow stick. Then place a glow stick in each cup of water and stir. After one minute of stirring, turn out the lights and compare their brightness.
4. Place the "ice" cup in the freezer, and put the "hot" cup in a warm place. Leave the other glow stick on the counter at room temperature. Which glow stick glowed the longest? Did the temperature affect the brightness?

What's Happening?

Glow stick insides are made of hydrogen peroxide and a tiny glass bottle of phenyl oxalate ester plus a fluorescent dye. When you break the glass bottle inside the tube, the two chemicals mix, which releases light. This is called chemiluminescence. Heat adds extra energy to the glow stick and speeds up the reaction, causing the stick to glow brighter, but for a shorter time. Cooling the glow stick slows down the reaction and the light is dimmer but lasts much longer.

320 Glowing Groceries

Did you know you probably have glow-in-the-dark food in your pantry right now?

ADULT NEEDED

Supplies

Dark closet, 2 clear plastic cups, Tonic water, Bleach, Black light (found at party stores), Dropper

Do It!

1. Pour some tonic water into both cups. Turn off the lights in your closet and turn on the black light. What happens to the tonic water under the black light?
2. Have an adult fill the dropper with the bleach. Warning: Be extra careful with bleach as it can stain anything it touches.
3. Add a drop or two of bleach into one cup of tonic water while it is still under the black light. What do you see? If nothing changes, add a few more drops. Also, do not drink the tonic water with bleach. Pour it down the drain when you are done.

What's Happening?

Tonic water gets its distinctive bitter taste from quinine, which absorbs light energy and re-emits it as lower-energy, blue, visible light. When you add bleach, it reacts with the quinine to break some of its chemical bonds so that it is no longer able to absorb the ultraviolet light.

Candy Crunch

Have you heard this urban myth? Well it's true! Biting wintergreen hard candies WILL make a spark!

═ Do It! ═

1. To make a closet completely dark, place a towel at the bottom of the door.
2. Go into the dark closet with the mirror and one of the hard candies. Wait about two minutes for your eyes to adjust to the darkness.
3. Facing the mirror, put the candy in your mouth and chomp down on the candy with your teeth while your mouth is open. Did you see a blue-green spark of light?
4. If you have braces or aren't able to chomp the candy with your teeth, put the candies in a plastic bag and use pliers to break them up instead.

Supplies

A completely dark closet, Mirror, 2 wintergreen flavored hard candies

What's Happening?

The flavoring used in wintergreen candies is wintergreen oil, a fluorescent chemical that absorbs light at a shorter wavelength and releases it at a longer wavelength. When you bite the candy, you create a small electrical charge that reacts with the sugar to cause a spark of ultraviolet light. That ultraviolet light is absorbed by the wintergreen oil, and another flash of light is created.

Tape Tear

Duct tape can fix anything, right? It turns out you can do some enlightening science with it too!

═ Do It! ═

1. Cut two 18-inch pieces of duct tape. Fold over 1 inch on one end of each piece. These will be handles. Match up the folded ends and stick the tape together, sticky side to sticky side.
2. Take the tape into the dark closet. Wait about two minutes for your eyes to adjust to the darkness.
3. Hold the folded handle ends and pull the stuck tape apart. Look where the two pieces of tape met. You might see a faint glow of light. Try the same thing with the other tapes. Which tapes produced a glow? What color was the glow?

Supplies

A completely dark closet, Duct tape, Masking tape, Electrical tape, Scotch tape, Scissors

What's Happening?

As you pulled apart the tapes, you may have observed triboluminescence. In this case, when the tapes are stuck together, the sticky parts make weak chemical bonds. When you pull them apart, energy is released in the form of light.

Cool Creations

Science allows you to play with some pretty neat stuff, including bubbles, crystals, plastics, slime, and even the properties of light and color!

Light & Color

323 Break a Pencil

Use the power of light and water to break a pencil into two pieces.

Supplies

Tall, clear glass of water; Pencil

Do It!

1. Hold the pencil straight up and down in the center of the glass of water. What do you see? Slowly move the pencil all the way to one side of the glass. What happens to the pencil in the water?

What's Happening?

Light travels faster in air than in water. Add that to the round shape of the glass, and you have an interesting result. When the pencil is right in the middle of the glass, the light travels straight from the pencil to your eyes without bending. The light hits the front of the glass straight on as it travels from the pencil through the water into the air to your eyes. You might notice that the pencil looks a little fatter in the water. The curve of the glass acts as a magnifying glass.

As you move the pencil to the side of the glass, the light from the pencil no longer goes straight to your eyes, but instead comes in at an angle. When the light passes through the water and comes out into the air, the light speeds up. But not all the light from the pencil speeds up at the same time. Because the light is coming out at an angle, some of the light will come out into the air first and the rest just after. This causes the light rays to bend, and the part of the pencil underwater appears closer to the side of the glass than the part of the pencil above the water. In fact, if you move the pencil all the way to the side of the glass, the part underwater disappears completely. The light is bent so much that it doesn't even get to your eyes.

What If?

What if you try other liquids, such as corn syrup or mineral oil? How does dissolving salt or sugar in the water change how the light is bent?

Color Explosion

Watch colors dance in milk.

Supplies

Plate, Whole milk, Food coloring, Cotton swab, Dish soap

Do It!

1. Fill the plate with milk.
2. Place two drops of each color in the center of the plate.
3. Dip the cotton swab in soap. Touch the swab to the center of the colors. Watch the colors explode! Touch the swab to the milk in other places on the plate to keep the colors moving.

What's Happening?

Milk is mostly water. Water molecules have positive and negative ends that stick to each other, creating a skin on the surface of the milk. Fats and proteins are mixed in with the water and interact differently with the soap. Soap has a negative end that latches onto the positive end of the water. This prevents the water from sticking to itself, and the skin rushes off the surface of the milk, carrying the colors with it. As the soap interacts with the fats and proteins, the water and colors swirl around.

Candy Chromatography

What dyes are in your candies?

Do It!

Supplies

Candy-coated chocolate pieces (such as M&Ms), Paper towel, Scissors, Pencil, Plate, Tall jar, Water, Salt, Clear tape

1. Cut the paper towel into strips 1 inch taller than the jar and 1 inch wide. Label the top of each strip with each candy's color. Draw a line 1 inch from the bottom of each strip.
2. Pour 1 inch of water into the jar. Add a pinch of salt.
3. Place each colored candy on the plate. Put a drop of water next to each, and then place the candy on the drop. Let the candies sit for three minutes, and then remove them. Place the matching filter strip on the colored drop above the line. Let it soak up the color.
4. Place the strips into the jar with the bottom, not the color, touching the water. Tape them in place.
5. Leave the strips in the jar until the water is 2 inches from the top. Let the strips dry. How many colors do you see?

What's Happening?

The water moves up the strips using capillary action. The water sticks to the paper towel more than it sticks to itself and moves up the strip. The dyes in the candies move with the water, but some colors move faster than others, so they separate on the filter.

Color-mixing Spinner

Mixing colors of light is very different from mixing colors of paint or ink.

Supplies

Cereal box,
White paper,
Cup, Scissors,
Glue, Markers,
String

= Do It! =

1. Trace the largest part of the cup onto the cereal box and cut out the circle. Cut out two circles of the same size from the white paper. Glue the white paper circles to each side of the cardboard circle. Use the markers to divide the circle into six wedges and color them using red, green, and blue.

2. Use the scissors to poke two holes about an inch apart on either side of the center of the circle. Cut a piece of string about 3 feet long. Thread the string through the two holes in the circle and tie the ends together.

3. Slide the circle to the middle of the string and hold one end of the string in each hand. Twirl the circle around so the string gets all twisted around. Then pull outward on the strings to watch the circle spin. What color do you see when the red, blue, and green colors mix? On a piece of scrap paper, mix red, blue, and green inks using the markers. How do these two colors compare?

4. Make color-mixing spinners with just red and green, red and blue, or blue and green. What colors do you see when they mix on the spinner?

What's Happening?

The spinning motion of the cardboard circle mixes the colored light you see reflected off the spinner. The primary colors of light are red, blue, and green. When you mix together these colors in light, you get white. The primary colors of paint or ink are yellow, cyan, and magenta. When you mix together these colors in paint or ink, you get black. Inks and light colors mix differently. Red and green light makes yellow, blue and green light makes cyan, and red and blue light makes magenta.

What If?

What if you color your color-mixing spinner with yellow, cyan, and magenta? What other color combinations can you try?

Crookes Radiometer

When William Crookes first built his radiometer in 1873, he thought that the black and white flags spun around because light pushes on shiny surfaces. It turns out he was wrong. Can you figure out what really happens?

Supplies

Clear jar with lid, Aluminum foil, Scissors, Ruler, Black paint, Glue stick, Thread, Toothpick, Tape, Black paper, Bright sun or lamp with incandescent bulb

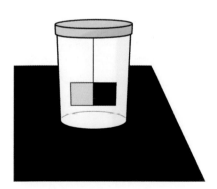

Do It!

1. Cut out two 1-inch square pieces of foil. Paint one side of each piece black.

2. Cut a piece of thread a few inches longer than the height of the jar. Tie one end to the center of the toothpick. Use the glue stick to attach the foil pieces to the toothpick so that they hang down like flags. The foil pieces should face in opposite directions so each side of the toothpick has a black and shiny foil flag.

3. Tape the other end of the thread to the inside lid of the jar. Adjust the length of the thread so that the toothpick flags hang about 1 inch from the bottom of the jar and don't touch the sides. Make sure the foil is completely flat before putting the lid on the jar.

4. Lay out some black paper in a bright, sunny spot outside or near a lamp with an incandescent bulb. Leave the jar on the black paper in the bright light. It will take several seconds for the toothpick to stop moving. As the light hits the paper, it will start to slowly turn around.

What's Happening?

Radiometer is a misleading name for this experiment. The spinning of the flags is not caused by the brightness of the light, but rather by the heat absorbed by the black flag compared to the white or shiny flag. The air molecules inside the jar flow between the warmer black flag and the cooler white flag, causing them to spin around. By placing the radiometer on black paper, the radiometer can heat up quicker to help it spin faster. Radiometers purchased at stores have a partial vacuum. That means most (but not all) of the air has been pulled out of the jar. Enough air remains inside to keep the flags spinning but not to slow them down. The radiometer you make will move slower because there is more air resistance in the jar.

328 Disappearing Bowl

How do you see things that are clear?

Supplies

Large glass bowl, Smaller glass bowl made of Pyrex, Vegetable oil

Do It!

1. Fill the large bowl ⅓ full of oil. Place the smaller bowl in the large bowl. Add oil until the level of the oil is almost level with the top of the small bowl. Can you see the large bowl? Can you see the smaller bowl? Pour oil into the smaller bowl. Can you see the small bowl now?

What's Happening?

Clear objects are visible because we can see the light bounce off (reflect) or bend through (refract). Light bends because it slows when it moves from the air to the glass, and then speeds up again when it moves out of the glass into the air. In this experiment, the speed of light in oil is the same as the speed of light in Pyrex glass. When the empty bowl is sitting in oil, you can see the bowl because the light bends when it enters the air inside the bowl. When you fill the bowl with oil, it disappears because the light does not bend as it moves from the oil to the Pyrex glass and back to the oil again.

329 Disappearing Coin

Make your money disappear by spending it, or use science!

Supplies

2 clear cups, 2 coins, Water, Table, Straw

Do It!

1. Sit at a table and place the cups a foot from the edge. Place a coin inside one cup and a coin underneath the other cup. Can you see both coins?
2. Fill both cups with water. Can you see the coins now? Use the straw to place two drops of water on the coin underneath the cup. Can you see the coin?

What's Happening?

Light bends when it hits a clear object because the speed of light is different inside the clear object than it is in the air. When light hits the empty clear cup, it bends and you can see the coin in and under the cup. When you fill both cups with water, the light travels through the water and to your eye. The air between the cup and the coin causes the light to bend just enough so that you can't see the coin under the cup when the cups are away from you. If you look down into the cup, you will see the coin underneath.

Reappearing Coin

First you don't see it ... and then you do!

== Do It! ==

Supplies

Paper cup,
Coin, Water

== Do It! ==

1. Place a coin in the empty cup. Look down in the cup to see the coin, and then move your head back until it is just out of view. Keep your head in place while you pour water into the cup. Can you see the coin now?

What's Happening?

When you view the coin in the cup, light reflects straight off the coin to your eye. When you move your head, the side of the cup gets in the way so the light reflected off the coin doesn't make it to your eye. However, when you pour water into the cup, the light reflected off the coin travels through the water and into the air. It then bends upward, as the speed of light is faster in air. This bending allows the light from your coin to reach your eye. What was hidden by the cup is now revealed!

Indoor Rainbow

The best part of a rainstorm is the rainbow afterward. Now you can make your own rainbow indoors whenever you want.

Supplies

Bowl, Water,
Mirror,
Flashlight,
White paper

== Do It! ==

1. Fill the bowl most of the way with water. Put the mirror in the bowl so that it leans against the side of the bowl at an angle and is at least halfway under the water.

2. Hold the paper above the bowl with one hand. Use the other hand to shine the flashlight onto the part of the mirror that is under the water. What do you see on the paper?

What's Happening?

The white light from a flashlight is made up of all the colors of the rainbow. When that light hits the water, it slows down. Because the flashlight is shining on the water at an angle, and not straight on, the light bends when it slows down. The different colors of the light bend different amounts, so they are spread out into a rainbow of colors. The mirror in the water reflects the rainbow up onto the paper so that you can see it.

Measure the Speed of Light

Light is incredibly fast. It travels at about 300 million meters every second! How can you measure something so fast? With the light-creating box in your kitchen—also known as a microwave oven.

═ Do It! ═

Supplies

Microwave oven, Large chocolate bar, Ruler, Calculator

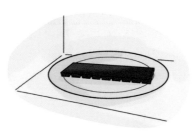

1. Take out the wheels inside your microwave that make your food spin around while it's cooking. We want the plate to stay still for this experiment.

2. Place the chocolate upside down on the plate so there is a long, smooth chocolate surface. Put the plate in the microwave and heat it on high for 15 seconds.

3. Remove the plate and look for the melted spots on the chocolate. Use the ruler to measure the distance between the close edges of two melted spots in centimeters. These two spots are where the light wave went into the chocolate bar and came back out again, and is equal to half of a wavelength. Use your calculator to divide that distance by 100. This is the distance in meters. Multiply that number by 2 to get the full wavelength in meters.

4. Look on the door or back of your microwave to find the frequency of the light waves it uses to cook your food. Most microwaves have a frequency of 2450 MHz, which is 2,450,000,000 waves per second! Multiply the full wavelength in meters by 2,450,000,000 waves/second to get the speed of light. You should get something close to 300,000,000 meters/second.

What's Happening?

Your microwave oven heats food by using light waves. Light is simply a form of energy, and when microwave light hits your food, that energy is converted from light into heat. Most microwaves have a plate that spins around to help the light waves heat your food evenly, but when we take it out, the light waves only heat the food where they pass through the food. This allows you to measure the wavelength of the light in your microwave, which can be used to calculate its speed.

What If?

What if you use other foods for this experiment? Try a tray full of marshmallows or bread with butter.

Does it matter how high up off the bottom of the microwave you place the food? Put a microwave-safe bowl upside down and put your plate of chocolate on top of that. Do you get better results?

Metamerism Matters

Have you ever put on a pair of socks that looked the same color, only to go out in the sunshine and discover that one is black and one is blue? When the light changes how you see the color of your socks, you have metamerism!

Supplies

Shoebox,
Flashlight,
Scissors, Balloons
of different colors,
Small objects of
different colors
(plastic brick toys
work well), Tape

Do It!

1. Cut a hole in the center of the lid of the shoebox that is the same size as the top of the flashlight. Cut a 1-inch square hole on a short end of the shoebox.

2. Put a red object in the box. Turn on the flashlight and shine it in the hole on top. Look through the small hole on the side. What color is the object?

3. Cut the bottom off a blue balloon and stretch it over the flashlight. Shine the blue light in the hole on top of the box and look in the small hole in the side. What color is the object now? Try other combinations of object and light colors. Does the color of an object depend on the color of light you use?

What's Happening?

When you look at an object, the color you see depends on the color reflected off the object. So, a red object reflects red light but absorbs all the other colors. If you look at a red object with a blue light, it will appear black. All the blue light is absorbed and there is no red light to reflect to your eye.

What If?

What if you use different "white" lights to look at the objects? Try bright sunlight, fluorescent lights, incandescent lights, and LED lights. Do the colors change? What if you test your black and blue socks? What kind of light makes them both look blue or both look black?

Kaleidoscope

Kaleidoscope means "beautiful shape" in Greek. What beautiful shapes will you see in yours?

Do It!

Supplies

Paper towel tube; Cardboard; Aluminum foil; Scissors; Ruler; Tape; Markers, paint, stickers (optional)

1. Cut three pieces of cardboard 1 inch wide and as long as your paper towel tube. Wrap each piece with foil, shiny side out and as smooth as possible.
2. Assemble the mirrors into a long triangle tube and tape them together. Slide the triangle tube into the paper towel tube and tape it down. Make sure you can still see through both ends. Decorate the tube with markers, paint, and stickers, if you like.
3. Look into the tube and point the other end at different objects. What do you see?

What's Happening?

Look at yourself in the mirror. What do you see? Light reflects to create an image. Turn your back to the mirror and use a handheld mirror to look behind you into the mirror. What do you see now? The mirrors reflect back and forth until the image becomes too small to see. This is what happens in the kaleidoscope, but with three mirrors, the pattern gets more interesting.

---

335 Rainbow Paper

Capture a rainbow on paper and hang it on the wall!

Do It!

Supplies

Clear nail polish, Black paper, Scissors, Shallow pan, Warm water

1. Pour 1 inch of warm water into the pan.
2. Cut a piece of black paper smaller than the pan. Place the paper into the water.
3. Pour three drops of clear nail polish onto the water. Lift the paper by its corners straight up so that the nail polish stays on the paper. Lay the paper flat and let it dry for 10 minutes. Tilt the dry paper as you look at it. Can you see the rainbow?

What's Happening?

The color of light can be described by its wavelength. Visible light with large wavelengths are red, orange, and yellow; short wavelengths are green, blue, and indigo. The nail polish forms a film on the paper that's so thin that the light reflecting off it and the light reflecting off the bottom of the film combine. Some colors in the light combine, and the color appears twice as bright. Other colors combine, the waves cancel out, and the color does not appear at all. All of this combining creates a rainbow of colors.

Sky Colors

Why is the sky blue and sunset orange?

Supplies

Clear, straight drinking glass; Water; Milk; Measuring spoon; Flashlight; Tabletop in a dark room

═ Do It! ═

1. Fill the glass with water and add 2 teaspoons of milk.
2. Shine the flashlight through the glass. Look at the milky water on the side next to the flashlight. The water appears blue! Look at the water on the opposite side of the flashlight. The water looks orange!

What's Happening?

When light shines through the sky, it bounces off tiny particles. Scientists call this scattering. The milky water acts like particles in the atmosphere. The light with the shortest wavelength (blue) is scattered the most. This is the color we see when the sun is high in the sky. When you look at the milky water from the side, you see scattered blue light.

At sunset, the sun is low and the sunlight travels through more atmosphere. By the time the sunlight reaches your eyes, the blue is scattered out. When you look at the water opposite the flashlight, you see the orange light with the blue scattered out.

Un-mixing Colors 337

With this experiment, you get to turn back time!

═ Do It! ═

1. Stir some corn syrup and a different color of food coloring together into each small cup.
2. Fill the large glass ⅓ full of corn syrup. Place the small glass inside and push it into the corn syrup. Fill the small glass with water. Clip the binder clips on the large glass to hold the center glass in place.
3. Place a large drop of each colored syrup into the syrup between the two glasses.
4. Hold the large glass, and then very slowly turn the small glass. The colored drops will appear to mix with the syrup. Turn the glass until the colors have gone all the way around. Then slowly turn the inside glass in the other direction. Watch the colored drops un-mix!

Supplies

Large clear glass, Small clear glass, Corn syrup, Water, 3 droppers, 3 small cups, Food coloring, 3 spoons, 4 large binder clips

What's Happening?

When you have a dense and slow-moving liquid, such as corn syrup, and you mix it slowly, then it has what scientists call laminar flow. These liquids don't actually mix. Instead, many thin, parallel layers move around the glass. When you turn the glass the other direction, the color drops stay in their layers and come back together.

Antibubbles

What is a bubble that's inside-out and under water? An antibubble!

Supplies

Tall, clear jar or vase; Water; Dish soap; Spoon; Sugar; Pipette or small syringe; Small bowl

= Do It! =

1. Fill the jar ¾ full of water. Add two squirts of dish soap and gently mix the soap in with a spoon. Try not to make any bubbles.

2. Pour a tablespoon or more of sugar into the jar. The amount depends on the size of your jar. You want a small layer of sugar on the bottom.

3. Fill the small bowl with water. Gently mix in one squirt of dish soap and a teaspoon of sugar.

4. Fill the pipette or syringe with the mixture in the bowl. Hold the tip of the syringe close, but just above the top surface of the water in the jar. Carefully release one drop at a time. Some of the water drops will briefly sit on the surface of the water before popping. With a little practice, you will be able to get drops that go under the surface of the water and slowly sink down to hover in the middle of the jar or rest on the sugar at the bottom. These are antibubbles!

5. If you cannot get the drops to go down into the water, add a little more dish soap and gently stir it in without disturbing the sugar at the bottom.

What's Happening?

A regular bubble is a drop of air surrounded by a shell of soap and water floating in the air. An antibubble is a drop of water surrounded by a shell of air floating in the water. To make an antibubble, you first must make the water less sticky. Water sticks to itself so strongly that it makes a skin on the top surface. Adding soap makes the water less sticky, which allows a water drop surrounded by air to break through the skin, also called surface tension. Sugar is added to water drops to make them heavier than water so that they sink instead of rising to the top and popping.

What If?

What if you add food coloring to the water in the bowl? Color will help you better see the antibubble and what happens to it when it pops.

Long-lasting Bubbles

A few tricks will make your bubbles stick around longer.

Supplies

Dish soap, Distilled water, Corn syrup, Bowl, Measuring cup, Measuring spoon, Bubble wand or straw

Do It!

1. In a bowl, mix 1 cup of water with ¼ cup of dish soap. Let the mixture sit for an hour.
2. Dip the bubble wand or straw into the bubble solution and blow some bubbles. Use the stopwatch to time how long the bubbles last before they pop.
3. Gently mix 1 tablespoon of corn syrup into the bubble solution. Use the bubble wand or straw to blow bubbles with the new solution. Do the bubbles last longer?

What's Happening?

A bubble is made of two layers of soap with water in between. The soap and water stick together, and when you blow a bubble, they stretch out and hold the air inside. When the water in the middle evaporates or the bubble is broken, it pops. Adding corn syrup creates thicker soap layers so the water doesn't evaporate as quickly and the bubble is harder to break. Using distilled water and letting the solution sit for an hour prevents impurities and gas bubbles in the solution that can cause your bubbles to pop. The result is longer-lasting bubbles!

Bouncing Bubbles 340

These bubbles will bounce off your hands!

Supplies

Dish soap, Distilled water, Glycerin, Refrigerator, Bowl, Measuring cup, Measuring spoon, Bubble wand or straw, Knit cotton glove or a clean sock

Do It!

1. In a bowl, mix 1 cup of water with ¼ cup of dish soap. Gently mix 1 tablespoon of glycerin into the bubble solution. Let the mixture sit in the refrigerator for at least 24 hours.
2. Put on a glove. With the other hand, use the bubble wand or straw to blow a bubble onto your gloved hand. Gently bounce the bubble around on your hand!

What's Happening?

The glycerin in the bubble solution makes the soap layers thicker, stronger, and less likely to pop. By cooling the solution, the water between the soap layers takes longer to evaporate, which also makes the bubbles harder to pop. The bubbles are strong enough to hold and bounce!

What If?

What if you don't cool your solution in the refrigerator? How does this affect the bounciness of the bubbles?

Giant Bubbles

Bubbles come in all sizes, but giant ones are always more fun!

Supplies

Bubble solution, 2 sticks (from outside or bamboo skewers), Cotton string, 2 rubber bands, Washer or nut, Bucket

Do It!

1. Cut an 18-inch-long piece of string. Tie the ends of the string to the end of each stick.

2. Cut a 36-inch-long piece of string. Thread the string through the washer. Tie these ends to the same ends of the sticks that you tied the other string. Wrap a rubber band several times around the sticks over the strings to hold them in place.

3. Pour 1 inch of bubble solution into the bucket. Hold the sticks together and dip the entire string into the bubble solution. Pull the string straight up and keep the sticks together. Hold the sticks high and slowly pull the sticks apart as you walk backward. A giant bubble will form as the air pushes through the bubble solution between the strings.

What's Happening?

Water is sticky. It sticks to almost everything, but it sticks to itself more. Water alone is too sticky to make bubbles. A mixture of soap and water — the basics of a bubble solution — is just sticky enough but not too sticky that it stretches out into a thin film. The bubble solution sticks to the cotton string, so when you pull it apart, you get a very thin sheet of bubble solution. Even the slightest breeze will stretch that sheet outward until it makes a giant, round bubble.

What If?

What if you make a bubble big enough to hold a person? Pour bubble solution into a kiddie pool and throw in a hula hoop. Have a friend stand in the center of the hula hoop, and then pull it slowly upward. The bubble solution will stick to the hoop as you pull it up, making a bubble around your friend!

Dry Ice Bubbles

These bubbles are spooky-looking! For safety's sake, ask a grown-up to help you with the dry ice.

ADULT NEEDED

Supplies

Wide-mouth jar,
Rubber hose,
Funnel (big enough
to cover the
top of the jar),
Bubble solution
(the Bouncing
Bubbles recipe is
recommended),
Dry ice (from the
grocery store or an
ice cream shop),
Tongs or leather
gloves, Water,
Cotton knit gloves

═ Do It! ═

1. Fill the jar about halfway with warm water.
2. Stick the end of the funnel onto one end of the rubber hose.
3. Ask an adult to put a few pieces of dry ice into the jar. Make sure they wear leather gloves or use tongs to pick up the dry ice. DO NOT touch dry ice with your bare hands.
4. Hold the funnel over the top of the jar so that the "smoke" flows into the rubber hose. Dip the other end of the hose into the bubble solution. Soon you will see smoke-filled bubbles dropping off the end of the hose. Put on the cotton gloves if you want to hold and bounce the smoky bubbles.

What's Happening?

Dry ice is frozen carbon dioxide. At room temperature, carbon dioxide is a gas, but if you cool that gas down to -110°F, it becomes solid. Dry ice is so cold that touching it immediately burns the skin. When you add dry ice to warm water, it warms up so quickly that it changes straight from the solid state to the gas state, called sublimation. The smoke that you see is carbon dioxide mixed with water as a gas, like your smoke-like breath on a very cold day.

What If?

What if you put food coloring in the water? Can you make colored "smoke" in the bubbles?

Why create one bubble when you can make many?

= Do It! =

Supplies

Bubble solution, Straw, Flat surface

1. Spread bubble solution on the flat surface with your hands.
2. Dip one end of the straw in the solution and hold it an inch above the soapy surface. Blow into the straw to make a large half bubble.
3. Dip your straw in the solution and stick it through the center of the bubble, an inch above the soapy surface. Blow into the straw to make another bubble slightly smaller than the first. It's a bubble within a bubble! Can you add a third bubble inside the second bubble?

What's Happening?

The soap and water in the bubble solution stick together. When you blow a bubble, it stretches out and holds the air on the soapy surface. Because the surface and straw are covered with solution, they become part of the bubble instead of popping it. When you blow a bubble inside a bubble, the outer bubble gets a little bigger. This is because you are blowing more air inside both bubbles.

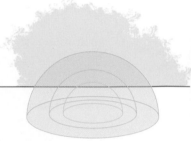

344 Square Bubbles

How do you create cubed bubbles?

= Do It! =

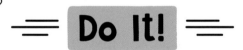

Supplies

7 straws, 7 12-inch pipe cleaners, Scissors, Bubble solution, Bucket

1. Bend the end of a pipe cleaner into a square wand. Dip it into the solution and blow. Does the wand make a square bubble?
2. Cut six straws and six pipe cleaners in half. Twist the ends of three pipe cleaners together. Bend them apart to make a pyramid. Twist the other pipe cleaners to make four pyramids.
3. Slide the straws over the pipe cleaners. Create a cube with the pyramids. Twist the ends to hold them together.
4. Pour solution into the bucket. Dip the cube completely into the solution. Slowly pull it out. What shape are the bubbles? Shake the cube gently and see how the shape changes. Use a straw to blow a bubble into the center of the cube. What shape is the bubble?

What's Happening?

Bubbles are round because a sphere requires only a little bubble solution to hold a lot of air. The cube wand changes that. The bubble solution sticks to the sides of the wand and stretches the shortest distance between sides. Blow a bubble in the middle, and the other bubbles in the cube push on it to create a square.

How Much Can You Blow?

Are you full of hot air? This experiment can help you find out.

Supplies

Bubble solution, Straw, Plastic garbage bag, Ruler, Calculator

Do It!

1. Lay the garbage bag flat on a table or other flat surface. Make sure the bag is smooth with very few wrinkles.

2. Pour a tiny amount of bubble solution on the bag and spread it out. Keep your ruler out and ready.

3. Dip the straw in the bubble solution and hold it just above the center of the bag. Take a deep breath and blow as much air as you possibly can out of your lungs to create a large bubble on the bag.

4. Use a ruler to quickly measure the diameter (width) of the bubble. If the bubble pops, measure the soapy outline of the bubble on the bag. Use a calculator to measure the volume of air in liters inside the bubble. If you measured in inches: diameter x diameter x diameter x .00429 = volume in liters. If you measured in centimeters: diameter x diameter x diameter x .000262 = volume in liters.

5. Repeat the process by breathing out normally as you blow up the bubble. Repeat again by breathing in normally, exhaling normally, and then blowing a bubble with all the air left in your lungs. Measure the diameter of both these bubbles and calculate the volume. A bubble 20 cm (8 inches) in diameter is about the same size as a 2-liter soda bottle!

What's Happening?

Lung capacity is the amount of air you can hold in your lungs. There are three types of lung capacity. Vital capacity is all the air your lungs can hold. Tidal volume is the air you normally have in your lungs. Expiratory reserve is the air you have left in your lungs after a normal breath. Which of these volumes was greatest, and which was smallest? Many factors affect your lung capacity, including your height, weight, and whether you live at high or low altitude.

To calculate the amount of air in the bubble, we used the equation for the volume of a sphere (4/3 (radius)^3), divided by 2 because there is only half a sphere on the garbage bag, adjusted for the units used and for the diameter of the sphere being twice the radius.

346 Alum Crystals

When you want large and impressive crystals, alum is your friend.

Supplies

Alum (find it in the spice section), Water, Measuring cup, 2 jars or cups, Mixing spoon, Pencil, Fishing line, Coffee filter

Do It!

1. Pour ½ cup of hot tap water into one of the jars. Stir in a small amount of alum at a time until no more alum will dissolve. Place a coffee filter over the jar and let it sit overnight.

2. Pour the alum water into the other jar. You will see some small crystals on the bottom of the first jar. Pour out the crystals and choose the biggest one.

3. Cut a piece of fishing line a few inches longer than the jar is tall. Tie one end around the crystal. Tie the other end around the middle of a pencil. Hang the seed crystal inside the jar by resting the pencil across the top of the jar. The crystal should hang in the middle of the alum water. If the line is too long, just turn the pencil so it wraps around to shorten the line. Place the jar in a warm, dry place and lay the coffee filter on top to keep dust out.

4. Check on the crystal several times each day to watch it grow. If you notice crystals on the bottom or sides of the jar, pour the alum water into a new, clean jar and move the crystal too. The other crystals in the jar will also act as seeds and slow down the growth of the crystal on the line. How large can you get the alum crystal to grow?

What's Happening?

Scientists call this process of growing crystals "nucleation." In nucleation, a couple of alum molecules in the water stick together and fall to the bottom of the jar. Soon, other alum molecules join the first two and a crystal starts to grow. This crystal becomes a seed for more crystals to grow. If you take the other seed crystals out of the jar, the only place for the molecules to stick is the seed crystal on the string. The larger this crystal gets, the faster it will grow because there is more room for the alum molecules in the water to join on.

Crystal Garden

Create your own garden of brilliantly colored crystal flowers.

Supplies

2 plastic containers, Charcoal briquettes, Water, Ammonia, Liquid bluing, Salt, Measuring spoon, Mixing spoon, Food coloring

= Do It! =

1. Cover the bottom of one of the plastic containers with charcoal.
2. In the other container, mix 4 tablespoons each of salt, water, and liquid bluing, and 1 tablespoon of ammonia.
3. Pour the mixture over the charcoal. Add drops of food coloring to the charcoal.
4. Place the container in a warm, dry spot. Crystals will form in a few hours.
5. To grow more crystals, add more liquid mixture as it evaporates. Pour the solution carefully down the side of the container, avoiding the crystals. If you get ammonia or bluing on your hands, wash it off immediately.

What's Happening?

Each ingredient plays a role in creating the crystals in the garden. The water and ammonia dissolve the bluing and salt. They carry the bluing and salt up through the holes in the charcoal. Ammonia helps the water evaporate quicker so smaller crystals are formed. Bluing is made of tiny particles suspended in the liquid. Salt sticks to those particles to form crystals.

Crystal Snowflakes

These snowflakes won't melt!

= Do It! =

1. Fill the jar ¾ full of hot tap water. Stir in several spoonfuls of Borax until it won't dissolve anymore.
2. Cut the pipe cleaner into three equal pieces. Twist the pieces together in the center and shape them into a star.
3. Cut a piece of string that's half as tall as the jar. Tie one end of the string to the pipe cleaner. Tie the other end to the pencil.
4. Lower the pipe cleaner into the jar. Rest the pencil across the top to hold it in place. The pipe cleaner should be submerged but not touching the bottom.
5. Place the jar in a cool spot. After 24 hours, pull your crystal snowflake out of the jar.

Supplies

Borax soap, Water, Tall jar, Mixing spoon, Pencil, String, Pipe cleaner, Scissors

What's Happening?

When you pour Borax into water, it dissolves into tiny particles that are suspended in the water. Hot water holds more Borax particles than cold water, and more particles mean more crystals. As the water cools, the Borax falls out of suspension and sticks to other Borax particles, forming crystals.

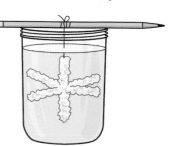

349 Eggshell Geode

Geodes usually take centuries to form. You can make one in just a couple of days!

Supplies

Large eggshell, White glue, Small paintbrush, Jar, Water, Alum, Measuring spoon, Measuring cup, Food coloring, Mixing spoon, Paper towel

Do It!

1. Clean and dry the eggshell.
2. Pour two drops of glue into the eggshell and paint it all over the inside surface.
3. Pour alum into the shell, turning it around so that the alum sticks to the glue and the inside is covered. Let it dry overnight.
4. In a jar, mix 1 cup of hot tap water, 6 tablespoons of alum, and 15 drops of food coloring. Submerge the eggshell in the liquid and leave it for 24 hours.
5. Remove the eggshell geode from the water. Lay it on a paper towel to dry. Your eggshell will be full of brightly colored crystals.

What's Happening?

On the outside, geodes look like regular rocks. When you break them open, you find sparkling crystals. Geodes are formed from decomposed fossils and bubbles trapped in molten rock. Water flows through the bubbles and leaves behind minerals that form crystals. Large geodes can take up to a million years to form.

350 Frost Crystals

You don't have to wait until winter for frost to grow on your window.

Supplies

Epsom salt, Water, Dish soap, Window, Bowl, Measuring cup, Mixing spoon, Paper towel

Do It!

1. In a bowl, dissolve ½ cup of hot tap water and ⅓ cup Epsom salt. If the salt won't dissolve, heat the bowl in the microwave for 30 seconds and stir.
2. Mix two drops of dish soap to the salt solution.
3. Dip a paper towel into the mixture and wipe it onto a window. In about five minutes, you will see crystals form!

What's Happening?

Epsom salt is made up of tiny crystals. When you pour salt into water, it dissolves. When the water evaporates, the salt forms crystals again. The salt solution on the window creates a thin layer of crystals, much like frost on a window. Real frost is formed when a thin layer of moisture freezes and forms water crystals.

You might be wondering what the dish soap was for. Without the soap, the water and salt would form droplets on the window instead of spreading out. The soap makes the saltwater stick to the window instead of sticking to itself.

Rock Candy

Rock candy is crystals you can eat!

Do It!

Supplies

Sugar, Water, Measuring cup, Microwave-safe bowl, Tall jar, Skewer, Clothespin

1. Pour 1 cup of water and 3 cups of sugar into a microwave-safe bowl. Heat the bowl in the microwave for two minutes. Stir to dissolve the sugar. Pour the hot sugar solution into a jar and let it cool for 20 minutes.
2. Dip one end of a skewer in the sugar solution, and then dip it in dry sugar. Lay the skewer flat to cool.
3. Clip a clothespin to the non-sugared end of the skewer. Place the sugared end into the sugar solution. Balance the clip on the jar. The skewer should not touch the bottom of the jar.
4. Set the jar in a cool place and cover with a paper towel.
5. Check the candy every day for a week, or until the crystals are the size you want. Admire the crystals before you eat them!

What's Happening?

As the hot sugar solution cools, the sugar leaves the solution to form sugar crystals on the skewer. The sugar on the skewer act as seeds on which the sugar crystals start to grow.

Salt Crystals

Not all crystals are the same. Look carefully to see different shapes and patterns.

Do It!

Supplies

Table salt, Epsom salt, Salt substitute, 3 plastic cups, Water, Mixing spoon, Measuring cup, Refrigerator, Marker

1. Pour ½ cup of each salt into a cup and label them.
2. Pour ½ cup of hot tap water into each cup. Stir until the salt is dissolved. Place the cups in the refrigerator where they won't be disturbed.
3. After 24 hours, the cups should be full of crystals. If not, put them back in the refrigerator one more day. Pour out any remaining liquid.
4. Look closely at the crystals. What shape are they? How are they similar? Different?

What's Happening?

When salt dissolves in water, the charged ions that make up the salt molecules split up and float in the water. For example, table salt is sodium chloride, so there are sodium ions and chlorine ions. As the water evaporates, fewer ions fit in the water, so they pair up to make sodium chloride again. This creates crystals. The crystals grow as more molecules are added. Table salt and salt substitute make square crystals. Epsom salt makes spiky crystals.

Speleothems

You don't need to live in a cave to create stalactites and stalagmites.

Supplies

2 jars or cups, Wool or cotton yarn, Tray or cookie sheet, Small paper plate, Washing soda, Water, Mixing spoon, Measuring spoon

Do It!

1. Fill the jars with hot tap water and stir in several spoonfuls of washing soda. Keep adding washing soda until it will no longer dissolve in the water. Place the two jars on a tray with the small paper plate between them.

2. Cut three pieces of yarn about 24 inches long. Twist the yarn together and put one end in each jar. Make sure the ends are pushed down into the solution. The section between the jars should droop a little.

3. Leave the jars in a warm, dry place where they will not be disturbed. Depending on the temperature and humidity, it could take from one to four days for speleothems to form. After an hour or so, you should see the solution drip from the yarn onto the plate. Too much dripping will dissolve the stalagmites before they form. Too little dripping, and they won't grow at all. Slide the jars closer or farther apart to adjust the dripping. Soon, you will have your very own speleothems!

What's Happening?

Stalactites and stalagmites form when water seeps through rocks above caves. As the water moves through the rock, it dissolves small amounts of minerals. When the water drips from the cave ceiling, small amounts of the mineral are left behind, eventually leaving an icicle-like stalactite. The water that drips onto the cave floor also contains minerals that build up to form stalagmites. It can take hundreds of years to form speleothems.

In this experiment, the water and the minerals in the washing soda (sodium carbonate) traveled along the yarn instead of through rock. These speleothems, stalactites, and stalagmites form in a few days instead of a hundred years!

What If?

What if you dissolve a crystal-making substance other than washing soda? Try baking soda, Epsom salt, table salt, or sugar.

Gelatin Plastic

Gelatin plastic is used for everything from pill capsules to makeup. It's also found in some of your favorite sweets, such as marshmallows.

Do It!

Supplies

Unflavored gelatin, Water, Bowl, Spoon, Measuring spoon, Jar lid, Food coloring

1. In a bowl, add 3 tablespoons of hot tap water, 2½ teaspoons of gelatin, and some drops of food coloring.
2. Mix the gelatin until it is dissolved. Before the gelatin cools, pour it into the jar lid. Use a spoon to push out any bubbles.
3. Leave the gelatin in a cool, dry spot for three to five days, until it is completely dry. Then remove it from the mold. How does the gelatin plastic feel? Can you bend it?

What's Happening?

All plastics are made of polymers, or chains of molecules. In gelatin plastic, that molecule is collagen. Collagen comes from the bones and skin of pigs and cows. When collagen is heated, it forms the chains that make plastic so strong and flexible.

Make a Bouncy Ball

Make your own bouncy ball at home with just a few household chemicals.

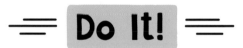

Do It!

Supplies

Borax soap, Water, School glue, Cornstarch, Measuring spoon, Measuring cup, 2 cups, Mixing spoon, Fork, Food coloring

1. In one cup, mix ½ cup of hot tap water and 1 teaspoon of Borax. Stir until dissolved.
2. In another cup, mix 1 tablespoon of glue, one tablespoon of cornstarch, and two drops of food coloring.
3. Pour the glue mixture into the Borax. Let it sit for 15 seconds. Use a fork to pull the glue out.
4. Knead the glue into a ball. If it's sticky, put it in the Borax for a few more seconds.
5. Roll it into a ball and start bouncing! How high does it bounce? Does it bounce better on hard floors or carpet? When you are done, store your ball in a sealed bag.

What's Happening?

Glue contains long chains of a molecule called polyvinyl acetate, or PVA. PVA makes the glue sticky. The Borax links these chains together to make a strong, stretchy mesh. Cornstarch binds the mesh together so that it holds a round shape. The stretchy mesh is flexible, so when it hits the ground, it squishes a bit. However, the ball is elastic, so it returns to its round shape as it bounces back up. The result is a bouncy plastic ball!

356 Plastic Milk

ADULT NEEDED

Before plastic was made from petroleum, it was made from milk. In the early 1900s, milk was used to make buttons, beads, and jewelry. You can make your very own buttons and beads from milk, too!

Supplies

Whole milk; Vinegar; Measuring spoon; Measuring cup; Bowl; Spoon; Strainer; Paper towels; Food coloring, glitter, cookie cutters (optional)

═ Do It! ═

1. Have a grown-up help you heat 1 cup of milk on the stove until it is hot but not boiling. You will see steam rise off the milk when it is ready. Pour the hot milk into a bowl.

2. Add 4 teaspoons of vinegar and stir for about one minute. The milk will get chunky.

3. Pour the chunky milk through a strainer and wait until the chunks are cool enough to touch. Rinse off the milk chunks in the sink under running water and press them together. How does the milk plastic feel? How much plastic did you get from one cup of milk?

4. After the plastic is rinsed, wrap it in paper towels and squeeze out any extra water. Mold the plastic into any shape you like. You can add food coloring, glitter, or use a cookie cutter to make shapes. Use a toothpick to make holes to make beads for a necklace. Leave the milk plastic on paper towels to dry for at least two days.

What's Happening?

Plastics can look and feel very different, but the one thing they have in common are the molecules they are made of. All plastics are made of polymers, or chains of molecules. In milk plastic, that molecule is casein. In a glass of milk, casein is a monomer, or single molecule. When you add an acid like vinegar to the milk, the casein molecules bunch together and form chains of casein molecules that look like slimy, white chunks. These chunks are milk plastic. When it is dry, the plastic is hard, shiny, and durable.

What If?

What if you make milk plastic from cold milk instead of hot? What if you use skim milk or cream? What if you use more vinegar, or less vinegar, or even a different acid, such as lemon juice?

Pencils Through a Plastic Bag

Add drama to this experiment by holding the bag of water over someone's head!

Supplies

Resealable plastic sandwich bag, 3 or more sharpened pencils, Water

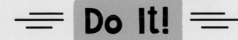 **Do It!**

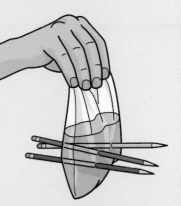

1. Fill the plastic bag about ¾ full of water and seal it tightly.
2. Poke the pointy end of a pencil into the bag. Without hesitating, slide the pencil the rest of the way through so that the pointy end is on one side of the bag and the eraser is on the other. Does the water leak out? Can you add more pencils? How many pencils can you poke through the bag?

What's Happening?

Polymers are simply long chains of molecules that are connected. Many common materials are made of polymers: rubber balloons, nylon pantyhose, paper, and plastic bags. When the pencils are pushed into the plastic bag, they simply slide between the polymer chains. The polymer chains are held together around the hole created by the pencil, preventing the water from leaking out.

Shrinking Plastic

Use thermoplastics to make some incredible shrinking creations. **ADULT NEEDED**

Supplies

Clear plastic takeout tray (make sure it has a #6 recycle symbol), Permanent markers, Ruler, Scissors, Aluminum foil, Cookie sheet, Oven, Hole punch (optional)

 **Do It!**

1. Preheat the oven to 325°F.
2. Cut a flat piece of plastic into a 4" x 4" square. Cut other shapes too, and color them with a permanent marker. Use a hole punch to make a hole for jewelry.
3. Line the cookie sheet with foil. Lay the plastic on the sheet. Make sure they are not touching.
4. Place the sheet in the oven for three minutes. Let the plastic cool completely (about five minutes) before removing them.
5. Measure the square. How much did it shrink?

What's Happening?

The clear plastic in this experiment is made of tangled chains of polystyrene molecules, or polymers. To make the thin, clear plastic, the polystyrene is heated and rolled out so that the polymer chains straighten out. The plastic is cooled very quickly so that it holds its shape. Plastics made in this way are called thermoplastics. If you reheat a thermoplastic, the polymer chains will curl back up to their original shape, and the thin plastic shrinks!

A Quick Lesson on Slime

All slimes are non-Newtonian fluids, which is just a fancy way of saying that they don't act how most liquids are supposed to act. Isaac Newton came up with a way to describe how liquids flow called viscosity. Thin liquids, such as water, have a low viscosity. Thick liquids, such as molasses or ketchup, have a high viscosity. Viscosity is not the same as density. For example, vegetable oil is more viscous (flows slower) but is less dense than water. A liquid is non-Newtonian when its viscosity can be changed by other factors, such as stirring, stretching, or squeezing.

How Do You Make a Slime?

Slimes are made of polymers, or chains of molecules like a long chain of paper clips. Slime happens when you add a cross-linking chemical that connects those chains. (Think attaching strings to different paper clip chains, and then tangling them together so they can't easily come apart.) All the slime recipes here have two ingredients: a polymer and a cross linker.

359 Soap Slime

Here's a soft slime that smells good, too!

Slime

Supplies

Cornstarch, Shampoo, Spoon, Bowl

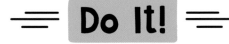

Do It!

1. Pour ¼ cup of cornstarch into the bowl, and then squirt a small amount of shampoo into the bowl. Mix them together.
2. Keep mixing in small amounts of shampoo until the mixture comes together. Take the slime out of the bowl and finish mixing it together with your hands. Add more cornstarch if the slime is too sticky or shampoo if it is too stiff.

What If?

What if you use other soaps like hand soap, body soap, or even shaving cream?

Oobleck

This slime is named after the ooey, gooey slime that falls from the sky in the Dr. Seuss book of the same name. It is simple, slimy fun, and the easiest slime to make.

Supplies

Cornstarch, Water, Measuring cup, Bowl, Spoon (optional), Food coloring (optional)

═ Do It! ═

1. Pour 1 cup of cornstarch into a bowl.
2. Add about ¼ cup of water and a few drops of food coloring. Use a spoon or your hands to mix the oobleck. If it is too dry, add more water. If it is too wet, add more cornstarch.
3. Put your finger on top of the oobleck and push down slowly. Then use your finger (or whole hand) to hit the oobleck hard. What happens?

What If?

What if you adjust the amount of water? What is the least amount of water needed to make oobleck? What is the most water you can add so that it still has slimy properties?

Snot

This slime bears a striking resemblance to the mucus that comes out of your nose!

═ Do It! ═

1. Pour ½ cup of glue (a 4-oz. bottle) and ½ cup of liquid starch into the bowl or bag.
2. If you use a bag, push the air out and seal the bag. Use your hands to squish the bag and mix the glue and starch. Once it's mixed, you can take it out and play with it over the bowl. Keep the bag for storage later.
3. If you use a bowl, use the spoon or your hands to mix the glue and starch. This is definitely the messier option, but that's the whole point of slime.
4. After the glue and starch are mixed, try rolling your slime into a ball and stretching it out. Grab a handful of slime, hold it high over the bowl, and let it flow from your hands. How long can the snotty slime flow before it breaks?

Supplies

Clear school glue, Liquid starch, Measuring cup, Bowl or quart-sized resealable freezer bag, Spoon

What If?

What if you add more glue than starch, or more starch than glue? Try to get the slime solid enough to roll it into a bouncing ball. How high can the ball bounce?

362 Sticky Slime

This is a classic slime recipe for the ooziest, stickiest, slimiest slime you can make. Add some food coloring to increase the slime factor even more!

Supplies

White school glue, Borax soap, Water, Measuring cup, Measuring spoon, 2 bowls, 2 mixing spoons, Food coloring (optional)

Do It!

1. In one bowl, add ½ cup of glue (a 4-oz. bottle) and ½ cup of water. Use a spoon to mix them together.

2. In another bowl, mix 1 cup of warm water with 1 teaspoon of Borax soap. Make sure the soap is completely dissolved.

3. Add the soap mixture to the glue mixture, and mix slowly with a spoon. Once the slime thickens, use your hands to knead it together until it is completely mixed. Now your slime is ready for sticky stretching and squishing!

What If?

What if you add more Borax to the soap solution? What if you add less? How does the amount of soap affect the stickiness or ooziness of your slime?

363 Edible Slime ADULT NEEDED

Yes, you can eat this version of slime, but it is probably more fun to play with than to eat.

Do It!

Supplies

Soluble fiber that contains psyllium, such as Metamucil; Water; Glass microwave-safe bowl; Measuring cup; Spoon

1. Pour 1 cup of water and 1 teaspoon of soluble fiber into a bowl. Stir well until the fiber is completely dissolved.

2. Heat the bowl in the microwave for four minutes. Stop heating as soon as you see the mixture boil.

3. Stir the mixture, and then microwave for another two minutes. Repeat this process four more times. Let the slime cool completely before playing with it.

What If?

What happens if you use more soluble fiber in the slime? How about less? What if you continue to heat the slime more than four times? What if you only heat the slime two times instead of four?

Magnetic Slime

Adding iron to the slime gives it surprising magnetic properties.

═ Do It! ═

1. Make Snot or Sticky Slime, except add ¼ cup of iron oxide powder to the soap or liquid starch before adding the glue.

2. Make a small ball of slime and put it on a Styrofoam plate. Put the magnet under the plate and drag it around under the slime. Can you move it with the magnet? Put all the slime on the plate and spread it out. What happens if you move the magnet underneath the plate now?

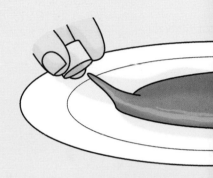

What If?

What if you try magnetizing different types of slime? Which one responds to the magnet the most?

Glow-in-the-Dark Slime

Create spooky slime with some glow-in-the-dark science.

═ Do It! ═

1. Make Oobleck, Sticky, or Edible Slime, but with tonic water instead of regular water.

2. Place the slime under a black light to see it glow. The tonic water will glow blue, but you can add green food coloring to give it a more traditional slimy color.

Index